BELL'S GUIDE

The
Comprehensive
Real Estate
Handbook

Second Edition

BELL'S GUIDE
THE COMPREHENSIVE
REAL ESTATE HANDBOOK
SECOND EDITION

RANDALL BELL, MAI, MBA

Research: Orell C. Anderson
Computer Layout: Rick Bell
Art Coordinator: Brent Hardwell

Reproduction or translation of any part of this work beyond that permitted by Sections 107 and 108 of the 1976 United States Copyright Act without the permission of the copyright owner is unlawful.

Library of Congress Catalog Card Number: 97-71983

Bell, Randall
Bell's Guide - The Comprehensive Real Estate Handbook
ISBN 1-886734-11-9

Printed in the United States of America

10 9 8 7 6 5 4 3 2

Preface

Utilizing charts, graphs, diagrams and checklists instead of voluminous text, this book was written with real estate students, home owners, tenants and long-time professionals in mind. It is designed to quickly yet comprehensively take the reader through the intricacies of a multitude of real estate topics, and to then provide practical directions for further research. This book evolved through the preparation of numerous court exhibits for the classroom and for jury trials. In court trials, as in the everyday world of real estate, it is important to present complex topics in a clear, concise manner. While this book covers a vast spectrum of topics, the issues important to home owners and real estate professionals are truly at one's fingertips.

Acknowledgments

In writing and compiling this book, I was fortunate to have the assistance of many recognized professionals. My special thanks are given to the following: Orell C. Anderson, A. Terrance Dickens, Duane L. King, Rick Bell and Brent Hardwell. I also wish to thank my parents, Preston and Frances Bell. My greatest thanks goes to my wonderful wife, Melanie, and our three beautiful children, Michael, Steve and Britten.

RANDALL BELL

Melange Media Corporation
Publishers of
Professional Reference Books and Directories
11757 West Ken Caryl Ave. #F329
Littleton, CO 80127
(800) 92 BELLS (922-3557)

Important Notice

Real estate laws and practices vary from state to state and are subject to change. While this information is believed to be correct at the time of publication, no warranty (expressed or implied) is given as to its accuracy. This book is not a substitute for obtaining professional assistance. ***Always consult with a reputable CPA, attorney, broker or appraiser when making real estate decisions.***

Table of Contents

Architecture
&
Development

**Land Development
Section Chart
Zoning
Architectural Styles
Window Styles
Roof Styles
Insulation
Construction Terms
Parking
Measurement Tables**

LAND DEVELOPMENT
An Overview

Who builds buildings? An architect or planner may claim that he does, as might a building contractor. City officials often act as if they are responsible, as do banks and lenders. Sub-contractors will assert that they actually construct the building; however, the construction worker will be quick to point out that none of the others ever pounds a single nail, only he does. Clearly it requires numerous professionals to construct any building, but the greatest risks and liabilities are those of the land developer.

Land development can be the most lucrative or the most disastrous of professions depending, as it does, not only upon the developer's expertise and financial stability but, at times, on elements of just plain luck.

Among the risks in land development is the necessity of organizing multiple tasks which must then be supervised and performed by others. Any one of these assignments has the potential, if mishandled, of destroying the profitability of an entire project.

The processes inherent in land development can be illustrated in flow-chart form. This chart details the flow of activities commonly undertaken in a typical land development project, which has four primary phases:

1. **Project Conception & Planning**
    This includes everything from the initial idea to permits being issued.

2. **Loans & Financing**
    This includes the selection of a lender and the processes to secure all the funds that are required for the project.

3. **Construction**

   This phase includes all building activities from site grading to final tenant improvements.

4. **Management**

   This final phase includes all the steps required to lease or sell the property, from selecting a broker to achieving a stabilized cash flow.

The most common pitfalls in the area of land development are:

1. failure to accurately and completely estimate all costs and contingencies;

2. selection of under-qualified contractors, or the poor supervision of contractors;

3. over-optimism of market conditions; and

4. lack of knowledge in obtaining entitlements (approvals) from government agencies.

Land Development

Land Development

Project Conception and Planning

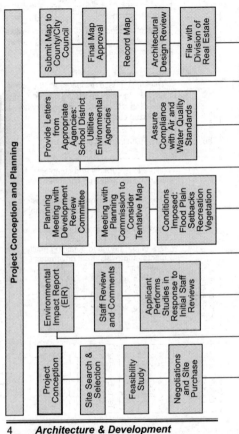

Project Conception and Planning			
Project Conception	Environmental Impact Report (EIR)	Planning Meeting with Development Review Committee	Provide Letters from Appropriate Agencies: School District Utilities Environmental Agencies	Submit Map to County/City Council
Site Search & Selection	Staff Review and Comments	Meeting with Planning Commission to Consider Tentative Map	Assure Compliance with Air and Water Quality Standards	Final Map Approval
Feasibility Study	Applicant Performs Studies in Response to Initial Staff Reviews	Conditions Imposed: Flood Plain Setbacks Recreation Vegetation		Record Map
Negotiations and Site Purchase				Architectural Design Review
				File with Division of Real Estate

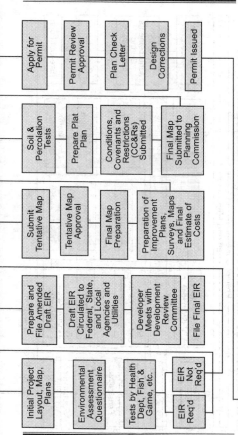

Land Development

To "Lender Selection"

Land Development

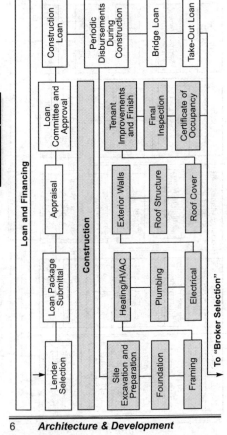

Loan and Financing

Lender Selection → Loan Package Submittal → Appraisal → Loan Committee and Approval → Construction Loan

Construction Loan → Periodic Disbursements During Construction → Bridge Loan → Take-Out Loan

Construction

Site Excavation and Preparation → Foundation → Framing

Heating/HVAC → Plumbing → Electrical

Exterior Walls → Roof Structure → Roof Cover

Tenant Improvements and Finish → Final Inspection → Certificate of Occupancy

To "Broker Selection"

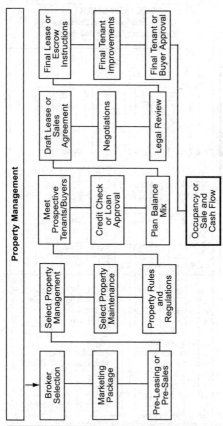

Land Development

SECTION CHART
One Section of Land Contains
One Square Mile or 640 Acres

W1/2 NW1/4 80 Acres	E1/2 NW1/4 80 Acres	NE1/4 160 Acres		
1320 Feet		2640 Feet		
NW1/4 SW1/4 40 Acres	WE1/4 SW1/4 40 Acres	N1/2 NW1/4 SE1/4 20 Acres / S1/2 NW1/4 SE1/4 20 Acres	W1/2 NE1/4 SE1/4 20 ACS	E1/2 NE1/4 SE1/4 10 Chains
SW1/4 SW1/4 40 Acres / 80 Rods	SE1/4 SW1/4 40 Acres / 440 Yards	NW1/4 SW1/4 SE1/4 / SW1/4 SW1/4 SE1/4	10 Acs / SE1/4 SW1/4 SE1/4	5 Acs / 10 Acs

1 Acre = 43,560 SqFt
1 Acre = 160 Sq Rods
1 Acre is approx 208.75 Feet Square
1 Acre is 8 Rods x 20 Rods (or any two numbers rods whose product is 160)
1 Chain = 66 Feet = 100 Links
1 Furlong = 660 Feet = 40 Rods
1 Link = 7.92 Inches

1 Mile = 8 Furlongs = 320 Rods = 80 Chains = 5,280 Feet
1 Rod = 16.5 Feet
1 Section = 1 Mile x 1 Mile
1 Section = 640 Acres
1 Sq Rod = 272.25 SqFt = 30.25 SqYards
1 Township = 6 Miles x 6 Miles
Township = 36 Sections

ZONING

Zoning designations are determined by cities or (in unincorporated areas) by counties. The designations can and do vary from city to city; however, these zoning designations are typical of those used in many areas.

R-1   Residential, One Family Dwelling

R-2   Residential, Duplex Family Dwelling

R-3

R-4   } These zoning designations are for multiple family dwellings (apartments) of various sizes and density

R-5

C   Commercial (Office and Retail)

M   Manufacturing (Industrial)

CM   Commercial/Manufacturing

A   Agricultural

OS   Open Space

RMP   Residential Mobilehome Park

PF   Public Facility

PB   Parking Building

P   Parking

Note that zoning designations include development constraints for setbacks, parking, building height limitations, lot coverage, floor area ratios, hillside restrictions, etc.

ARCHITECTURAL STYLES

Architecture, a profession in and of itself, revolves around developments and styles that have developed and evolved literally over centuries. In many cultures, the quality of a society's architecture is a direct reflection upon the status and sophistication of that society. Much like art and artists, architectural works last well beyond the life of the architect. Of course, many well-known architects receive much of the same admiration of society as do artists and musicians.

Architecture may very well have the same effect upon individual property owners. Some make their priorities of architectural styles a main criteria in selecting a property and insist upon a specific architectural style that reflects their outlooks and life-styles. Others simply desire a functional property. Recognizing these traits and addressing them is important to any real estate professional.

To assist in making these issues simpler, numerous architectural styles are illustrated which reflect the predominate and typical features of the major categories of architecture. In addition, numerous roof and window types are illustrated which detail and reflect further architectural choices that are available.

These drawings are also useful for brokers, agents and appraisers as a guide to categorizing and describing properties in listings and reports. Further, they are useful when consulting with clients about personal preferences.

French Provincial

Mission

Split Level

Dutch Colonial

A - Frame

Bungalow

Condominium

Contemporary

New England

Cape Cod

Town Home

Ranch

Regency

Early Georgian

Victorian

Modern American

Architecture Styles

Georgian

Architecture Styles

Southern Colonial

Tudor

Cottage

WINDOW STYLES

Basement

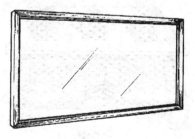

Picture

Window Styles

Manual Awning

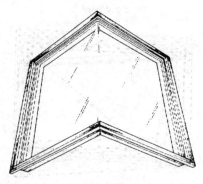

Corner Picture

Window Styles

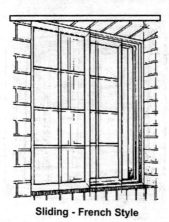

Sliding - French Style

Transom

Casement - French Style

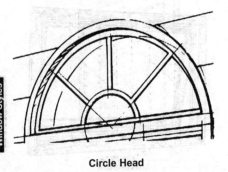

Circle Head

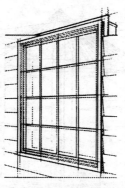

French Picture

Traverse

Window Styles

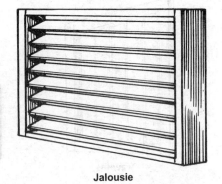

Fixed Bow

Jalousie

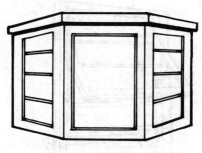

Fixed Bay

Double Hung

Window Styles

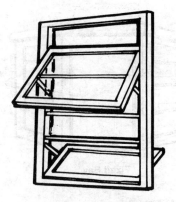

Projected Intermediate

Intermediate Combination

ROOF STYLES

Gable Roof

Parapet

Roof Styles

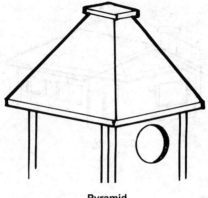

Pyramid

Saw-Tooth

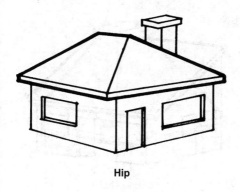

Hip

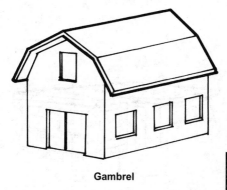

Gambrel

Roof Styles

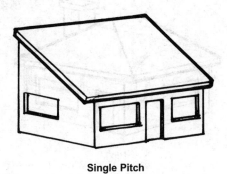

Single Pitch

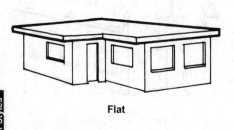

Flat

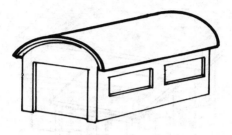

Semi-Circular

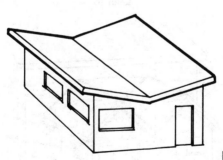

Butterfly or Double-Pitch

Roof Styles

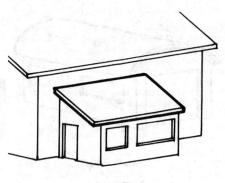

Lean To

M-Style

INSULATION

R-Value for Equivalent Building Materials

Each of these insulating and building materials is equivalent to R-19, which is a standard minimum within the construction industry. As the illustration depicts, only six inches of fiberglass batt will insulate the same as 18 feet of concrete or stone.

Proper insulation may save significant amounts on heating and cooling costs.

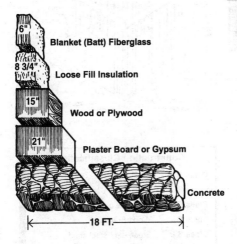

6" Blanket (Batt) Fiberglass

8 3/4" Loose Fill Insulation

15" Wood or Plywood

21" Plaster Board or Gypsum

Concrete

18 FT.

CONSTRUCTION TERMS

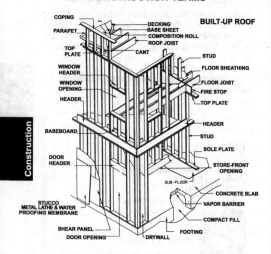

Construction Classification	
Class A	Steel Frame
Class B	Reinforced Concrete Frame
Class C	Concrete or Brick
Class D	Wood Frame
Class S	Steel, e.g., steel shed

Construction

Quality Classification

Class A--Excellent

Class B--Good

Class C--Low End

Class D--Near Obsolete

Class R--Renovated

Building Group Use Summary

A **Assembly**--Theaters, auditoriums, stadiums

B **Business**--Offices, retail, restaurants

E **Educational**--Schools, day care

F **Factories**--Mills, manufacturing plants

H **Hazardous**--Plants of explosive materials

I **Institutional**--Hospitals, nursing homes

R **Residential**--Homes, apartments, hotels

S **Storage**--Warehouse facilities

Construction

Fire Type Range

Type I--Most strict (non-combustible)

to

Type V--Least strict (combustible)

PARKING

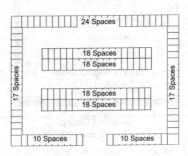

| 24 Spaces |
| 18 Spaces |
| 18 Spaces |

17 Spaces   17 Spaces

| 18 Spaces |
| 18 Spaces |

| 10 Spaces | | 10 Spaces |

Standard Parking Space

8' 6"   17' 0"

Compact Parking Space

8' 0"   15' 0"

Parking "Rule of Thumb"

Approximately 1 acre of parking = 150 parking spaces. (Assume 8'6" x 17'0" spaces and 25'+ aisles).

Note that the parking spaces may vary due to site configuration and/or mix of compact car spaces.

MEASUREMENT TABLES

English System - Linear Measure

12 Inches (In Or ")	= 1 Foot (Ft Or ')
3 Feet	= 1 Yard (Yd)
40 Rods	= 1 Furlong (Fur)
	= 220 Yards
	= 660 Feet
5½ Yards	= 1 Rod (Rd), Pole, Or Perch (16½ Feet)
1 International Nautical Mile	= 6076.1549 Feet

English System - Area Measure

144 Sq Inches	= 1 SqFt (Ft^2)
	= 1,296 Sq Inches
30¼ Sq Yards	= 1 Square Rod (Rd^2)
	= 272¼ SqFt
160 Sq Rods	= 1 Acre
	= 4,840 Sq Yards
	= 43,560 Square Feet
640 Acres	= 1 Square Mile (Mi^2)
1 Mile Sq	= 1 Section (Of Land)
6 Miles Sq	= 1 Township
	= 36 Sections
	= 36 Sq Miles

Note: Squares and Cubes may be abbreviated with *superscript* figures, i.e. Ft^2 = Square Foot and Ft^3 = Cubic Foot.

Measurement Tables

Gunter's or Surveyor's Chain Measure

7.92 Inches (In)	= 1 Link
100 Links	= 1 Chain (Ch)
	= 4 Rods
	= 66 Feet
80 Chains	= 1 Statute Mile (Mi)
	= 320 Rods
	= 5,280 Feet

Metric System - Linear Measure

10 Millimeters (Mm)	= 1 Centimeter (Cm)
10 Centimeters	= 1 Decimeter (Dm)
	= 100 Millimeters
10 Decimeters	= 1 Meter (M)
	= 1,000 Millimeters
10 Meters	= 1 Dekameter (Dam)
10 Dekameters	= 1 Hectometer (Hm)
	= 100 Meters
10 Hectometers	= 1 Kilometer (Km)
	= 1,000 Meters

Metric System - Area Measure

100 Sq Millimeters	= 1 Sq Centimeter (Cm^2)
10,000 Sq Centimeters	= 1 Square Meter (M^2)
	= 1,000,000 Sq Millimeters
100 Sq Meters	= 1 Are (A)
100 Ares	= 1 Hectare (Ha)
	= 10,000 Sq Meters
100 Hectares	= 1 Sq Kilometer (Km^2)
	= 1,000,000 Sq Meters

Surface Areas

1 Acre	= 43,560 Sq Feet
	= 4,840 Sq Yards
	= 0.405 Hectare
	= 160 Sq Rods
	= Apx 208.7 Sq Feet
1 Section	= 1 Mile^2
	= 640 Acres
1 Sq Rod	= 272.25 SqFt
	= 30.25 SqYards
1 Township	= 6 Miles^2
Township	= 36 Sections
1 Sq Centimeter (Cm^2)	= 0.155 Square Inch
1 Sq Decimeter (Dm^2)	= 15.500 Square Inches
1 Sq Foot (Ft^2)	= 929.030 Sq Centimeters
1 Sq Inch (In^2)	= 6.452 Square Centimeters
1 Sq Kilometer (Km^2)	= 247.105 Acres
	= 0.386 Square Mile
	= 1,196 Square Yards
1 Sq Meter (M^2)	= 10.764 Sq Feet
1 Sq Mile (Mi^2)	= 640 Acres
1 Sq Millimeter (Mm^2)	= 0.002 Sq Inch
1 Sq Rod (Rd^2), Sq Pole, Or Sq Perch	= 25.293 Sq Meters
1 Square Yard (Yd^2)	= 0.836 Sq Meter

Measurement Formulas

Area of a Circle	= Diameter^2 x .785398
Area of a Rectangle	= Length x Height
Area of Square	= Length^2
Area of Surface on Sphere	= Radius^2 x 3.1416 x 4
Area of Triangle	= 1/2 x Base x Height
Circumference of a Circle	= PI (3.14159) x Diameter

English And Metric Equivalents

Angstrom	= 0.1 Nanometer (Exactly)
	= 0.000 1 Micron (Exactly)
	= 0.000 000 1 Millimeter (Exactly)
	= 0.000 000 004 Inch
1 Cable's Length	= 120 Fathoms
	= 720 Feet
	= 219.456 Meters (Exactly)
1 Centimeter (Cm)	= 0.3937 Inch
1 Chain (Ch)	= 66 Feet
	= 20.1168 Meters (Exactly)
1 Chain (Engineers)	= 100 Feet
	= 30.48 Meters (Exactly)
1 Decimeter (Dm)	= 3.937 Inches
1 Dekameter (Dam)	= 32.808 Feet
1 Fathom	= 6 Feet
	= 1.8288 Meters (Exactly)
1 Foot (Ft)	= 0.3048 Meters (Exactly)
1 Inch (In)	= 2.54 Centimeters (Exactly)
1 Kilometer (Km)	= 0.621 Mile = 3,280.8 Feet
1 League (Land)	= 3 Statute Miles
	= 4.828 Kilometers
1 Link	= 7.92 Inches
	= 0.201 Meter
1 Link (engineers)	= 1 Foot
	= 0.305 Meter
1 Meter (M)	= 39.37 Inches
	= 1.094 Yards
1 Mile (Mi) (Statute Or Land)	= 5,280 Feet
	= 1.609 Kilometers
1 International Nautical Mile (INM)	= 1,852 Kilometers (Exactly)
	= 1.150779 Statute Miles
	= 6,076.11549 Feet
1 Rod (Rd), Pole, Or Perch	= 16½ Feet
	= 5½ Yards
	= 5.029 Meters
1 Yard (Yd)	= 0.9144 Meter (Exactly)

Legal & Title

Ownership Interests
Bundle of Rights
Escrow Flow Chart
Taxes
Eminent Domain
Legal & Title Glossary

OWNERSHIP INTERESTS

Note: <u>Always</u> *consult an attorney or CPA in title decisions. Specific laws may differ from state to state.*

	TENANCY IN COMMON
Parties	Any number of persons (can be husband and wife)
Division	Ownership can be divided into any number of interests equal or unequal.
Title	Each co-owner has a separate legal title to his undivided interest.
Possession	Equal right of possession
Conveyance	Each co-owner's interest may be conveyed separately by its owner.
Purchaser's Status	Purchaser will become a tenant in common with the other co-owners in the property.
Death	On co-owner's death his interest passes by will to his devisees or his heirs (no survivorship right).
Successor's Status	Devisees or heirs become tenants in common.
Creditor's Rights	Co-owner's interest may be sold at execution sale to satisfy creditor. Creditor becomes a tenant in common.
Presumption	Favored in doubtful cases except husband and wife cases

OWNERSHIP INTERESTS
(continued)

Note: <u>*Always*</u> *consult an attorney or CPA in title decisions.
Specific laws may differ from state to state.*

JOINT TENANCY

Any number of persons
(can be husband and wife)

Ownership interests must be equal.

There is only one title to the whole property.

Equal right of possession

Conveyance by one co-owner without
the others breaks his joint tenancy.

Purchaser will become a tenant in common
with the other co-owners in the property.

On co-owner's death his interest ends and
cannot be disposed of by will. The survivor owns
the property by survivorship.

The last survivor owns property in severally.

Co-owner's interest may be sold at execution
sale to satisfy creditor, breaking the joint tenancy
and allowing the creditor to become a tenant in
common.

Must be expressly stated; not favored

	COMMUNITY PROPERTY
Parties	Only husband and wife
Division	Ownership and managerial interests are equal except control of business is solely with managing spouse.
Title	Title is in the "community." Each interest is separate but management is united.
Possession	Both co-owners have equal management and control.
Conveyance	Personal property (except "necessities") may be conveyed for valuable consideration without consent of other spouse; real property requires written consent of other spouse, and separate interest cannot be conveyed except upon death.
Purchaser's Status	Purchase can acquire only whole title of community, cannot acquire a part.
Death	On co-owner's death ½ belongs to survivor in severally; ½ goes by will to descendant devisees or by succession to survivor.
Successor's Status	If passing by will, tenancy in common between devisee and survivor results.
Creditor's Rights	Property of community is liable for contracts of either spouse which are made after marriage. Co-owner's interest can't be sold separately. Whole property may be sold on execution to satisfy creditor.
Presumption	A strong presumption exists that property acquired by husband and wife is community

TENANCY IN PARTNERSHIP

Only partners (any number)

Ownership interest is in relation to interest in partnership.

Title is in the "partnership."

Equal right of possession exists, but only for partnership purposes.

Any authorized partner may convey whole partnership property. No partner may sell his interest in the partnership without the consent of his co-partners.

Purchaser can only acquire the whole title.

On partner's death, his partnership interest passes to the surviving partner pending liquidation of the partnership. Share of deceased partner then goes to his estate.

Heirs or devisees have rights in partnership interest but not in specific property.

Partner's interest cannot be seized or sold separately by his personal creditor, but his share of profits may be obtained by a personal creditor. Whole property may be sold on execution sale to satisfy partnership creditor.

Based upon the partnership status

BUNDLE OF RIGHTS

The most complete ownership of real estate is the "fee simple estate", which is the total and complete "bundle of rights", subject only to taxes (i.e. property taxes), police powers (i.e. zoning and land use regulations), eminent domain (the right for the government to take property for the public good, i.e. roads) and escheat (probate). All other forms of ownership are something less than this.

The Complete "Bundle of Rights"
Fee Simple Estate

ESCROW FLOW CHART
The Mechanics of Escrow

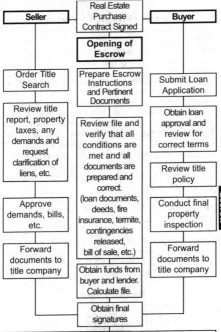

Seller		Buyer
	Real Estate Purchase Contract Signed	
	Opening of Escrow	
Order Title Search	Prepare Escrow Instructions and Pertinent Documents	Submit Loan Application
Review title report, property taxes, any demands and request clarification of liens, etc.	Review file and verify that all conditions are met and all documents are prepared and correct. (loan documents, deeds, fire insurance, termite, contingencies released, bill of sale, etc.)	Obtain loan approval and review for correct terms
		Review title policy
Approve demands, bills, etc.		Conduct final property inspection
Forward documents to title company	Obtain funds from buyer and lender. Calculate file.	Forward documents to title company
	Obtain final signatures	

Escrow

Authorize recording, prepare statements and disburse funds. Forward final documents to all parties: buyer, seller and lender. Close file.

Escrow Closed

TAXES

Interest - Primary Residence

Tax Facts: In most cases, the interest portion of residential loan payments is tax deductible. Some limitations apply, such as the home must be a primary or secondary residence; also, total capital improvements and acquisition loan amount cannot be greater than $1,000,000. To illustrate the effect of this tax deduction, assume a $100,000 loan, at 10% interest with a term of 30 years. This loan has annual payments that total $10,531, of which $9,975 is a tax deduction on the first year of the loan. The interest on home equity loans may also be deductible.

Tax Tip: Be careful of buying a home with a large amount of cash, and then planning to finance the home later. The house must be financed within 90 days of closing escrow, or the interest deduction will be limited to any acquisition loan balance plus $100,000. Acquisition debt interest may be deducted for loans up to $1,000,000. Limitations apply, consult with a tax advisor.

Property Taxes

Tax Facts: Real estate property taxes and certain points are tax deductible. If you bought or sold a home, you may have paid pro-rated property taxes. Refer to your closing escrow statement.

Depreciation

Tax Facts: If a property qualifies as a rental property, depreciation can be deducted in addition to property taxes and loan interest costs. Depreciation is a significant deduction and is often the incentive to convert a second home into a rental property.

Residential properties that were rented after December 31, 1986 are depreciated over 27 1/2 years on a "straight-line basis". (Rental properties being rented prior to this date continue the depreciation method already in use). This means that a depreciation deduction in the amount of approximately 3.36% of the depreciable capital investment may be taken each 12 month period.

Tax Tip: Depreciation is a particularly complex tax issue, so always consult with a qualified tax advisor. There is often confusion regarding what constitutes a capital improvement versus a repair, and the rules involving depreciation often change.

Tax Rates - 1997

Tax Facts: Home owners receive significant benefits and deductions on their income taxes. The major advantage not available to renters is the allowance to deduct mortgage interest payments, which makes up most of the total loan payment in the early years of a conventional loan. There are other important deductions as well, such as property taxes. Following are the tax rates for various taxable incomes for 1997:

Tax Rates - Single

Income			Tax Rate
$0	to	$ 24,650	15.0%
$ 24,650	to	$ 59,750	28.0%
$ 59,750	to	$124,650	31.0%
$124,650	to	$271,050	36.0%
$271,050 +			39.6%

Tax Rates - Married Filing Jointly

Income			Tax Rate
$0	to	$ 40,100	15.0%
$ 40,100	to	$ 96,900	28.0%
$ 96,900	to	$147,700	31.0%
$147,700	to	$263,750	36.0%
$263,750 +			39.6%

Tax Tip: Tax rates vary for married couples who file separately and for heads of households. Persons or couples with high incomes have limits on itemized deductions. State taxes, if any, are paid in addition to these Federal Income Taxes.

Always refer to a current tax guide or consult with an accountant to insure that you take all allowable deductions.

Equity Loans

Tax Facts: Home equity loans are second mortgages or trust deeds that are secured by a primary or secondary residence. Interest may be tax deductible on home equity loans up to $100,000. To be deductible, the total of the home equity debt and the primary mortgage cannot exceed the market value of the residence. Subject to the fair market value of the house and other debt, the first $100,000 of proceeds of equity loans may be used for any purpose.

Tax Tip: While the interest paid on home equity loans is generally deductible, the interest paid on consumer debt (credit cards and unsecured loans) is not. Some home owners refinance their consumer debt with equity loans in order to receive the tax benefits. Note that some states restrict home equity loans. Consult with your accountant.

Rollover

Taxes

Tax Facts: Capital gains taxes may be deferred if the seller purchases another home that costs the same or more than the "adjusted sales price" (sales price less sales expenses) of the home sold. The new home must be purchased within two years of the sale of the old home, and each time a residence is sold, any profits may be "rolled over". Certain improvements to the new home can be applied to its cost.

Tax Tip: While attempting to sell your property, in order to use your residence as a rental property to defer capital gains, you may rent it for up to two years before you sell it and buy a new home or return to live in the property. There is a limit on multiple rollovers within a two year period. Check with your tax advisor.

File Form 2119 "Sale or Exchange of Principal Residence" with your tax return.

Capital Gains

Tax Facts: Capital gains taxes may be applicable for a home that is sold that was owned for over one year, and if (a) the seller does not intend to buy another home, or (b) the replacement home is less than the sales price of the home that was sold. Capital gains are subject to a maximum rate of 28%, but exceptions apply. Capital

Capital Gain Computation		
1.		Sales Price
	-	<u>Sales Expenses</u>
	=	Adjusted Sales Price
2.		Cost Basis
		(Original Cost less Prior Deferrals)
	+	Capital Improvements
	-	<u>Depreciation</u>
	=	Adjusted Cost Basis
3.		Adjusted Sales Price
	-	<u>Adjusted Cost Basis</u>
	=	Capital Gain

Taxes

gains are computed as follows:

Tax Tip: Ask your tax preparer for a list of qualifying home improvements for capital gains purposes. Always keep an itemized list of all home improvements and receipts, as they may reduce tax liability. While listing fees, sales commissions, attorney's fees and other closing costs are not tax deductible, these costs are deductible for capital gains purposes, since they may be added to the cost basis or used to reduce the adjusted sales price.

Refer to IRS Publication 530, "Tax Information for First Time Homeowners."

55+ Tax Exemption

Tax Facts: Homeowners who are 55 or older have a once-in-a-lifetime exclusion that allows no capital gains taxes for up to $125,000 in profits resulting in the sale of their home. The home must have been occupied by the seller for at least 3 of the prior 5 years. This exception can only be used once, even if the limit was not met. In other words, if a sale results in a $50,000 exemption, the taxpayer may not later claim any portion of the $75,000 "remainder".

Tax Tip: The 55 Age Exemption may be used in conjunction with the Capital Gains Rollover, which may serve to further enhance the tax benefits. If contemplating or planning to marry, be sure to consult with a tax consultant in regards to claiming exemptions prior to the marriage as they may not exist after.

Taxes

Moving

Tax Facts: Certain moving related expenses may be a tax deduction if the move was a result of a new job or a job transfer. To deduct expenses incurred beginning in 1994, your new job location must be at least 50 miles farther from your former home than your old job location. (The location of your new home is not considered). Both homeowners and renters may deduct qualified moving expenses.

Tax Tip: Qualified moving costs include the reasonable costs of moving household goods and personal effects (including in-transit or foreign-move storage expenses) and travel (including lodging) to your new home.

You cannot deduct for meals while moving from your old residence to your new residence; travel expenses, meals, and lodging for pre-move house-hunting trips; meals and lodging while occupying temporary quarters in the area of your new job; or qualified residence sale, purchase, and lease expenses.

Taxes

Second Homes

Tax Facts: The tax implications of second homes may differ from a primary residence. A second residence is considered to be a second home, when rented, if it is occupied by the owner for the greater of <u>more than</u> 14 days per year, or more than 10% of the days it is rented. (If personal use is less than this, it is considered to be a vacation or rental property.) If the house is not rented at all during the year, no personal use is required.

Using this "test", all loan interest payments and property taxes are tax deductible for a second home.

Tax Tip: If the property is also rented, related property expenses (in addition to taxes and interest) may be deducted; however, the deduction may not exceed the total amount of rental income. In other words, losses are not permitted for tax calculations involving second homes.

Vacation or Rental Homes

Tax Facts: The tax implications of a vacation home differ from a primary or secondary residence. A home is considered to be a vacation home if it is occupied by the owner for <u>less than</u> 14 days per year, or if it is occupied less than 10% of the days it is rented, if it is rented for more than 140 days per year. (If personal use is more than this, it is considered to be a second home.)

If a residence passes the "test" of being a vacation or rental home then loan interest and property taxes may be deducted. In addition, depreciation and other rent related expenses may also be deducted, and losses up to $25,000 may be allowed. (Losses involve certain requirements of income and "active management".) If the home is occupied by the owner during the year, then deductions are prorated for the period of owner use.

Tax Tip: If the home is vacant for a portion of the year, use this formula to determine what portion of the loan interest and property taxes are deductible:

(total interest + taxes)
X *(percent of total rent days/365).*

If adjusted gross income before rental income is more than $100,000, consult with your tax advisor.

Points

Tax Facts: Points are up-front loan charges that are paid to the lender when the loan is originated. One point equals 1% of the principal loan amount. In 1994, the IRS announced that points paid by sellers are tax deductible by the buyer if they are used for the use of the loaned funds, not for services, and include settlement charges. Both seller and buyer points may be deducted by the buyer the year the house is purchased.

Tax Tip: Points may be deducted by buyers on Schedule A mortgage expenses. Buyers who closed escrow after December 31, 1990, can claim this deduction, amending their return by filing Form 1040X. Amended returns must be filed within three years from the date of original filing. There are also tax benefits with refinancing. Check with your tax advisor.

IRS Publications

The IRS provides free publications and forms that explain the tax aspects of real estate transactions. Request those publications that apply to your situation:

Publications

521 Moving Expenses
523 Selling Your Home
527 Residential Rental Property (Including Rental or Vacation Homes)
530 Tax Information for First-Time Homeowners
544 Sales and Other Dispositions of Assets
551 Basics of Assets

Forms

W-2 Wages and Tax Statement
2119 Sale of Your Home
3903 Moving Expenses
3903 Foreign Moving Expenses
4782 Employee Moving Expense Information
8822 Change of Address

You can order any of these publications or forms by calling 1-(800)TAX-FORM (1(800)829-3676). These publications and instructions are updated annually to reflect changes in the tax law. Be sure you get the

Taxes

EMINENT DOMAIN

Eminent Domain is the right of government to take or condemn a property from the property owner for the good of the general public (i.e. roadways, fire stations, road widening). When taking a property, the government is obligated to pay *"just compensation"*.

Value of Partial Acquisitions

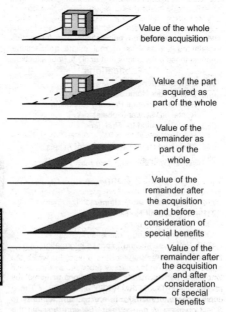

Value of the whole before acquisition

Value of the part acquired as part of the whole

Value of the remainder as part of the whole

Value of the remainder after the acquisition and before consideration of special benefits

Value of the remainder after the acquisition and after consideration of special benefits

Eminent Domain

Legal Definitions for Eminent Domain

Fair Market Value

The fair market value of the property taken is the highest price (or most likely price, depending on the jurisdiction) on the date of valuation that would be agreed to by a seller (being willing to sell but under no particular or urgent necessity for so doing, nor obliged to sell) and a buyer (being ready, willing, and able to buy but under no particular necessity for so doing), each dealing with the other with full knowledge of all the uses and purposes for which the property is reasonably adaptable and available.

The fair market value of property taken for which there is no relevant market is its value on the date of valuation as determined by any method of valuation that is just and equitable.

Damage to Remainder

Damage to the remainder is the damage, if any, caused to the remainder by either or both of the following:

• the severance of the remainder from the part taken

• the construction and use of the project for which the property is taken in the manner proposed by the plaintiff whether or not the damage is caused by a portion of the project located on the part taken

Benefit to Remainder

Benefit to the remainder is the benefit, if any, caused by the construction and use of the project for which the property is taken in the manner proposed by the plaintiff whether or not the benefit is caused by a portion of the project located on the part taken.

Note: Definitions differ in various jurisdictions. Consult with an eminent domain attorney.

Eminent Domain

Summation Method

A: Value of the whole before acquisition:
$\qquad$ \$_____

    Land: \$_____
    Improvements \$_____

B: Value of the part acquired as part of
the whole: \$_____
    Land: \$_____
    Improvements \$_____

C: Value of the remainder as part of
the whole: (A - B)   \$_____
    Land: \$_____
    Improvements \$_____

D: Value of the remainder after the
acquisition, disregarding special benefits.
    \$_____
    Land: \$_____
    Improvements \$_____

E: Severance Damages: (C - D) \$_____
    Land: \$_____
    Improvements \$_____

F: Value of the remainder after the
acquisition, considering special
benefits: \$_____
    Land: \$_____
    Improvements \$_____

G: Special Benefits: (F - D)   \$_____
    Land: \$_____
    Improvements \$_____

H: Net Damages or Net Special
Benefits (E - G):   \$_____
Note: Cannot be less than 0.

I: Total Just Compensations (B + H):
    \$_____

Note: If no special benefits, A - D = I

Summation Method - Cost to Cure (CTC)

A: Value of the whole before acquisition:
$$\$ \underline{\hspace{4cm}}$$
Land: $ \underline{\hspace{3cm}}
Improvements $ \underline{\hspace{3cm}}

B: Value of the part acquired as part of the whole:
$$\$ \underline{\hspace{4cm}}$$
Land: $ \underline{\hspace{3cm}}
Improvements $ \underline{\hspace{3cm}}

C: Value of the remainder as part of the whole (A - B)
$$\$ \underline{\hspace{4cm}}$$
Land: $ \underline{\hspace{3cm}}
Improvements $ \underline{\hspace{3cm}}

D_1: Value of the remainder after the acquisition, disregarding special benefits (uncured):
$$\$ \underline{\hspace{4cm}}$$
Land: $ \underline{\hspace{3cm}}
Improvements $ \underline{\hspace{3cm}}

E_1: Severance Damages (uncured):
$(C - D_1)$ $ \underline{\hspace{3cm}}
Land: $ \underline{\hspace{3cm}}
Improvements $ \underline{\hspace{3cm}}

D_2: Value of the remainder after the acquisition, disregarding special benefits (cured):
$$\$ \underline{\hspace{4cm}}$$
Land: $ \underline{\hspace{3cm}}
Improvements $ \underline{\hspace{3cm}}

E_2: Severance Damages (cured):
$(C - D_2 + CTC)$ $ \underline{\hspace{3cm}}
Land: $ \underline{\hspace{3cm}}
Improvements $ \underline{\hspace{3cm}}
Cost to Cure $ \underline{\hspace{3cm}}

F: Value of the remainder after the acquisition, considering special benefits: $ \underline{\hspace{3cm}}
Land: $ \underline{\hspace{3cm}}
Improvements $ \underline{\hspace{3cm}}

G: Special Benefits: $(F - D_2)$ $ \underline{\hspace{3cm}}
Land: $ \underline{\hspace{3cm}}
Improvements $ \underline{\hspace{3cm}}

H: Net Damages or Net Special Benefits $(E_2 - G)$.
Note: Cannot be less than 0. $ \underline{\hspace{3cm}}

I: Total Just Compensations (B + H):
$$\$ \underline{\hspace{4cm}}$$
Note: If no special benefits, $A - D_2 + CTC = I$

Eminent Domain

EMINENT DOMAIN GLOSSARY

Abutter's Rights -- a property owner's rights, by virtue of sharing a common property line, i.e. rights to view and to be viewed

Access Rights -- a property owner's right of ingress and egress on a street or highway

Acquisition or Taking -- the process of purchasing or condemning a property by a public agency

Air Rights -- the right to use airspace, usually at stated elevations, above the property

Benefit, general -- the gain obtained by the general public as a result of a public improvement

Benefit, special -- the gain obtained by a specific property owner as a result of a public improvement

Bundle of Rights -- the right to use a property, subject to taxation, police powers (i.e. zoning), eminent domain and escheat (state's rights if owner has no will)

Compensable Damages -- any loss in value caused by the taking, to be paid by the public agency under applicable law

Condemnation -- the legal proceedings to acquire property for public use

Condemnation, inverse -- a property owner's right to compel payment for damages or a taking, as a result of a public project

Condemnee -- the property owner

Condemner -- the public agency

Damages -- in a partial taking, the loss in value to the remainder parcel as a result of the taking; usually this is computed as the value of the property prior to the taking, less the value of the property in the "after condition"

Dedication -- a property owner's conferring, and the acceptance by a public agency, of property for public use (i.e. streets) without compensation paid to the property owner

Direct Compensation -- payment for land or improvements acquired for public use

Easement -- the right to use another's property for a stated use, i.e. a driveway, utility lines, drainage, access, etc.

Easement, aviation -- the right to fly over a property. These rights are generally associated with lands surrounding airports for take-off and landings, with specific elevations stated

Easement, drainage -- an easement for the flow of water

Easement, subsurface -- the right to utilize below grade portions of a property, for uses such as pipelines or cables

Egress -- the right and ability to exit a property

Eminent Domain -- the right of public agencies (or quasi-public agencies) to take private property for public use upon payment of just compensation

Expressway -- a main arterial or highway with intersections at grade

Highest and Best Use -- he physically possible, legally permissible, financially feasible and maximally productive use of a property

Ingress -- the right and ability to enter a property

Eminent Domain

Just Compensation -- the payment by a public agency to the property owner, as required by law, for the loss incurred resulting from taking or damaging the property for public purposes

Larger Parcel --the portion of a property that has unity of ownership, contiguity, and use

Partial Taking -- the condemnation of a portion of a property

Plottage -- the value added from the combining of two or more parcels into a single larger parcel that has greater development potential, as compared with the use of the individual smaller parcels

Proximity Damage -- the damages caused by proximity to a highway or other public project

Relocation Assistance -- advisory or financial assistance to persons or businesses displaced by a public program, to assist them in relocating to comparable areas

Remainder -- the portion of a property retained by the owner after a partial taking

Right of Way -- the land, such as a street or highway, utilized for transportation

Take -- the actual property (or portion of a property) that the condemner obtains for public use

Condemnation Appraisal Format

I. TITLE PAGE:

A. Property Identification
B. Case name and number, parcel number
C. Dates of value, condition (if different) and report
D. To whom submitted
E. Appraiser's name and address

II. LETTER OF TRANSMITTAL:

A. Date of report
B. Client or addressee
C. Identification of property
D. Case name, number and parcel number
E. Source and date of authorization to appraise
F. Dates of value and condition
G. Conclusions of value, gross severance damages, and special benefits
H. Reference to report which follows
I. Certification
J. Appraiser's signature

III. TABLE OF CONTENTS:

A. Important sections and subsections
B. Location of exhibits

IV. LIMITING CONDITIONS:

A. Limiting conditions and assumptions
B. Standardized and unique premises

V. SUMMARY OF CONCLUSIONS:

A. Value of Total Larger Parcel Before Taking
B. Value of Part Taken
C. Value Remainder Before Taking
D. Value Remainder After but Before Special Benefits

E. Gross Severance Damages
F. Value Remainder After Taking, Including Special Benefits
G. Special Benefits
H. Estimated Just Compensation

VI. INTRODUCTION AND PURPOSE OF APPRAISAL:

A. Nature of the appraisal problem with brief description of larger parcel, proposed acquisition and improvement, and remainder
B. Purpose of appraisal noting dates of value and condition (if different)
C. Definition of fair market value

VII. DETERMINATION OF LARGER PARCEL:

A. Unity of ownership
B. Physical contiguity
C. Unity of use

VIII. DESCRIPTION OF LARGER PARCEL:

Standard appraisal format and content with special concentration on factors most pertinent to proposed acquisition and improvement, i.e. access, drainage, view, site prominence, utilities, zoning and reasonable probability of change, current use, highest and best use

IX. VALUATION OF LARGER PARCEL:

Comprehensive valuation with three approaches, if applicable

X. THE PROPOSED ACQUISITION:

A. Location within Larger Parcel
B. Legal Description
C. Nature of interest being acquired
D. Size and shape - dimensions and area

Eminent Domain

E. Character of property within acquisition

F. Value of property within taking

XI. THE PROPOSED IMPROVEMENTS:

A. Source of information identifying engineers, architect, or others, and date interviewed

B. Titles of maps, plans, profiles, or renderings showing proposed improvement; general description of improvement; relationship of improvement to subject and its current and highest and best use

XII. EFFECT OF TAKING AND PROPOSED IMPROVEMENT ON REMAINDER PROPERTY:

A. Physical characteristics of property:

1. Size	5. View
2. Shape	6. Site prominence
3. Access	7. Drainage
4. Frontage Ratio	8. etc.

B. Property Efficiency and Developability:
   1. Yield
   2. Development costs (direct and indirect)
   3. Ability to contour
   4. Contiguity of developable area
   5. Proration of dedicated areas and arterials

C. Use:
   1. Current use
   2. Permitted use (zoning)
   3. Highest and best use

D. Marketability and Value:
   Must show how above changes in remainder's physical and utility characteristics manifest themselves in review of salability and value; first excluding effect of special benefits, if any, then with this enhancement

Eminent Domain

E. Market Data Approach-Support:
   Comparison with sales or previously severed
   and/or specially benefitted property

F. Method-Support:
   Reference to special engineering studies to
   reflect expenditures necessary to correct
   property deficiencies brought about by taking
   and construction; appraiser must show
   economic justification; limitations of method

G. Reconciliation:
   From above information, form final opinion of
   value of remainder with and without special
   benefits

XIII. FINAL COMPUTATION/CONCLUSIONS:

A. Value Total Larger Parcel Before Taking
B. Value Part Taken
C. Value Remainder Before Taking
D. Value Remainder After Taking, excluding
   Special Benefits
E. Gross Severance Damages
F. Value Remainder After Taking, with Special
   Benefits
G. Special Benefit
H. Estimated Just Compensation

XIV. EXHIBITS:
(Addenda or throughout report)

Photos - aerial and ground shots, Vicinity Map,
Neighborhood Map, Contour Parcel Map, Before
and After Maps, Proposed Improvement, Zoning
Map, Master Plan of Highways.

XV. ADDENDA:

• Market data sheets and maps
• List of persons interviewed with date
• Title Report and Legal Description, if lengthy
• Special studies, zoning information, etc.
• Qualifications

Eminent Domain

Legal & Title Glossary

AITD--all inclusive trust deed or "wrap loan"

ALTA--title insurance policy that expands risk

Basis Point--1/100th of 1% annually

Beneficiary--the lender, utilizing a trust deed

Fiduciary--a party having the duty to act in trust and good faith on behalf of another

Fixed Rate Mortgage--interest rate set for term

Graduated Mortgage--increased payments over time

Grant Deed--deed which transfers property

Grantee--one who receives a deed, the buyer

Grantor--one who gives a deed, the seller

Joint Tenancy--undivided, equal interest, survivorship to other tenant(s), may not be willed

Loan Type--e.g., construction, bridge, take-out, re-finance

Mortgage--creates lien as security for debt

Mortgagee-the borrower, utilizing a mortgage

Mortgagor--the lender, utilizing a mortgage

Optionee--one who purchases/receives an option

Optionor--one who sells/gives an option

Points--1 point = 1% of loan, effectively increases the interest rate

Prepayment--right to prepay loan

Recording--filing of deed with county office

Sale Leaseback--owner sells property and then leases from new owner

Seller Financing--seller takes note rather than cash

Stocker Exchange--tax-deferred exchange

Straight Note-interest only, principal paid at term

Teaser Rate--low initial rate to entice borrowers

Tenant in Severity--one who owns property alone

Tenants in Common--undivided ownership, may be unequal interests, no survivorship, may be willed

Title Insurance--protection from defects in title

Trust Deed--security for a loan

Trustee--the party who holds a property "in trust" for the benefit of another party (beneficiary); owes a fiduciary responsibility

Trustor--one who creates a trust

Variable Rate Mortgage--rate "floats" with index

Yield Maintenance--prepayment penalty on fixed loan

Income
Properties

Apartment
Office
Retail
Industrial
Lodging & Recreation

APARTMENT
Features

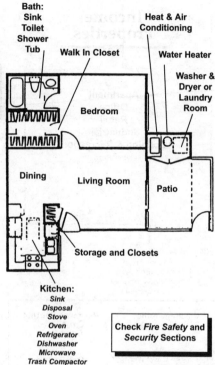

Bath:
Sink
Toilet
Shower
Tub

Walk In Closet

Heat & Air
Conditioning

Water Heater

Washer &
Dryer or
Laundry
Room

Apartment

Bedroom

Dining

Living Room

Patio

Storage and Closets

Kitchen:
Sink
Disposal
Stove
Oven
Refrigerator
Dishwasher
Microwave
Trash Compactor

Check *Fire Safety* and
***Security* Sections**

Apartment Measurement Guidelines

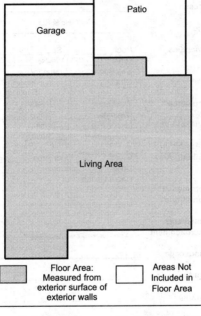

| Garage | Patio |
| Living Area | |

Floor Area:
Measured from
exterior surface of
exterior walls

Areas Not
Included in
Floor Area

Apartment

Coverage Ratio	**Revenues Per Unit**
Ground Floor Area	Gross Sales
Land Area	Gross SqFt
Floor Area Ratio (FAR)	**Occupancy**
Gross Building Area	Occupied Units
Land Area	Total Units

APARTMENT BUILDING FEATURES

Access _____

Age _____

Amenities
Pool _____ Spa _____
Tennis _____ Views: _____
Rec Room _____ Laundry _____
Other _____

Appliances
Washers _____ Dryers _____
Disposals _____ Range _____
Microwave _____ Trash _____
Refrigerators _____ Stove _____

Building Area
Gross_____ Floor Area_____
Units _____ Stories_____
Room Counts _____

Detrimental Conditions _____

Easements/ Encroachment _____

Landscape _____

Lighting _____

Parking _____

Permits _____

Signage _____

Termite Inspection _____

Utilities _____

Asbestos _____
ADA Compliance _____

Emergency Shutoff Controls

Electrical Panel _____

Gas Shutoff _____

Sewer Cleanout _____

Water Shut-off _____

Other _____

Energy Conservation

Door
Weather-stripping _____

Window
Weather-stripping _____

Insulation - Floor _____

Insulation - Wall _____

Insulation - Piping _____

Insulation - Ceiling _____

Energy Saving
Devices _____

Low - Flow Toilets _____

Other _____

Apartment Inspection

This checklist is designed to assist a prospective apartment building buyer in organizing the task of making a preliminary property inspection. A careful examination prior to making an offer or closing escrow can assist in revealing the real condition of the property and negotiating price. Make a visual inspection of all applicable items on this checklist, and categorize their priority. Note that this checklist is intended for preliminary use only and is not to be considered a substitute for a professional property inspection.

Repair/Replacement Priority

H = **High Priority** - These items must be repaired immediately and include any issues related to safety or significant non-performance.

M = **Medium Priority** - These items include deferred maintenance items that will soon require repair or replacement.

L = **Low Priority** - These items include cosmetics and upgrades. They are not required for safety but may enhance the appeal of the property.

Apartment Checklist

	Appears Serviceable	Not Applicable	Repair	Repair Priority H	M	L

Foundation

	Appears Serviceable	Not Applicable	Repair	H	M	L
Anchor Bolts	☐	☐	☐	☐	☐	☐
Basement	☐	☐	☐	☐	☐	☐
Crawlspace	☐	☐	☐	☐	☐	☐
Grading	☐	☐	☐	☐	☐	☐
Mud-sill	☐	☐	☐	☐	☐	☐
Sheer Panel	☐	☐	☐	☐	☐	☐
Soil Conditions	☐	☐	☐	☐	☐	☐
Slab on Grade	☐	☐	☐	☐	☐	☐
Other _____	☐	☐	☐	☐	☐	☐

Grounds/Site

	Appears Serviceable	Not Applicable	Repair	H	M	L
Exterior Stairs	☐	☐	☐	☐	☐	☐
Fences & Gates	☐	☐	☐	☐	☐	☐
Decks	☐	☐	☐	☐	☐	☐
Driveway	☐	☐	☐	☐	☐	☐
Retaining Walls	☐	☐	☐	☐	☐	☐
Sidewalks	☐	☐	☐	☐	☐	☐
Trip Hazards	☐	☐	☐	☐	☐	☐
Other _____	☐	☐	☐	☐	☐	☐

Restrooms

	Appears Serviceable	Not Applicable	Repair	H	M	L
Bathtub	☐	☐	☐	☐	☐	☐
Cabinets	☐	☐	☐	☐	☐	☐
Electrical	☐	☐	☐	☐	☐	☐
Heater	☐	☐	☐	☐	☐	☐
Sink	☐	☐	☐	☐	☐	☐
Shower	☐	☐	☐	☐	☐	☐
Toilet	☐	☐	☐	☐	☐	☐
Ventilation	☐	☐	☐	☐	☐	☐
Other _____	☐	☐	☐	☐	☐	☐

Apartment

	Appears Serviceable	Not Applicable	Repair	Repair Priority H M L

Roof

	Appears Serviceable	Not Applicable	Repair	H	M	L
Attic	☐	☐	☐	☐	☐	☐
Exposed Flashing	☐	☐	☐	☐	☐	☐
Gutters & Downspout	☐	☐	☐	☐	☐	☐
Main Roof	☐	☐	☐	☐	☐	☐
Vents	☐	☐	☐	☐	☐	☐
Other _____	☐	☐	☐	☐	☐	☐

Exterior

Exterior Walls	☐	☐	☐	☐	☐	☐
Trim	☐	☐	☐	☐	☐	☐
Other _____	☐	☐	☐	☐	☐	☐

Interior

Ceilings	☐	☐	☐	☐	☐	☐
Entry Doors	☐	☐	☐	☐	☐	☐
Exterior Doors	☐	☐	☐	☐	☐	☐
Fire Alarms	☐	☐	☐	☐	☐	☐
Fire Sprinklers	☐	☐	☐	☐	☐	☐
Floors	☐	☐	☐	☐	☐	☐
Interior Doors	☐	☐	☐	☐	☐	☐
Interior Walls	☐	☐	☐	☐	☐	☐
Lighting	☐	☐	☐	☐	☐	☐
Stairs	☐	☐	☐	☐	☐	☐
Stair Rails	☐	☐	☐	☐	☐	☐
Windows	☐	☐	☐	☐	☐	☐
Other _____	☐	☐	☐	☐	☐	☐

Kitchen & Appliances

Dishwasher	☐	☐	☐	☐	☐	☐
Disposal	☐	☐	☐	☐	☐	☐
Hood	☐	☐	☐	☐	☐	☐
Microwave	☐	☐	☐	☐	☐	☐
Refrigerator	☐	☐	☐	☐	☐	☐
Sink	☐	☐	☐	☐	☐	☐
Stove/Range	☐	☐	☐	☐	☐	☐
Washer/Dryer	☐	☐	☐	☐	☐	☐
Other _____	☐	☐	☐	☐	☐	☐

Apartment

	Appears Serviceable	Not Applicable	Repair	Repair Priority		
				H	M	L
Heating & Cooling						
Air Conditioner	☐	☐	☐	☐	☐	☐
Air Filters	☐	☐	☐	☐	☐	☐
Burners	☐	☐	☐	☐	☐	☐
Controls	☐	☐	☐	☐	☐	☐
Combustion Air	☐	☐	☐	☐	☐	☐
Distribution	☐	☐	☐	☐	☐	☐
Overall System	☐	☐	☐	☐	☐	☐
Venting	☐	☐	☐	☐	☐	☐
Other _____	☐	☐	☐	☐	☐	☐
Plumbing						
Fuel System	☐	☐	☐	☐	☐	☐
Hose Faucets	☐	☐	☐	☐	☐	☐
Main Line	☐	☐	☐	☐	☐	☐
Sprinklers	☐	☐	☐	☐	☐	☐
Supply Lines	☐	☐	☐	☐	☐	☐
Waste Lines	☐	☐	☐	☐	☐	☐
Water Heater	☐	☐	☐	☐	☐	☐
Water Heater Brackets	☐	☐	☐	☐	☐	☐
Water Heater T/P Valve	☐	☐	☐	☐	☐	☐
Other _____	☐	☐	☐	☐	☐	☐
Electrical						
Conductors	☐	☐	☐	☐	☐	☐
Main Panel	☐	☐	☐	☐	☐	☐
Outlets	☐	☐	☐	☐	☐	☐
Sub-Panels	☐	☐	☐	☐	☐	☐
Wiring	☐	☐	☐	☐	☐	☐
Other _____	☐	☐	☐	☐	☐	☐
Amenities						
Laundry Room	☐	☐	☐	☐	☐	☐
Pool/Spa	☐	☐	☐	☐	☐	☐
Rec Room	☐	☐	☐	☐	☐	☐
Tennis	☐	☐	☐	☐	☐	☐
Other _____	☐	☐	☐	☐	☐	☐

Apartment

Office

OFFICE
Building Features

Labels (clockwise from top):
- Building Mounted Signage
- Convenient Street Access
- ADA Parking
- Convenient
- Ample Parking
- Lighted
- Street Front-
- Surface Parking
- Landscape Buffer
- Drop Off & Delivery Area
- Mid-Block Entry
- Fenestration
- Landscape Irrigation
- Landscaping
- Street Set-Back
- Corner Location
- ADA Compliance Path of
- Appealing Design
- Subterranean Parking
- View Amenities
- Overall Design Appearance
- HVAC & Elevator
- Adequate Elevator Service
- Roof-Top Parking
- Street Exposure
- Demising Walls

Office Building Measurement Guidelines

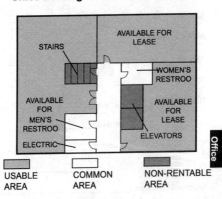

RENTABLE AREA = USABLE AREA + COMMON AREA

Note: Measurements are made from the inside surface of exterior walls and middle line of interior partitions. Columns which support building are not deducted.

CONSTRUCTION AREA = Total floor area, measured from the exterior walls, includes the basement

Add on (Load) Factor
$$\frac{\text{Rentable Area} - \text{Usable Area}}{\text{Usable Area}}$$

Coverage Ratio
$$\frac{\text{Ground Floor Area}}{\text{Land Area}}$$

Effective Ratio
$$\frac{\text{Net Rentable Area}}{\text{Gross Building Area}}$$

Floor Area Ratio (FAR)
$$\frac{\text{Gross Building Area}}{\text{Land Area}}$$

Vacancy Factor
$$\frac{\text{Vacant Area}}{\text{Rentable Area}}$$

OFFICE BUILDING FEATURES

Access _____

ADA Compliance _____

Age _____

Asbestos _____

Building Area   Gross _____

Rentable _____

Usable _____

No of Tenants _____

Corner/Mid-block _____

Easements _____

**Detrimental
Conditions** _____

Encroachment _____

Front Feet _____

Landscape _____

Lighting _____

Permits _____

Signage _____

Termite _____

Office

Emergency Shutoff Control

Electrical Panel _____

Gas Shutoff _____

Sewer Clean _____

Water Shutoff _____

Other _____

Energy Conservation

Door
Weather-stripping _____

Window
Weather-stripping _____

Insulation - Floor _____

Insulation - Wall _____

Insulation - Piping _____

Insulation - Ceiling _____

Energy Savings
Devices _____

Low - Flow Toilets _____

Other _____

Office

Office Checklist

Office Inspection

This checklist is designed to assist a prospective office building buyer in organizing the task of making a preliminary property inspection. A careful examination prior to making an offer or closing escrow can assist in revealing the real condition of the property and negotiating price. Make a visual inspection of all applicable items on this checklist, and categorize their priority. Note that this checklist is intended for preliminary use only and is not to be considered a substitute for a professional property inspection.

Repair/Replacement Priority

H = High Priority - These items must be repaired immediately and include any issues related to safety or significant non-performance.

M = Medium Priority - These items include deferred maintenance items that will soon require repair or replacement.

L = Low Priority - These items include cosmetics and upgrades. They are not required for safety but may enhance the appeal of the property.

Foundation	Appears Serviceable	Not Applicable	Repair	Repair Priority H	M	L
Anchor Bolts	☐	☐	☐	☐	☐	☐
Basement	☐	☐	☐	☐	☐	☐
Crawl Space	☐	☐	☐	☐	☐	☐
Grading	☐	☐	☐	☐	☐	☐
Mud-sill	☐	☐	☐	☐	☐	☐
Sheer Panel	☐	☐	☐	☐	☐	☐
Soil Conditions	☐	☐	☐	☐	☐	☐
Slab on Grade	☐	☐	☐	☐	☐	☐
Other _____	☐	☐	☐	☐	☐	☐

Grounds/Site						
Exterior Stairs	☐	☐	☐	☐	☐	☐
Fences & Gates	☐	☐	☐	☐	☐	☐
Decks	☐	☐	☐	☐	☐	☐
Driveway	☐	☐	☐	☐	☐	☐
Parking (Structure)	☐	☐	☐	☐	☐	☐
Retaining Walls	☐	☐	☐	☐	☐	☐
Sidewalks	☐	☐	☐	☐	☐	☐
Trip Hazards	☐	☐	☐	☐	☐	☐
Other _____	☐	☐	☐	☐	☐	☐

Restrooms						
Bathtub	☐	☐	☐	☐	☐	☐
Cabinets	☐	☐	☐	☐	☐	☐
Electrical	☐	☐	☐	☐	☐	☐
Heater	☐	☐	☐	☐	☐	☐
Sink	☐	☐	☐	☐	☐	☐
Shower	☐	☐	☐	☐	☐	☐
Toilet	☐	☐	☐	☐	☐	☐
Ventilation	☐	☐	☐	☐	☐	☐
Other _____	☐	☐	☐	☐	☐	☐

Office

	Appears Serviceable	Not Applicable	Repair	Repair Priority		
				H	M	L
Roof						
Attic	☐	☐	☐	☐	☐	☐
Exposed Flashing	☐	☐	☐	☐	☐	☐
Gutters & Downspout	☐	☐	☐	☐	☐	☐
Main Roof	☐	☐	☐	☐	☐	☐
Vents	☐	☐	☐	☐	☐	☐
Other _____	☐	☐	☐	☐	☐	☐
Exterior						
Exterior Walls	☐	☐	☐	☐	☐	☐
Trim	☐	☐	☐	☐	☐	☐
Other _____	☐	☐	☐	☐	☐	☐
Interior						
Ceilings	☐	☐	☐	☐	☐	☐
Elevator	☐	☐	☐	☐	☐	☐
Entry Doors	☐	☐	☐	☐	☐	☐
Exterior Doors	☐	☐	☐	☐	☐	☐
Fire Alarms	☐	☐	☐	☐	☐	☐
Fire Sprinklers	☐	☐	☐	☐	☐	☐
Floors	☐	☐	☐	☐	☐	☐
Interior Doors	☐	☐	☐	☐	☐	☐
Interior Walls	☐	☐	☐	☐	☐	☐
Lighting	☐	☐	☐	☐	☐	☐
Stairs	☐	☐	☐	☐	☐	☐
Stair Rails	☐	☐	☐	☐	☐	☐
Windows	☐	☐	☐	☐	☐	☐
Other _____	☐	☐	☐	☐	☐	☐
Kitchenette & Lunchroom						
Dishwasher	☐	☐	☐	☐	☐	☐
Disposal	☐	☐	☐	☐	☐	☐
Hood	☐	☐	☐	☐	☐	☐
Microwave	☐	☐	☐	☐	☐	☐
Refrigerator	☐	☐	☐	☐	☐	☐
Sink	☐	☐	☐	☐	☐	☐
Stove/Range	☐	☐	☐	☐	☐	☐
Other _____	☐	☐	☐	☐	☐	☐

Office

	Appears Serviceable	Not Applicable	Repair	Repair Priority		
				H	M	L
Heating & Cooling						
Air Conditioner	❏	❏	❏	❏	❏	❏
Air Filters	❏	❏	❏	❏	❏	❏
Burners	❏	❏	❏	❏	❏	❏
Controls	❏	❏	❏	❏	❏	❏
Combustion Air	❏	❏	❏	❏	❏	❏
Distribution	❏	❏	❏	❏	❏	❏
Overall System	❏	❏	❏	❏	❏	❏
Venting	❏	❏	❏	❏	❏	❏
Other _____	❏	❏	❏	❏	❏	❏
Plumbing						
Fuel System	❏	❏	❏	❏	❏	❏
Hose Faucets	❏	❏	❏	❏	❏	❏
Main Line	❏	❏	❏	❏	❏	❏
Sprinklers	❏	❏	❏	❏	❏	❏
Supply Lines	❏	❏	❏	❏	❏	❏
Waste Lines	❏	❏	❏	❏	❏	❏
Water Heater	❏	❏	❏	❏	❏	❏
Water Heater Brackets	❏	❏	❏	❏	❏	❏
Water Heater T/P Valve	❏	❏	❏	❏	❏	❏
Other _____	❏	❏	❏	❏	❏	❏
Electrical						
Conductors	❏	❏	❏	❏	❏	❏
Main Panel	❏	❏	❏	❏	❏	❏
Outlets	❏	❏	❏	❏	❏	❏
Sub-Panels	❏	❏	❏	❏	❏	❏
Wiring	❏	❏	❏	❏	❏	❏
Other _____	❏	❏	❏	❏	❏	❏
Amenities						
Exercise Room	❏	❏	❏	❏	❏	❏
Fountain	❏	❏	❏	❏	❏	❏
Other _____	❏	❏	❏	❏	❏	❏

Office

Center Features

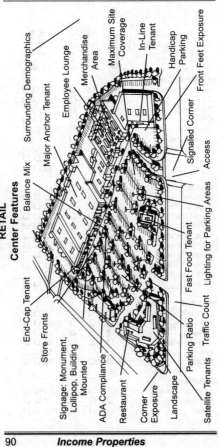

Surrounding Demographics

Maximum Site Coverage

In-Line Tenant

Handicap Parking

Front Feet Exposure

Employee Lounge

Merchandise Area

Signaled Corner

Access

Major Anchor Tenant

Balance Mix

Fast Food Tenant

Lighting for Parking Areas

End-Cap Tenant

Store Fronts

Signage: Monument, Lollipop, Building Mounted

ADA Compliance

Restaurant

Corner Exposure

Landscape

Parking Ratio

Satellite Tenants

Traffic Count

Retail Measurement Guidelines

| STORAGE & EMPLOYEES' LOUNGE | MEN'S RESTROO | WOMEN'S RESTROO |

RETAIL FLOOR

CHECK-OUT AREA

RETAIL FLOOR · NON RETAIL FLOOR

Add On (Load) Factor	**Floor Area Ratio (FAR)**
$\dfrac{\text{Rentable Area - Usable Area}}{\text{Usable Area}}$	$\dfrac{\text{Gross Building Area}}{\text{Land Area}}$
Coverage Ratio	**Sales Per SqFt**
$\dfrac{\text{Ground Floor Area}}{\text{Land Area}}$	$\dfrac{\text{Gross Sales}}{\text{Gross SqFt}}$
Effective Ratio	**Vacancy Factor**
$\dfrac{\text{Net Rentable Area}}{\text{Gross Building Area}}$	$\dfrac{\text{Vacant Area}}{\text{Rentable Area}}$

RETAIL GROSS LEASABLE AREA (GLA)

Measurements are made from the exterior surface of exterior walls and the middle line of interior partitions. Columns which support building are not deducted.

RETAIL BUILDING FEATURES

Access _____

ADA Compliance _____

Age _____

Anchor Tenant _____

Asbestos _____

Balance Mix _____

Building Area
Gross _____
Rentable _____
Usable _____
No. of Tenants _____

Commercial Business District _____

Co-Op Ads _____

Corner/Mid-block _____

Easements _____

Detrimental Conditions _____

Encroachment _____

Front Feet _____

Landscape _____

Lighting _____

Merchant Assoc. _____

Retail

Permits _____

Retail Windows _____

Rules & Regs _____

Satellite Tenants _____

Signage _____

SKUs _____

Termite _____

Traffic Counts _____

Emergency Shutoff Control

Electrical Panel _____
Gas Shutoff _____
Sewer Clean _____
Water Shutoff _____
Other _____

Energy Conservation

Door
Weather-strip _____
Window
Weather-stripping _____
Insulation - Floor _____
Insulation - Wall _____
Insulation - Piping _____
Insulation - Ceiling _____
Savings Devices _____
Low - Flow Toilets _____

Other _____

Retail

Retail Inspection

This checklist is designed to assist a prospective retail building buyer in organizing the task of making a preliminary property inspection. A careful examination prior to making an offer or closing escrow can assist in revealing the real condition of the property and negotiating price. Make a visual inspection of all applicable items on this checklist, and categorize their priority. Note that this checklist is intended to be for preliminary use only and is not to be considered a substitute for a professional property inspection.

Repair/Replacement Priority

H = **High Priority** - These items must be repaired immediately and include any issues related to safety or significant non-performance.

M = **Medium Priority** - These items include deferred maintenance items that will soon require repair or replacement.

L = **Low Priority** - These items include cosmetics and upgrades. They are not required for safety but may enhance the appeal of the property.

Retail

Retail Checklist

	Appears Serviceable	Not Applicable	Repair	Repair Priority		
				H	M	L
Foundation						
Anchor Bolts	❑	❑	❑	❑	❑	❑
Basement	❑	❑	❑	❑	❑	❑
Crawl Space	❑	❑	❑	❑	❑	❑
Grading	❑	❑	❑	❑	❑	❑
Mud-sill	❑	❑	❑	❑	❑	❑
Sheer Panel	❑	❑	❑	❑	❑	❑
Soil Conditions	❑	❑	❑	❑	❑	❑
Slab on Grade	❑	❑	❑	❑	❑	❑
Other _____	❑	❑	❑	❑	❑	❑
Grounds/Site						
Exterior Stairs	❑	❑	❑	❑	❑	❑
Fences & Gates	❑	❑	❑	❑	❑	❑
Decks	❑	❑	❑	❑	❑	❑
Driveway	❑	❑	❑	❑	❑	❑
Parking (Structure)	❑	❑	❑	❑	❑	❑
Retaining Walls	❑	❑	❑	❑	❑	❑
Sidewalks	❑	❑	❑	❑	❑	❑
Trip Hazards	❑	❑	❑	❑	❑	❑
Other _____	❑	❑	❑	❑	❑	❑
Restrooms						
Bathtub	❑	❑	❑	❑	❑	❑
Cabinets	❑	❑	❑	❑	❑	❑
Electrical	❑	❑	❑	❑	❑	❑
Heater	❑	❑	❑	❑	❑	❑
Sink	❑	❑	❑	❑	❑	❑
Shower	❑	❑	❑	❑	❑	❑
Toilet	❑	❑	❑	❑	❑	❑
Ventilation	❑	❑	❑	❑	❑	❑
Other _____	❑	❑	❑	❑	❑	❑

Retail

	Appears Serviceable	Not Applicable	Repair	Repair Priority		
				H	M	L
Roof						
Attic	☐	☐	☐	☐	☐	☐
Exposed Flashing	☐	☐	☐	☐	☐	☐
Gutters & Downspout	☐	☐	☐	☐	☐	☐
Main Roof	☐	☐	☐	☐	☐	☐
Vents	☐	☐	☐	☐	☐	☐
Other _____	☐		☐	☐	☐	☐
Exterior						
Exterior Walls	☐	☐	☐	☐	☐	☐
Trim	☐	☐	☐	☐	☐	☐
Other _____	☐	☐	☐	☐	☐	☐
Interior						
Ceilings	☐	☐	☐	☐	☐	☐
Elevator	☐	☐	☐	☐	☐	☐
Entry Doors	☐	☐	☐	☐	☐	☐
Exterior Doors	☐	☐	☐	☐	☐	☐
Fire Alarms	☐	☐	☐	☐	☐	☐
Fire Sprinklers	☐	☐	☐	☐	☐	☐
Floors	☐	☐	☐	☐	☐	☐
Interior Doors	☐	☐	☐	☐	☐	☐
Interior Walls	☐	☐	☐	☐	☐	☐
Lighting	☐	☐	☐	☐	☐	☐
Stairs	☐	☐	☐	☐	☐	☐
Stair Rails	☐	☐	☐	☐	☐	☐
Windows	☐	☐	☐	☐	☐	☐
Other _____	☐	☐	☐	☐	☐	☐
Kitchenette & Lunchroom						
Dishwasher	☐	☐	☐	☐	☐	☐
Disposal	☐	☐	☐	☐	☐	☐
Hood	☐	☐	☐	☐	☐	☐
Microwave	☐	☐	☐	☐	☐	☐
Refrigerator	☐	☐	☐	☐	☐	☐
Sink	☐	☐	☐	☐	☐	☐
Stove/Range	☐	☐	☐	☐	☐	☐
Other _____	☐	☐	☐	☐	☐	☐

Retail

	Appears Serviceable	Not Applicable	Repair	Repair Priority		
				H	M	L
Heating & Cooling						
Air Conditioner	☐	☐	☐	☐	☐	☐
Air Filters	☐	☐	☐	☐	☐	☐
Burners	☐	☐	☐	☐	☐	☐
Controls	☐	☐	☐	☐	☐	☐
Combustion Air	☐	☐	☐	☐	☐	☐
Distribution	☐	☐	☐	☐	☐	☐
Overall System	☐	☐	☐	☐	☐	☐
Venting	☐	☐	☐	☐	☐	☐
Other _____			☐	☐	☐	☐
Plumbing						
Fuel System	☐	☐	☐	☐	☐	☐
Hose Faucets	☐	☐	☐	☐	☐	☐
Main Line	☐	☐	☐	☐	☐	☐
Sprinklers	☐	☐	☐	☐	☐	☐
Supply Lines	☐	☐	☐	☐	☐	☐
Waste Lines	☐	☐	☐	☐	☐	☐
Water Heater	☐	☐	☐	☐	☐	☐
Water Heater Brackets	☐	☐	☐	☐	☐	☐
Water Heater T/P Valve	☐	☐	☐	☐	☐	☐
Other _____			☐	☐	☐	☐
Electrical						
Conductors	☐	☐	☐	☐	☐	☐
Main Panel	☐	☐	☐	☐	☐	☐
Outlets	☐	☐	☐	☐	☐	☐
Sub-Panels	☐	☐	☐	☐	☐	☐
Wiring	☐	☐	☐	☐	☐	☐
Other _____			☐	☐	☐	☐
Amenities						
Exercise Room	☐	☐	☐	☐	☐	☐
Other _____			☐	☐	☐	☐

Retail

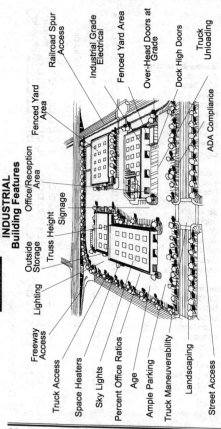

INDUSTRIAL
Building Features

Railroad Spur Access

Industrial Grade Electrical

Fenced Yard Area

Over-Head Doors at Grade

Truck Unloading

Dock High Doors

ADA Compliance

Fenced Yard Area

Office/Reception Area

Truss Height

Signage

Outside Storage

Lighting

Freeway Access

Truck Access

Space Heaters

Sky Lights

Percent Office Ratios

Age

Ample Parking

Truck Maneuverability

Landscaping

Street Access

Industrial

Industrial Measurement Guidelines

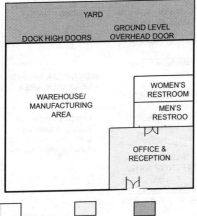

WAREHOUSE FLOOR — OFFICE — YARD/STORAGE

RENTABLE AREA = USABLE AREA + COMMON AREA

Note: Measurements are made from the inside surface of exterior walls and the middle line of interior partitions. Columns that support the building are not deducted.

CONSTRUCTION AREA = Total Floor Area, measured from the exterior walls and includes any basement

Industrial Building Measurement Ratios

INDUSTRIAL ADD-ON (LOAD) FACTOR:

$$\frac{\text{Gross Area} - \text{Warehouse Area}}{\text{Warehouse Area}}$$

COVERAGE RATIO:

$$\frac{\text{Ground Floor Area}}{\text{Land Area}}$$

INDUSTRIAL EFFECTIVE RATIO:

$$\frac{\text{Net Warehouse Area}}{\text{Gross Building Area}}$$

FLOOR AREA RATIO (FAR):

$$\frac{\text{Gross Building Area}}{\text{Land Area}}$$

VACANCY FACTOR:

$$\frac{\text{Vacant Area}}{\text{Rentable Area}}$$

PERCENT OFFICE:

$$\frac{\text{Office Area}}{\text{Total Area}}$$

INDUSTRIAL GROSS LEASABLE AREA (GLA):

Measured from the exterior center wall (outside surface) to center of joint partition walls

Inches to Decimals	
1"	= 0.083
2"	= 0.167
3"	= 0.250
4"	= 0.333
5"	= 0.417
6"	= 0.500
7"	= 0.583
8"	= 0.667
9"	= 0.750
10"	= 0.833
11"	= 0.917
12"	= 1.000

Industrial

INDUSTRIAL BUILDING FEATURES

Access _____

Age _____

Building Area Gross _____ Rentable _____
Usable_____

Corner/Midblock _____

Dock High Doors _____

Easement _____

Electrical _____

Encroachment _____

Front Feet _____

Landscape _____

Lighting _____

Overhead Doors _____

**Permits for
Additions, etc.** _____

Rail Served _____

Signage _____

Termite Inspection _____

Truss Height _____

Yard Area _____

Industrial

Asbestos _____

ADA Compliance _____

Emergency Shutoff Controls

Electrical Panel _____

Gas Shutoff _____

Sewer Cleanout _____

Water Shut-off _____

Other _____

Energy Conservation

Door
Weather-stripping _____

Window
Weather-stripping _____

Insulation - Floor _____

Insulation - Wall _____

Insulation - Piping _____

Insulation - Ceiling _____

Energy Saving
Devices _____

Low - Flow Toilets _____

Other _____

Industrial

Industrial Inspection

This checklist is designed to assist a prospective industrial building buyer in organizing the task of making a preliminary property inspection. A careful examination prior to making an offer or closing escrow can assist in revealing the real condition of the property and negotiating price. Make a visual inspection of all applicable items on this checklist, and categorize their priority. Note that this checklist is intended for preliminary use only and is not to be considered a substitute for a professional property inspection.

Repair/Replacement Priority

H = **High Priority** - These items must be repaired immediately and include any issues related to safety or significant non-performance.

M = **Medium Priority** - These items include deferred maintenance items that will require repair or replacement soon.

L = **Low Priority** - These items include cosmetics and upgrades. They are not required for safety but may enhance the appeal of the property.

Industrial

Industrial Checklist

	Appears Serviceable	Not Applicable	Repair	Repair Priority		
				H	M	L
Foundation						
Anchor Bolts	❏	❏	❏	❏	❏	❏
Basement	❏	❏	❏	❏	❏	❏
Crawl Space	❏	❏	❏	❏	❏	❏
Grading	❏	❏	❏	❏	❏	❏
Mud-sill	❏	❏	❏	❏	❏	❏
Sheer Panel	❏	❏	❏	❏	❏	❏
Soil Conditions	❏	❏	❏	❏	❏	❏
Slab on Grade	❏	❏	❏	❏	❏	❏
Other _____	❏	❏	❏	❏	❏	❏
Grounds/Site						
Exterior Stairs	❏	❏	❏	❏	❏	❏
Fences & Gates	❏	❏	❏	❏	❏	❏
Decks	❏	❏	❏	❏	❏	❏
Driveway	❏	❏	❏	❏	❏	❏
Parking (Structure)	❏	❏	❏	❏	❏	❏
Retaining Walls	❏	❏	❏	❏	❏	❏
Sidewalks	❏	❏	❏	❏	❏	❏
Trip Hazards	❏	❏	❏	❏	❏	❏
Yard Area	❏	❏	❏	❏	❏	❏
Other _____	❏	❏	❏	❏	❏	❏
Restrooms						
Bathtub	❏	❏	❏	❏	❏	❏
Cabinets	❏	❏	❏	❏	❏	❏
Electrical	❏	❏	❏	❏	❏	❏
Heater	❏	❏	❏	❏	❏	❏
Sink	❏	❏	❏	❏	❏	❏
Shower	❏	❏	❏	❏	❏	❏
Toilet	❏	❏	❏	❏	❏	❏
Ventilation	❏	❏	❏	❏	❏	❏
Other _____	❏	❏	❏	❏	❏	❏

Industrial

	Appears Serviceable	Not Applicable	Repair	Repair Priority		
				H	M	L
Roof						
Attic	☐	☐	☐	☐	☐	☐
Exposed Flashing	☐	☐	☐	☐	☐	☐
Gutters & Downspout	☐	☐	☐	☐	☐	☐
Main Roof	☐	☐	☐	☐	☐	☐
Vents	☐	☐	☐	☐	☐	☐
Other _____	☐	☐	☐	☐	☐	☐
Exterior						
Exterior Walls	☐	☐	☐	☐	☐	☐
Trim	☐	☐	☐	☐	☐	☐
Other _____	☐	☐	☐	☐	☐	☐
Interior						
Ceilings	☐	☐	☐	☐	☐	☐
Elevator	☐	☐	☐	☐	☐	☐
Entry Doors	☐	☐	☐	☐	☐	☐
Exterior Doors	☐	☐	☐	☐	☐	☐
Fire Alarms	☐	☐	☐	☐	☐	☐
Fire Sprinklers	☐	☐	☐	☐	☐	☐
Floors	☐	☐	☐	☐	☐	☐
Interior Doors	☐	☐	☐	☐	☐	☐
Interior Walls	☐	☐	☐	☐	☐	☐
Lighting	☐	☐	☐	☐	☐	☐
Stairs	☐	☐	☐	☐	☐	☐
Stair Rails	☐	☐	☐	☐	☐	☐
Windows	☐	☐	☐	☐	☐	☐
Other _____	☐	☐	☐	☐	☐	☐
Kitchenette & Lunchroom						
Dishwasher	☐	☐	☐	☐	☐	☐
Disposal	☐	☐	☐	☐	☐	☐
Hood	☐	☐	☐	☐	☐	☐
Microwave	☐	☐	☐	☐	☐	☐
Refrigerator	☐	☐	☐	☐	☐	☐
Sink	☐	☐	☐	☐	☐	☐
Stove/Range	☐	☐	☐	☐	☐	☐
Other _____	☐	☐	☐	☐	☐	☐

Industrial

	Appears Serviceable	Not Applicable	Repair	Repair Priority H M L

Heating & Cooling

	Appears Serviceable	Not Applicable	Repair	H	M	L
Air Conditioner	☐	☐	☐	☐	☐	☐
Air Filters	☐	☐	☐	☐	☐	☐
Burners	☐	☐	☐	☐	☐	☐
Controls	☐	☐	☐	☐	☐	☐
Combustion Air	☐	☐	☐	☐	☐	☐
Distribution	☐	☐	☐	☐	☐	☐
Overall System	☐	☐	☐	☐	☐	☐
Venting	☐	☐	☐	☐	☐	☐
Other _____	☐	☐	☐	☐	☐	☐

Plumbing

	Appears Serviceable	Not Applicable	Repair	H	M	L
Fuel System	☐	☐	☐	☐	☐	☐
Hose Faucets	☐	☐	☐	☐	☐	☐
Main Line	☐	☐	☐	☐	☐	☐
Sprinklers	☐	☐	☐	☐	☐	☐
Supply Lines	☐	☐	☐	☐	☐	☐
Waste Lines	☐	☐	☐	☐	☐	☐
Water Heater	☐	☐	☐	☐	☐	☐
Water Heater Brackets	☐	☐	☐	☐	☐	☐
Water Heater T/P Valve	☐	☐	☐	☐	☐	☐
Other _____	☐	☐	☐	☐	☐	☐

Electrical

	Appears Serviceable	Not Applicable	Repair	H	M	L
Conductors	☐	☐	☐	☐	☐	☐
Main Panel	☐	☐	☐	☐	☐	☐
Outlets	☐	☐	☐	☐	☐	☐
Sub Panels	☐	☐	☐	☐	☐	☐
Wiring	☐	☐	☐	☐	☐	☐
Other _____	☐	☐	☐	☐	☐	☐

Amenities

	Appears Serviceable	Not Applicable	Repair	H	M	L
Crane/Lifts	☐	☐	☐	☐	☐	☐
Exercise Room	☐	☐	☐	☐	☐	☐
Other _____	☐	☐	☐	☐	☐	☐

Industrial

LODGING & RECREATION
Hotel Features

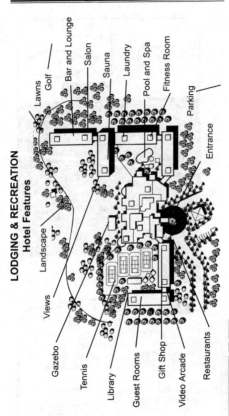

Lawns
Golf
Bar and Lounge
Salon
Sauna
Laundry
Pool and Spa
Fitness Room
Parking
Entrance
Landscape
Views
Gazebo
Tennis
Library
Guest Rooms
Gift Shop
Video Arcade
Restaurants

Lodging & Recreation

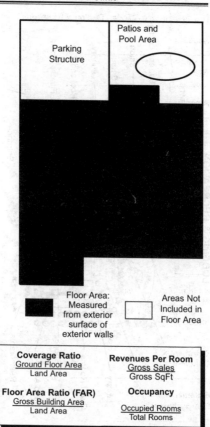

Floor Area:
Measured
from exterior
surface of
exterior walls

Areas Not
Included in
Floor Area

Coverage Ratio
Ground Floor Area
Land Area

Revenues Per Room
Gross Sales
Gross SqFt

Floor Area Ratio (FAR)
Gross Building Area
Land Area

Occupancy
Occupied Rooms
Total Rooms

Lodging & Recreation

HOTEL AND MOTEL BUILDING FEATURES

Access
_____

Age
_____

Amenities	Pool _____	Spa
_____	Tennis _____	Views
	Rec Room _____	Laundry
_____	Other	
_____		

Appliances	Washers _____	Dryers
_____	Disposals _____	Ranges
_____	Microwaves _____	Trash
_____	Refrigerators _____	Stoves
_____		

Building Area	Gross _____ Floor	
Area_____	Rooms _____	
Stories_____	Room Counts	
	_____	

Detrimental Conditions
_____

Easements/ Encroachment
_____

Lodging & Recreation

Landscape

Lighting

Parking

Permits

Signage

Termite Inspection

Utilities

Asbestos

ADA Compliance

Emergency Shutoff Controls

Electrical Panel

Gas Shutoff

Sewer Cleanout

Water Shut-off

Other

Hotel and Motel Inspection

This checklist is designed to assist a prospective motel or hotel buyer in organizing the task of making a preliminary property inspection. A careful examination prior to making an offer or closing escrow can assist in revealing the real condition of the property and negotiating price. Make a visual inspection of all applicable items on this checklist, and categorize their priority. Note that this checklist is intended for preliminary use only and is not to be considered a substitute for a professional property inspection.

Repair/Replacement Priority

H = **High Priority** - These items must be repaired immediately and include any issues related to safety or significant non-performance.

M = **Medium Priority** - These items include deferred maintenance items that will soon require repair or replacement.

L = **Low Priority** - These items include cosmetics and upgrades. They are not required for safety but may enhance the appeal of the property.

Lodging & Recreation

Hotel & Motel Checklist

	Appears Serviceable	Not Applicable	Repair	Repair Priority H M L

Foundation

	Appears Serviceable	Not Applicable	Repair	H	M	L
Anchor Bolts	❑	❑	❑	❑	❑	❑
Basement	❑	❑	❑	❑	❑	❑
Crawl Space	❑	❑	❑	❑	❑	❑
Grading	❑	❑	❑	❑	❑	❑
Mud-sill	❑	❑	❑	❑	❑	❑
Sheer Panel	❑	❑	❑	❑	❑	❑
Soil Conditions	❑	❑	❑	❑	❑	❑
Slab on Grade	❑	❑	❑	❑	❑	❑
Other _____	❑	❑	❑	❑	❑	❑

Grounds/Site

Exterior Stairs	❑	❑	❑	❑	❑	❑
Fences & Gates	❑	❑	❑	❑	❑	❑
Decks	❑	❑	❑	❑	❑	❑
Driveway	❑	❑	❑	❑	❑	❑
Retaining Walls	❑	❑	❑	❑	❑	❑
Sidewalks	❑	❑	❑	❑	❑	❑
Trip Hazards	❑	❑	❑	❑	❑	❑
Other _____	❑	❑	❑	❑	❑	❑

Restrooms

Bathtub	❑	❑	❑	❑	❑	❑
Cabinets	❑	❑	❑	❑	❑	❑
Electrical	❑	❑	❑	❑	❑	❑
Heater	❑	❑	❑	❑	❑	❑
Sink	❑	❑	❑	❑	❑	❑
Shower	❑	❑	❑	❑	❑	❑
Toilet	❑	❑	❑	❑	❑	❑
Ventilation	❑	❑	❑	❑	❑	❑
Other _____	❑	❑	❑	❑	❑	❑

Lodging & Recreation

	Appears Serviceable	Not Applicable	Repair	Repair Priority H	M	L
Roof						
Attic	❏	❏	❏	❏	❏	❏
Exposed Flashing	❏	❏	❏	❏	❏	❏
Gutters & Downspout	❏	❏	❏	❏	❏	❏
Main Roof	❏	❏	❏	❏	❏	❏
Vents	❏	❏	❏	❏	❏	❏
Other _____	❏	❏	❏	❏	❏	❏
Exterior						
Exterior Walls	❏	❏	❏	❏	❏	❏
Trim	❏	❏	❏	❏	❏	❏
Other _____	❏	❏	❏	❏	❏	❏
Interior						
Ceilings	❏	❏	❏	❏	❏	❏
Entry Doors	❏	❏	❏	❏	❏	❏
Exterior Doors	❏	❏	❏	❏	❏	❏
Fire Alarms	❏	❏	❏	❏	❏	❏
Fire Sprinklers	❏	❏	❏	❏	❏	❏
Floors	❏	❏	❏	❏	❏	❏
Interior Doors	❏	❏	❏	❏	❏	❏
Interior Walls	❏	❏	❏	❏	❏	❏
Lighting	❏	❏	❏	❏	❏	❏
Stairs	❏	❏	❏	❏	❏	❏
Stair Rails	❏	❏	❏	❏	❏	❏
Windows	❏	❏	❏	❏	❏	❏
Other _____	❏	❏	❏	❏	❏	❏
Restaurant Kitchen & Appliances						
Dishwasher	❏	❏	❏	❏	❏	❏
Disposal	❏	❏	❏	❏	❏	❏
Hood	❏	❏	❏	❏	❏	❏
Microwave	❏	❏	❏	❏	❏	❏
Refrigerator	❏	❏	❏	❏	❏	❏
Sink	❏	❏	❏	❏	❏	❏
Stove/Range	❏	❏	❏	❏	❏	❏
Washer/Dryer	❏	❏	❏	❏	❏	❏
Other _____	❏	❏	❏	❏	❏	❏

Lodging & Recreation

	Appears Serviceable	Not Applicable	Repair	Repair Priority H	M	L
Heating & Cooling						
Air Conditioner	☐	☐	☐	☐	☐	☐
Air Filters	☐	☐	☐	☐	☐	☐
Burners	☐	☐	☐	☐	☐	☐
Controls	☐	☐	☐	☐	☐	☐
Combustion Air	☐	☐	☐	☐	☐	☐
Distribution	☐	☐	☐	☐	☐	☐
Overall System	☐	☐	☐	☐	☐	☐
Venting	☐	☐	☐	☐	☐	☐
Other _____	☐	☐	☐	☐	☐	☐
Plumbing						
Fuel System	☐	☐	☐	☐	☐	☐
Hose Faucets	☐	☐	☐	☐	☐	☐
Main Line	☐	☐	☐	☐	☐	☐
Sprinklers	☐	☐	☐	☐	☐	☐
Supply Lines	☐	☐	☐	☐	☐	☐
Waste Lines	☐	☐	☐	☐	☐	☐
Water Heater	☐	☐	☐	☐	☐	☐
Water Heater Brackets	☐	☐	☐	☐	☐	☐
Water Heater T/P Valve	☐	☐	☐	☐	☐	☐
Other _____	☐	☐	☐	☐	☐	☐
Electrical						
Conductors	☐	☐	☐	☐	☐	☐
Main Panel	☐	☐	☐	☐	☐	☐
Outlets	☐	☐	☐	☐	☐	☐
Sub Panels	☐	☐	☐	☐	☐	☐
Wiring	☐	☐	☐	☐	☐	☐
Other _____	☐	☐	☐	☐	☐	☐
Amenities						
Laundry Facilities	☐	☐	☐	☐	☐	☐
Pool/Spa	☐	☐	☐	☐	☐	☐
Rec Room	☐	☐	☐	☐	☐	☐
Sauna	☐	☐	☐	☐	☐	☐
Tennis	☐	☐	☐	☐	☐	☐
Other _____	☐	☐	☐	☐	☐	☐

Lodging & Recreation

Tennis Court Dimensions

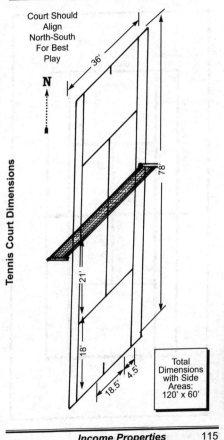

Court Should
Align
North-South
For Best
Play

N

36'

78'

21'

18'

18.5'

4.5'

Total
Dimensions
with Side
Areas:
120' x 60'

Lodging & Recreation

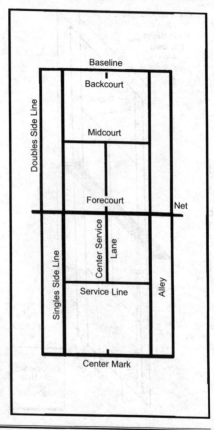

Income Properties

Lodging & Recreation

GOLF COURSE TERMS

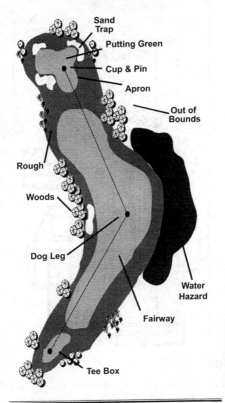

Sand Trap

Putting Green

Cup & Pin

Apron

Out of Bounds

Rough

Woods

Dog Leg

Water Hazard

Fairway

Tee Box

Lodging & Recreation

Pool Water Flow - With Solar Heater

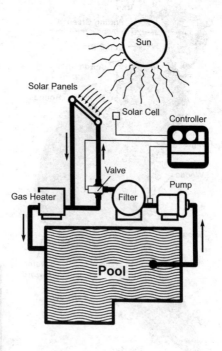

Property Management

Property Inspection
Real Estate Organizations
ADA Guidelines
Glossary of Management Terms
Real Estate Abbreviations

PROPERTY INSPECTION

Measurement Guidelines

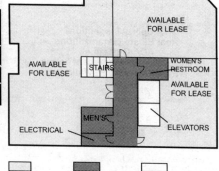

RENTABLE AREA = USABLE AREA + COMMON AREA

NOTE: Measurements are made from the inside surface of exterior walls and middle line of interior partitions. Columns which support building are not deducted.

CONSTRUCTION AREA = Total floor area, measured from the exterior walls, includes the basement

MEASUREMENT GUIDELINES BY PROPERTY TYPE

Apartments, Total Floor Area--Measured from exterior walls*

Condominiums, Total Living Area--Measured from the inside surface of exterior walls

Industrial, Gross Leasable Area (GLA)-- Measured from the exterior wall* to center of joint partition walls

Office, Gross, Rentable and Usable Area -- See chart to left

Residential, Gross Living Area--Total area of finished, above grade area measured from exterior walls*

Residential, Gross Building Area--Gross Living Area, plus basement area, measured from exterior walls†

Retail, Gross Leasable Area (GLA)--Measured from exterior wall* to center of joint partition walls

Property Inspection

*Outside surface † Inside surface

Inches to Decimals	
1"	= 0.083
2"	= 0.167
3"	= 0.250
4"	= 0.333
5"	= 0.417
6"	= 0.500
7"	= 0.583
8"	= 0.667
9"	= 0.750
10"	= 0.833
11"	= 0.917
12"	= 1.000

1 Acre	=	43,560 SqFt
1 Mile	=	5,280 Feet
1 Sq. Mile	=	640 Acres
1 Section	=	640 Acres
1 Township	=	36 Sections

BUILDING FEATURES

Access _____

Age _____

Building Area   Gross _____

               Rentable _____

               Usable _____

Corner/Midblock _____

Dock High Doors _____

Easement _____

Electrical _____

Encroachment _____

Front Feet _____

Landscape _____

Lighting _____

Overhead Doors _____

Permits for
Additions, etc. _____

Rail Served _____

Signage _____

Termite Inspection _____

Truss Height _____

Yard Area _____

Asbestos _____

ADA Compliance _____

Emergency Shutoff Controls

  Electrical Panel _____

  Gas Shutoff _____

  Sewer Cleanout _____

  Water Shut-off _____

  Other _____

Energy Conservation

  Door
  Weather-stripping _____

  Window
  Weather-stripping _____

  Insulation - Floor _____

  Insulation - Wall _____

  Insulation - Piping _____

  Insulation - Ceiling _____

  Energy Saving
  Devices _____

  Low - Flow Toilets _____

Other _____

Property Inspection

General Property Inspection

This checklist is designed to assist a prospective buyer in organizing the task of making a preliminary property inspection. A careful examination prior to making an offer or closing escrow can assist in revealing the real condition of the property and negotiating price. Make a visual inspection of all applicable items on this checklist, and categorize their priority. Note that this checklist is intended for preliminary use only and is not to be considered a substitute for a professional property inspection.

Repair/Replacement Priority

H = **High Priority** - These items must be repaired immediately and include any issues related to safety or significant non-performance.

M = **Medium Priority** - These items include deferred maintenance items that will require repair or replacement soon.

L = **Low Priority** - These items include cosmetics and upgrades. They are not required for safety but may enhance the appeal of the property.

General Property Checklist

	Appears Serviceable	Not Applicable	Repair	Repair Priority H	M	L
Foundation						
Anchor Bolts	☐	☐	☐	☐	☐	☐
Basement	☐	☐	☐	☐	☐	☐
Crawl Space	☐	☐	☐	☐	☐	☐
Grading	☐	☐	☐	☐	☐	☐
Mud-sill	☐	☐	☐	☐	☐	☐
Sheer Panel	☐	☐	☐	☐	☐	☐
Soil Conditions	☐	☐	☐	☐	☐	☐
Slab on Grade	☐	☐	☐	☐	☐	☐
Other _____	☐	☐	☐	☐	☐	☐
Grounds/Site						
Exterior Stairs	☐	☐	☐	☐	☐	☐
Fences & Gates	☐	☐	☐	☐	☐	☐
Decks	☐	☐	☐	☐	☐	☐
Driveway	☐	☐	☐	☐	☐	☐
Retaining Walls	☐	☐	☐	☐	☐	☐
Sidewalks	☐	☐	☐	☐	☐	☐
Trip Hazards	☐	☐	☐	☐	☐	☐
Other _____	☐	☐	☐	☐	☐	☐
Restrooms						
Bathtub	☐	☐	☐	☐	☐	☐
Cabinets	☐	☐	☐	☐	☐	☐
Electrical	☐	☐	☐	☐	☐	☐
Heater	☐	☐	☐	☐	☐	☐
Sink	☐	☐	☐	☐	☐	☐
Shower	☐	☐	☐	☐	☐	☐
Toilet	☐	☐	☐	☐	☐	☐
Ventilation	☐	☐	☐	☐	☐	☐
Other _____	☐	☐	☐	☐	☐	☐

Property Inspection

	Appears Serviceable	Not Applicable	Repair	Repair Priority		
				H	M	L
Roof						
Attic	☐	☐	☐	☐	☐	☐
Exposed Flashing	☐	☐	☐	☐	☐	☐
Gutters & Downspout	☐	☐	☐	☐	☐	☐
Main Roof	☐	☐	☐	☐	☐	☐
Vents	☐	☐	☐	☐	☐	☐
Other _____	☐	☐	☐	☐	☐	☐
Exterior						
Exterior Walls	☐	☐	☐	☐	☐	☐
Trim	☐	☐	☐	☐	☐	☐
Other _____	☐	☐	☐	☐	☐	☐
Interior						
Ceilings	☐	☐	☐	☐	☐	☐
Entry Doors	☐	☐	☐	☐	☐	☐
Exterior Doors	☐	☐	☐	☐	☐	☐
Fire Alarms	☐	☐	☐	☐	☐	☐
Fire Sprinklers	☐	☐	☐	☐	☐	☐
Floors	☐	☐	☐	☐	☐	☐
Interior Doors	☐	☐	☐	☐	☐	☐
Interior Walls	☐	☐	☐	☐	☐	☐
Lighting	☐	☐	☐	☐	☐	☐
Stairs	☐	☐	☐	☐	☐	☐
Stair Rails	☐	☐	☐	☐	☐	☐
Windows	☐	☐	☐	☐	☐	☐
Other _____	☐	☐	☐	☐	☐	☐
Restaurant Kitchen & Appliances						
Dishwasher	☐	☐	☐	☐	☐	☐
Disposal	☐	☐	☐	☐	☐	☐
Hood	☐	☐	☐	☐	☐	☐
Microwave	☐	☐	☐	☐	☐	☐
Refrigerator	☐	☐	☐	☐	☐	☐
Sink	☐	☐	☐	☐	☐	☐
Stove/Range	☐	☐	☐	☐	☐	☐
Washer/Dryer	☐	☐	☐	☐	☐	☐
Other _____	☐	☐	☐	☐	☐	☐

	Appears Serviceable	Not Applicable	Repair	Repair Priority		
				H	M	L
Heating & Cooling						
Air Conditioner	☐	☐	☐	☐	☐	☐
Air Filters	☐	☐	☐	☐	☐	☐
Burners	☐	☐	☐	☐	☐	☐
Controls	☐	☐	☐	☐	☐	☐
Combustion Air	☐	☐	☐	☐	☐	☐
Distribution	☐	☐	☐	☐	☐	☐
Overall System	☐	☐	☐	☐	☐	☐
Venting	☐	☐	☐	☐	☐	☐
Other _____	☐	☐	☐	☐	☐	☐
Plumbing						
Fuel System	☐	☐	☐	☐	☐	☐
Hose Faucets	☐	☐	☐	☐	☐	☐
Main Line	☐	☐	☐	☐	☐	☐
Sprinklers	☐	☐	☐	☐	☐	☐
Supply Lines	☐	☐	☐	☐	☐	☐
Waste Lines	☐	☐	☐	☐	☐	☐
Water Heater	☐	☐	☐	☐	☐	☐
Water Heater Brackets	☐	☐	☐	☐	☐	☐
Water Heater T/P Valve	☐	☐	☐	☐	☐	☐
Other _____	☐	☐	☐	☐	☐	☐
Electrical						
Conductors	☐	☐	☐	☐	☐	☐
Main Panel	☐	☐	☐	☐	☐	☐
Outlets	☐	☐	☐	☐	☐	☐
Sub Panels	☐	☐	☐	☐	☐	☐
Wiring	☐	☐	☐	☐	☐	☐
Other _____	☐	☐	☐	☐	☐	☐
Amenities						
Laundry Facilities	☐	☐	☐	☐	☐	☐
Pool/Spa	☐	☐	☐	☐	☐	☐
Rec Room	☐	☐	☐	☐	☐	☐
Sauna	☐	☐	☐	☐	☐	☐
Tennis	☐	☐	☐	☐	☐	☐
Other _____	☐	☐	☐	☐	☐	☐

Property Inspection

REAL ESTATE ORGANIZATIONS*

American Association of Certified Appraisers
800 Compton Road, Suite 10
Cincinnati, OH 45231
(800) 543-2222 Fax: (513) 729-1401

American Zoo and Aquariums Association
Oglebay Park
Wheeling, WV 26003
(304) 242-2160

American Bankers Association
1120 Connecticut Avenue, N.W.
Washington, D.C. 20036
(202) 663-5000 Fax: (202) 828-4548

American Bar Association
750 North Lakeshore Drive
Chicago, IL 60611
(312) 988-5000

American Hotel and Motel Association
1201 New York Avenue, N.W., Suite 600
Washington, D.C. 20005-3931
(202) 289-3100

American Institute of Architects
1735 New York Avenue, N.W.
Washington, D.C. 20006
(202) 626-7300 or (202) 626-7492

American Institute of C.P.A.s
1211 Avenue of the Americas
New York, NY 10036-8775
(212) 596-6200

*Note: May not be real estate specific but of interest or value

Real Estate Organizations

American Resort Development Association
1220 "L" Street, Suite 500
Washington, D.C.
(202) 371-6700

American Planning Association
122 S. Michigan Ave., Suite 1600
Chicago, IL 60603
(312) 955-9100
Or
1776 Massachusetts Ave, Suite 400
Washington, D.C. 20036
(202) 872-0611

American Real Estate & Urban Economics Association
Indiana University School of Business
Room 428
1309 E. 10th St.
Bloomington, Indiana 47405
(812) 850-7794

American Society of Appraisers
555 Herndon Parkway, Suite 125
Herndon, VA 20170
(703) 478-2228 Fax: (703) 742-8471

American Society of Farm Managers & Rural Appraisers
950 South Cherry Street, Suite 508
Denver, CO 80222
(303) 758-3513 Fax: (303) 758-0190

American Society of Golf Course Architects
221 North La Salle Street, Suite 3500
Chicago, IL 60601-1520
(312) 372-7090

Real Estate Organizations

Amusement and Music Operators Association
401 North Michigan Avenue, Suite 2200
Chicago, IL 60611
(312) 644-6610

Appraisal Institute
875 North Michigan Avenue, Suite 2400
Chicago, IL 60611-1980
(312) 335-4100 Fax: (312) 335-4400

Black's Guide
818 West Diamond Avenue, Suite 300
Gaithersburg, MD 20878
(301) 948-0995, CA - (800) 500-2450

Bowling Proprietors' Association
615 Six Flags Drive
Arlington, TX 76011
(817) 649-5105

Building Owners and Managers Assoc. Int. (BOMA)
1201 New York Avenue, N.W., Suite 300
Washington, D.C. 20005
(202) 408-2662

Conservation International Foundation
2501 M Street, N.W., Suite 200
Washington, D.C. 20037
(202) 429-5660

Employee Relocation Council
1720 N Street, N.W.
Washington DC 20036
(202) 857-0857 Fax (202) 467-4012

Farm Credit Council
7100 East Belleview, Suite 205
Englewood, CO 80111
(303) 740-4200 Fax: (303) 741-4202

Institute for Real Estate Management
430 North Michigan Avenue
Chicago, IL 60611
(312) 329-8200

International Association of Assessing Officers
130 East Randolph Street, Suite 850 Chicago, IL 60601
(312) 819-6100 Fax: (312) 819-6149

International Council of Shopping Centers
665 Fifth Avenue
New York, NY 10022-5370
(212) 421-8181 Fax (212) 489-0849

International Right of Way Association
13650 South Gramercy Place, Suite 100
Gardena, CA 90249
(310) 538-0233 Fax: (310) 538-1471

Lender's Service, Inc.
700 Cherrington Parkway
Coraopolis, PA 15108
(412) 299-4000 Fax (412) 299-4049

Marshall & Swift Cost Publications
1617 Wilshire Boulevard
Los Angeles, CA 90017
(213) 250-2222

Real Estate Organizations

Mortgage Bankers Association
1125 15th Street, N.W., Suite 700 Washington, D.C. 20005
(202) 861-6500 Fax: (202) 785-8357

Mortgage Guaranty Insurance Corporation
270 E. Kilbourn Avenue
Milwaukee, WI 53202
(800) 558-9900 Fax: (414) 347-6696

Mortgage Insurance Companies of America
727 15th Street, N.W., 12th Floor
Washington, D.C. 20005
(202) 393-5566 Fax: (202) 393-5557

National Apartment Association
1111 14th Street, N.W., Suite 900
Washington, D.C. 20005
(202) 842-4050

National Association of Independent Fee Appraisers
7501 Murdoch Avenue
St. Louis, MO 63119
(314) 781-6688 Fax: (314) 781-2872

National Association of Industrial and Office Parks
2201 Cooperative Way, 3rd Floor
Herndon, VA 20171
(703) 904-7100 Fax: (703) 904-7942

National Association of Industrial and Office Properties
1215 Cameron Street
Alexandria, VA 22314
(703) 356-5858 Fax: (703) 739-2991

Real Estate Organizations

National Association of Master Appraisers
303 West Cypress Street
San Antonio, TX 78212
(210) 271-0781 Fax: (210) 225-8450

National Association of Realtors (DC Offices)
700 11th Street, N.W.
Washington, D.C. 20001
(202) 383-1000 Fax: (202) 383-1035

National Association of Realtors (Chicago Offices)
430 North Michigan Avenue
Chicago, IL 60611
(312) 329-8200 Fax: (312) 329-8756

National Association of
State Development Agencies
750 1st Street, N.E., Suite 710
Washington, D.C. 20002
(202) 898-1302 Fax: (202) 898-1312

National Council for Urban Economic Development
1730 K Street, N.W., Suite 700
Washington, D.C. 20006
(202) 223-4735 Fax: (202) 223-4745

National Golf Foundation
1150 S. U.S. Highway 1, Suite 401
Jupiter, FL 33477
(561) 744-6006 Fax: (561) 744-6107

National League of Cities
1301 Pennsylvania Avenue, N.W., Suite 550
Washington, D.C. 20004
(202) 626-3000 Fax: (202) 626-3043

Real Estate Organizations

National Retail Federation
575 Fifth Avenue
New York, NY 10017
(212) 551-9260

National Retail Federation
325 7th Street, N.W., Suite 1000
Washington D.C. 20004
(202) 783-7971 Fax: (202) 737-2849

Real Estate Educators Association
10565 Lee Highway, Suite 104
Fairfax, VA 22030
(703) 352-6688

Real Estate Research Corporation
2 North La Salle Street, Suite 730
Chicago, IL 60602
(312) 346-5885 Fax: (312) 364-9825

Recreational Vehicle Industry Association
1896 Preston White Drive
Reston, VA 20191-4363
(703) 620-6003 Fax: (703) 620-5071

Savings & Community Bankers of America
900 19TH Street, N.W., Suite 400
Washington, D.C. 20006
(202) 857-3100 Fax: (202) 296-8716

Society of Industrial and Office Realtors
700 11th Street, N.W., Suite 510
Washington, D.C. 20001
(202) 737-1150 Fax: (202) 737-8796

Real Estate Organizations

Society of Industrial Realtors
700 11th Street, N.W.
Washington, D.C. 20001
(202) 383-1150

United States Tennis Association/National Tennis Center
Flushing Meadow Corona Park
Flushing, NY 11368
(718) 592-8000 Ticket/Info: (718) 271-5100

USA Roller Skating
4730 South Street
Lincoln, NE 68506
(402) 483-7551

U.S. Department of Commerce
Economic Development Administration
14th and Constitution
Washington, D.C. 20230
(202) 482-5081

Urban Land Institute
1025 Thomas Jefferson St., N.W., Suite 500W
Washington, D.C. 20007
(202) 624-7000

The organizations listed are for informational purposes only. No endorsement of any organization or their services is given or implied.

Real Estate Organizations

AMERICANS WITH DISABILITIES ACT (ADA)

INTRODUCTION

The Americans with Disabilities Act (ADA) is a law passed in 1990 with the objective of bringing persons with disabilities into mainstream life. It is actually an extension of the 1964 Civil Rights Act. That law states that an employer cannot discriminate on a basis of race, color, sex, national origin or religion. Simply stated, the ADA adds "disability" to that list. The ADA involves employment issues as well as physical building features.

With regard to real estate, the ADA Accessibility Guidelines are issued by the Architectural and Transportation Barriers Compliance Board and have been adopted by the Justice Department. The ADA affects the following places of Public Accommodation:

❑ **Places of Lodging:** Hotels, Motels and Inns unless the building in which establishment is located contains no more than five rooms for rent or hire and the proprietor resides on the premises, e.g. small boarding houses

❑ **Establishments Serving Food or Drink:** Bars, Nightclubs, Restaurants, etc.

❑ **Places of Exhibition or Entertainment:** Concert Halls, Movie and Live Theaters, Stadiums, etc.

❑ **Places of Public Gathering:** Auditoriums, Convention Centers, Lecture Halls, etc.

❑ **Sales or Rental Establishments:** Bakeries, Bookstores, Car Rental Establishments, Clothing Stores, Grocery Stores, Hardware Stores, Jewelry Stores, Pet Stores, Shopping Centers, Videotape Rental Stores, etc.

❑ **Service Establishments:** Banks, Barber/Beauty Shops, Funeral Parlors, Hospitals, Insurance Offices, Laundromats, Offices of Lawyers, Accountants and Health Care Providers, Pharmacies, Travel Services, etc.

❑ **Specified Public Transportation Stations:** Depots, Terminals, etc.

❑ **Places of Public Display or Collection:** Galleries, Libraries, Museums, etc.

❑ **Places of Recreation:** Amusement Parks, Parks, Zoos, etc.

❑ **Places of Education:** Colleges, Nurseries, Private Schools, Trade Schools, etc.

❑ **Social Service Center Establishments:** Adoption Agencies, Day Care Centers, Food Banks, Halfway Houses, Homeless Shelters, Rape Crisis Centers, Senior Citizen Centers, Substance Abuse Treatment Centers, etc.

❑ **Places of Exercise or Recreation**

ADA Guidelines

BASIC CONDITIONS

Space Allowance

Minimum clear width is 32" at a point (doorways) and 36" continuously. Wheelchairs must be able to pass at least every 200'. The width for two wheel chairs to pass is 60". Turning requires a width of 60" also.

Accessible Route

Minimum clear width of accessible route shall be 36", except at doors. Maximum level change is 1/2".

Protruding Objects

Objects, such as telephones, over 27" high may protrude on the accessible walkway a maximum of 4".

Ground and Floor Surfaces

Changes up to 1/4" may be vertical. From 1/4" to 1/2" must be beveled. Gratings must have spaces no larger than 1/2" in direction of travel. Maximum carpet pile of 1/2".

Parking and Passenger Loading Zones

Accessible parking is to be located at the shortest distance from the parking area to the accessible entrance. Accessible spaces to be designated with a sign.

ADA Guidelines

CHART OF ADA ACCESSIBLE PARKING REQUIREMENTS

Total Parking In Lot	Required Minimum Number of "Accessible Spaces"	Required Minimum Number of "Van Accessible Spaces"
	(Spaces 96" Wide, 60" Access Aisle)	(Spaces 96" Wide, 96" Access Aisle)
1 - 25	1	1
26 - 50	2	1
51 - 75	3	1
76 - 100	4	1
101 - 150	5	1
151 - 200	6	1
201 - 300	7	1
301 - 400	8	1
401 - 500	9	1
501 - 1000	2% of Total Accessible	1 in Every 8 Spaces
1001+	20, +1 for Each 100 Over 1000	1 in Every 8 Accessible Spaces

Note: The Designated Van Accessible spaces are not required of all the accessible spaces to comply with the Universal Parking Design. The Universal Parking Space Design has parking spaces 132" wide and 60" aisles at every other parking stall.

ADA Guidelines

Curb Ramps

Maximum slope of 1:12, minimum width of 36". If there are no hand rails, the curb ramp must have flared sides with a maximum slope of 1:10.

Ramps

Ramps are needed on any part of an accessible route with a slope greater than 1:20. Maximum ramp slope of 1:12. Maximum rise of 30". Minimum clear width of 36". If rise is greater than 6", handrails are required on both sides.

Stairs

Stair tread minimum of 11". Handrails required on both sides.

Elevators

Call buttons raised or flush. Up button to be on top. Minimum fully open response time is 3 seconds. Braille required for buttons.

Platform Lifts (Wheelchair Lifts)

Must comply with ASME Safety Code for Elevators and Escalators.

Windows

The ADA has reserved this category for possible further guidelines.

ADA Guidelines

Doors

Minimum clear opening of 32". Thresholds are to be beveled with a maximum of 3/4" for exterior sliding doors and 1/2" for other doors. Hardware shall not require tight grasping or twisting of wrist. Lever and push-types are acceptable.

Entrances

One to accompany each accessible route.

Drinking Fountains and Water Coolers

Spouts no higher than 36". Water flow at least 4" high.

Water Closets

Height of seat to be 17" to 19" from the finished floor.

Toilet Stalls

Minimum depth of 56" for wall-mounted toilets. Minimum depth 59" for floor-mounted toilets. Grab bars to be provided.

Urinals

Rim a maximum of 17" above the finished floor.

Lavatories and Mirrors

Rim or counter 34" maximum above floor. Hot pipes and drains to be insulated. Faucets to be lever-operated, push-type or electronic. Bottom of mirror to be a maximum of 40" high.

ADA Guidelines

Bathtubs

In-tub seat provided. Grab-bars provided. Controls that do not require twisting of wrist. A shower unit with a minimum of 60" of hose.

Shower Stalls

Stall to be minimum of 36" x 36". Seat to be provided. Grab-bars provided. Controls that do not require twisting of wrist.

Toilet Rooms

Provided on accessible route.

Bathrooms, Bathing Facilities and Showers

Provided on accessible route.

Sinks

Maximum of 34" to counter or rim. Knee clearance of 27" minimum. Sink to be 6 1/2" deep maximum. Exposed hot pipes and drains to be insulated. Faucets to be lever-operated, push-type or electronically controlled.

Storage

Fixed storage such as cabinets, shelves, closets and drawers to have a clear floor space of 30" x 48" minimum. 48" height maximum.

ADA Guidelines

Handrails, Grab Bars, Tub and Shower Seats

Diameter of grab bar to be 1 1/4" to 1 1/2". Grab bars may not rotate in their fittings. Structural strength to meet ADA guidelines.

Controls and Operating Mechanisms

Controls, such as light switches, must be operable with one hand. Controls must not require tight grasping, pinching or twisting of the wrist. Maximum forward reach of 48". Wall-mounted electrical and communication receptacles must be at least 15" high.

Alarms

Audible and visual alarms are to be provided.

Detectable Warnings

Warnings are required at hazardous vehicular areas and reflecting pools.

Signage

3" minimum character height. Raised and Braille characters and pictorial signs to comply with ADA standards.

Telephones

Clear floor space of 30" x 48" minimum. 48" maximum height to highest operable portion of phone. Push-button controls where available. Telephone handset cords to be 29" minimum. Hearing aid and TDD as required by the ADA.

ADA Guidelines

Fixed or Built-in Seating and Tables

Knee space of 27" minimum. Table tops to be 28" to 34" above finished floor or ground.

Assembly Areas

Wheelchair Location Requirements (Area 30" x 48")

An accessible route shall connect wheelchair seating with performing areas and dressing rooms. Seating areas are to be within 50' of stage or playing area and have a complete view.

Capacity of Seating In Assembly Area

4 to 25	1
26 to 50	2
51 to 300	4
301 to 500	6
Over 500	6, plus 1 additional space for each total seating capacity increase of 100.

Automated Teller Machines

To be provided on an accessible route. Controls, clearances, reach range and vision impairment equipment to comply with ADA standards.

Dressing and Fitting Rooms

Must allow a 180 degree wheelchair turn. Doors may not swing inward. Benches required that are 24" x 48" and 17" to 19" above the finished floor. Mirrors provided with a minimum of 18" wide and 54" high.

SPECIAL ADA CATEGORIES

The ADA has additional specific guidelines for restaurants and cafeterias, medical care facilities, businesses and mercantile, libraries, accessible transient lodging and transportation facilities. Refer to the ADA guidelines for details.

This description of ADA Guidelines is to be considered to be only a brief overview of selected issues. It is not designed or intended to be comprehensive. For current and detailed information, contact the U.S. Department of Justice, Civil Rights Department, Washington DC 20530. They may be contacted through the Division's ADA Information Line at (202) 514-0301 (Voice) or (202) 514-0381 (TDD) or (202) 514-0383 (TDD).

The ADA Accessibility Guidelines are issued by the Architectural and Transportation Barriers Compliance Board (202) 272-5434 (Voice).

ADA Guidelines

International Symbol of Accessibility

International Symbol of Access for Hearing Loss

International TDD Symbol

GLOSSARY OF MANAGEMENT TERMS

Abatement--Increases/decreases, e.g., property taxes

Absence--Terms to notify lessor if absent

Ad Valorem Tax -- A property tax that is based upon a fixed percentage of the property's value

Additional Rent--e.g. percentage rents, increases

Alteration -- Changing the use of the interior of the property while leaving the exterior as is

Alterations/Additions--Terms if lease is altered

Anchor Tenant -- A large, well-known credit tenant that is a main attraction to the property

Apportionment -- An insurance policy clause stating that all companies insuring a property will divide any loss in proportion to the amount of insurance coverage

Base Expense Year--Lessee pays prorated expenses above the base year (year lease starts) expense

Base Rent--Rent paid at start of lease

Book Value -- The original cost of a property, plus capital additions and less accrued depreciation

Brokerage Clause -- A lease clause stating the brokerage commissions are only paid if the tenant actually takes possession and pays rent

Commence--Date lease starts

Commissions--Payments to brokers for services

Common Area--Areas used by all tenants

Common Area Charges -- A lease clause that allows the landlord to "pass-through" prorated common area expenses to the tenant

Concessions--e.g. free rent, moving allowances

Condemnation--Terms if property is condemned

Continuous Occupancy and Operation -- Lease clauses that stipulate that the tenant will actually occupy the premises and/or maintain inventory levels through the term of the lease

Contract Rent--Rent as stated in the lease.

Covenants & Conditions--Rules of property

CPI--Rents increase with the *Consumer Price Index*

Default--Terms in case of default of rent payment

Effective Rent--Rent adjusted for concessions

Escalations--Increase in rent over initial lease terms

Estoppel--Statement verifying lease terms

Excess Rent--Rent paid over market

Exclusive -- A lease clause that stipulates the exclusion of tenants in a similar business

Expense Stop--Tenant pays expense over stated amount

Fire--Responsible party if fire occurs

Fixed--Set rent increase, e.g., 5% per year

Free Rent--e.g. one free month per year

Gross--Lessor pays all property expenses (see Net)

Hold Harmless -- A lease clause that indemnifies the landlord from actions arising from a tenant's operations

Insurance--e.g. liability, fire

Industrial Gross--Definition varies, often lessor pays all property taxes, insurance maintenance

Lease -- A written agreement whereby the landlord transfers the right of occupancy to the tenant for a specified term and rental rate

Lessee--Tenant

Lessor--Landlord

Location--e.g. within office or retail center

Loss Leader -- A product sold below cost in order to attract customers into the store

Management Assessments--A premium paid based on a percentage of building expenses

Modified Gross--A mixture between net and gross

Moving Allowance--Incentive to prospective tenants

Net--Lessee pays all property expenses (see Gross)

NNN--Definition varies, often denotes a net lease

Notice -- The method and time requirements for a tenant to give notice before vacating

Occupancy -- The level of occupancy expressed as occupied space divided by total rentable space

Off-Site Management -- The property management that deals with the administration issues

On-Site Management -- The property management that maintains an office on the premises and deals directly with the tenants

Operating Hours--Rules of hours of operation

Option--Extend term e.g., at lessee's option

Overage Rents--Rent paid over base amount

Owner's Inspection--Right of owner to inspect

Parking Allowance--Parking allotted to lessee

Percentage Lease--Lessee pays a percentage of business sales, in addition to rent

Prime Tenant--A large, well-known tenant

Prospect -- A possible tenant

Purchase Option--Lessee's option to buy

Quiet Title--Lessee's right to non-interference concerning title issues

Radius Clause--Lessee may not operate another business within a specified radius

Re-Appraisal--Rental increase based on appraised value

Recording--Filing of lease or deed with county office

Renewal -- A lease clause setting forth terms for renewal

Rent Roll--Summary of tenants, rates and terms

Rider--Additional lease terms, addendum

Satellite - A tenant that is secondary in size and location to the anchor tenant

Security Deposit--Amount and terms

Signs--Regulations governing signage

Size (Usable v. Rentable)--See diagram.

Subletting--Terms governing subleasing

Subordination--Lease takes a position behind future trust deeds or mortgages

Taxes--Rules governing who pays property taxes

Tenant Improvements (TI's)--e.g. carpet, demising walls, paint, ceiling, lighting

Term--Duration of lease in months or years

Terminate--Date lease ends

Use--Allowed uses of property, e.g. fast food

REAL ESTATE ABBREVIATIONS

A/C	Air Conditioning
ACRS	Accelerated Cost Recovery System
AD VALOREM	In Proportion To The Value
ADR	Asset Depreciation Range
AEK	All Electric Kitchen
AIREA	American Institute Of Real Estate Appraisers
AKA	Also Known As
ALTA	American Land Title Association (Policy)
AMI	Alternative Mortgage Instrument
AML	Adjustable Mortgage Loan
APA	American Planning Association
APP	Appreciation (In Appraisal Terminology)
APR	Annual Percentage Rate
AREUEA	American Real Estate And Urban Economics
ARM	Adjustable Rate Mortgage
ASA	American Society Of Appraisers
ASREC	American Society Of Real Estate Counselors
B&P	Business And Professions (Code)
BOMA	Building Owners And Managers Association
BONA FIDE	In Good Faith
BTU	British Thermal Unit
CAI	Community Associations Institute
CAL	Cash Above Loan
CBD	Central Business District
CCIM	Certified Commercial-Investment Member (Rnmi)
CD	Certificate Of Deposit
CLEAR	Free And Clear Of Loans

CLO	Call Listing Office
COE	Close Of Escrow
COL	Cash Over Loan
CPA	Certified Public Accountant
CPI	Consumer Price Index (See Cost Of Living Index)
CPM	Certified Property Manager (IREM)
CPM	Certified Property Manager
CRB	Certified Real Estate Brokerage Manager (RNMI)
CRE	Counselor In Real Estate (ASREC)
CRS	Certified Residential Specialist (RNMI)
CRV	Certificate Of Reasonable Value
DBA	Doing Business As
DCR	Debt Coverage Ratio
DEP	Depreciation
DOS	Due On Sale
EIS	Environmental Impact Statement
EPA	Environmental Protection Agency
ET AL	And Others
ET UX	And Wife
F/A	Forced Air Heater
FAR	Floor-Area Ratio
FDIC	Federal Deposit Insurance Corporation
FHA	Federal Housing Administration
FHLB	Federal Home Loan Bank
FHLMC	Federal Home Loan Mortgage Corporation (Freddie Mac)
FMHA	Farmers Home Administration
FMRR	Financial Management Rate Of Return
FMV	Fair Market Value
FNMA	Federal National Mortgage Association (Fannie Mae)

FPM	Flexible Payment Mortgage
FSLIC	Federal Savings And Loan Insurance Corporation
FTC	Federal Trade Commission
FY	Fiscal Year
GEM	Growing Equity Mortgage
GI	Government Issue, Veteran's Administration
GIM	Gross Income Multiplier
GNMA	Government National Mortgage Association, "Ginny Mae"
GNP	Gross National Product
GPM	Graduated Payment Mortgage
GRI	Graduate, Realtors® Institute
GRM	Gross Rent Multiplier
HOW	Homeowners Warranty
HUD	Department Of Housing And Urban Development
HVAC	Heating, Ventilation, And Air Conditioning
IAAO	International Association Of Assessing Officers
IRA	Individual Retirement Account
IREM	Institute Of Real Estate Management
IRR	Internal Rate Of Return
IRS	Internal Revenue Service
IRWA	International Right-Of-Way Association
KILO	Key In Listing Office
L/V	Loan-To-Value Ratio
M/M	Month To Month
MAI	Member of Appraisal Institute
MBA	Mortgage Bankers Association Of America
MGIC	Mortgage Guaranty Insurance Corporation

MLS	Multiple Listing Service
MMC	Money Market Certificate Of Deposit
MO	Make Offer
NAA	National Apartment Association
NACORE	National Association Of Corporate Real Estate Executives
NAHB	National Association Of Home Builders
NAR	National Association Of Realtors®
NAREB	National Association Of Real Estate Brokers
NARELLO	National Association Of Real Estate Licensing Law Officials
NOI	Net Operating Income
NOW	Negotiable Order Of Withdrawal (Account)
NPV	Net Present Value
OAR	Overall Rate
OBO	Occupied By Owner
OILSR	Office Of Interstate Land Sales Registration
OT	Over Tub (Shower)
OWC	Owner Will Carry (Loan)
P&I	Principal And Interest (Payment)
PAM	Pledged Account Mortgage
PITI	Principal, Interest, Taxes And Insurance (Payment)
PMI	Private Mortgage Insurance
PRIMA FACIE	At First Sight
PUD	Planned Unit Development
R/W	Right-Of-Way
RAM	Reverse Annuity Mortgage
REIT	Real Estate Investment Trust
RESPA	Real Estate Settlement Procedures Act
RESSI	Real Estate Securities And

	Syndication Institute
RM	Residential Member (Appraisal Institute)
RNMI	Realtors® National Marketing Institute
RRM	Renegotiated Rate Mortgage
S&L	Savings And Loan Association
SAM	Shared Appreciation Mortgage
SBA	Small Business Administration
SEC	Securities And Exchange Commission
SET OFF	Square Away A Debt By Mutual Deductions
SHORT RATE	Extra Payment For Canceling Insurance
SIR	Society Of Industrial Realtors®
SMSA	Standard Metropolitan Statistical Area
SRA	Senior Residential Appraiser (Appraisal Institute)
SREA	Senior Real Estate Analyst (Appraisal Institute)
SREA	Society Of Real Estate Appraisers (Now merged with the Appraisal Institute)
SRPA	Senior Real Property Appraiser (Appraisal Institute)
SYD	Sum-Of-The-Years-Digits (Depreciation)
T/G	Tongue And Groove (Construction)
TDR	Transferable Development Rights
TIL	Truth-In-Lending Law
UCC	Uniform Commercial Code
ULI	Urban Land Institute
VA	Veterans Administration
VRM	Variable Rate Mortgage
VW	View

Real Estate Abbreviations

W/W	Wall To Wall (Carpet)
WCR	Women's Council Of Realtors
YTM	Yield To Maturity

Home Ownership

Buying a Home
Selling a Home
Home Inspection
Condominiums & Townhouses
Home Financing
Moving
Renting vs. Buying
Common Repairs

BUYING A HOME
7 TIPS FOR A BULL'S EYE

Buying a home is the largest and single most important investment that many people make in their lifetime. The task should be approached carefully. In order to assist with this effort, the following checklists will help the homebuyer in the decision-making process.

❑ **AGENT:** Select a reputable licensed broker or agent. The right broker or agent can be a major advantage in a home buying decision. A reputable broker or agent will not hesitate to answer all your questions and discuss your concerns. Discuss each potential broker or agent's background, years in the business, years in the area, and request (and check) referrals. Ask what the agent or broker is *specifically* going to do to assist you.

❑ **AFFORDABILITY:** With your broker or agent, determine the amount of house that you can afford. Utilize the section on *Home Financing* and consult with a loan officer or mortgage broker in determining your loan limit. Loan applications can often be submitted well in advance of making offers. In fact, having preliminary loan approval can be a major incentive for a seller to accept your offer over others.

❑ **AREA/NEIGHBORHOOD:** Use the following checklist to help determine the area and neighborhood that are most suitable for your general life style.

❑ **POTENTIAL HOMES:** Use the checklists that follow to make a list of "must have" features in your desired home.

❑ **INSPECTION:** Utilizing the *Home Inspection* section, make a preliminary inspection of homes that you are seriously considering. Listing defects or items requiring repair in the offer may help in negotiating the price and help resolve who is responsible for their repair. Note that this preliminary inspection is not a substitute for a professional home inspection prior to the close of escrow.

❑ **OFFERS:** Submit offers only on homes that meet all of your "must have" features. Consider all the factors, including the motivation of the seller, and submit offers that are high enough to be taken seriously but low enough to "play out the market".

❑ **ESCROW:** Select a reputable escrow company with a reputation for excellent and prompt service to its clients. Responding quickly to the requests of the escrow officer can help assure a timely closing.

LOCATION & PROXIMITY FEATURES

Start the home search with specific goals in mind, and decide in advance which features you "must have". When looking at homes, remember that cosmetic features are usually more easily corrected than fundamental features, such as size or layout. Consider only those homes that have all the "must have" items, and then compare the other features that you desire.

1 = Must Have
2 = Desirable
3 = Low Priority
4 = Not Desired

Work Proximity	1	2	3	4
Area Pride of Ownership	1	2	3	4
Schools/Child Care Close-By	1	2	3	4
School Quality	1	2	3	4
Friends/Relatives in Area	1	2	3	4
Other Children in Area	1	2	3	4
Church/Synagogue	1	2	3	4
Cul-de-sac Location	1	2	3	4
Parks/Recreation Close-By	1	2	3	4
Corner Location	1	2	3	4
Shopping Proximity	1	2	3	4
Community Groups in Area	1	2	3	4

HOME FEATURES

(Circle All "Must Have" Items)

Architectural Style	*(Select from Architectural Chapter)*

_____

Age/Condition	New
	Excellent
	Good
	Average
	Fixer-Upper

Bedrooms   Must Have _____ Desired _____

Bathrooms   Must Have _____ Desired _____

Rooms	Family Living
	Dining
	Den/Study
	Work Room or Area
	Game Room
	Basement
	Home Office

Lot Size	Very Large
	Large
	Medium
	Small

Grounds	Landscape
	Patio
	Patio Cover
	Play Area
	BBQ

Special Features	Fireplace
	Fencing
	View
	Pool
	Spa
	RV Parking

LOG OF HOMES VISITED

No:_____ Address: _____

_____

Asking Price: _____

Bedrooms: _____ Bathrooms: _____

House SqFt: _____ Lot SqFt: _____ Age: _____

Desirable Features: _____

_____

Undesirable Features: _____

_____

Assumable Loan: Yes No

Seller Motivation: _____

Comments: _____

_____

No:_____ Address: _____

_____

Asking Price: _____

Bedrooms: _____ Bathrooms: _____

House SqFt: _____ Lot SqFt: _____ Age: _____

Desirable Features: _____

_____

Undesirable Features: _____

_____

Assumable Loan: Yes No

Seller Motivation: _____

Comments: _____

_____

LOG OF HOMES VISITED

No:_____ Address: _____

_____

Asking Price: _____

Bedrooms: _____ Bathrooms: _____

House SqFt: _____ Lot SqFt: _____ Age: _____

Desirable Features: _____

_____

Undesirable Features: _____

_____

Assumable Loan: Yes No

Seller Motivation: _____

Comments: _____

_____

No:_____ Address: _____

_____

Asking Price: _____

Bedrooms: _____ Bathrooms: _____

House SqFt: _____ Lot SqFt: _____ Age: _____

Desirable Features: _____

_____

Undesirable Features: _____

_____

Assumable Loan: Yes No

Seller Motivation: _____

Comments: _____

_____

SELLING A HOUSE

TEN TIPS FOR A SUCCESSFUL SALE

SOLD

10. Closing
    Escrow

9. Negotiating
   Offers

8. Marketing
   Plan

7. Establishing
   Sales Price

6. Cosmetic
   Upgrades &
   Repairs

5. Cleaning

4. Curb Appeal

3. Top-Priority
   Repairs

2. Property
   Inspection

1. Agent/Broker
   Selection

1. Agent/Broker Selection:

The foundation of a successful sale is often selecting a qualified and licensed agent or broker. Because their business is selling homes, they can provide an invaluable service in all of the next steps.

2. Property Inspection:

Utilizing the *Home Inspection* section that follows, inspect your property with your broker or agent, and make notes of all repairs needed.

3. Top-Priority Repairs:

Make top priority repairs, including any issues related to safety.

4. Curb Appeal:

Take steps to maximize the "curb-appeal" of the property. Consider the following suggestions as well as the advice from your broker or agent.

5. Cleaning:

Consider having a yard sale to dispose of any unwanted clutter. Thoroughly clean the house and manicure the landscaping.

6. Cosmetic Upgrades & Repairs:

Not all upgrades will increase the sales price "dollar for dollar." Consult with your broker or agent about what upgrades would maximize your sales price.

7. Establishing Sales Price:

Your broker or agent can perform a market study of other homes in the neighborhood that have sold. Using these "comparable sales", set a sales price that is high enough to "play out the market" but low enough to be realistic.

8. Marketing Plan:

Discuss the marketing plan with your broker or agent. This may include open houses, brochures or flyers, advertising, MLS listings or other approaches/efforts.

9. Negotiating Offers:

Consider all offers with your broker or agent. Pay attention to all contingencies. Negotiation is an art, and your broker or agent should have experience in this area. Always fully disclose all relevant issues related to the property.

10. Closing Escrow:

Be attentive to the requests of your escrow officer. Keep a calendar with the deadlines of any agreements you have made. Prompt attention can greatly assist in a timely escrow closing.

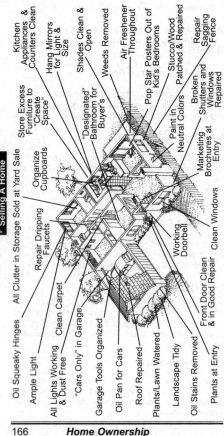

Kitchen Appliances & Counters Clean
Hang Mirrors for Light & Size
Shades Clean & Open
Weeds Removed
Air Freshener Throughout
Pop Star Posters Out of Kid's Bedrooms
Stucco/Wood Patched & Repaired
Repair Sagging Fence
Store Excess Furniture to "Create Space"
"Designated" Bathroom for Buyer's
Paint in Neutral Colors
Broken Shutters and Windows Repaired
Organize Cupboards
Marketing Brochures at Entry
Repair Dripping Faucets
Working Doorbell
Clean Windows
Oil Squeaky Hinges
All Clutter in Storage Sold at Yard Sale
Clean Carpet
Front Door Clean & in Good Repair
Ample Light
"Cars Only" in Garage
Plants at Entry
All Lights Working & Dust Free
Oil Pan for Cars
Oil Stains Removed
Garage Tools Organized
Roof Repaired
Plants/Lawn Watered
Landscape Tidy

HOME INSPECTION

The following checklists are designed to assist a prospective home buyer or seller in organizing the task of making a preliminary home inspection. The checklist should be followed by a seller to assist in bringing the property to optimum condition before listing it for sale. Conversely, a careful examination by a prospective buyer prior to making an offer will assist in revealing the real condition of the house and negotiating price. Make a visual inspection of all applicable items on this checklist, and categorize their priority. Note that this checklist is intended to be for preliminary use only and is not considered a substitute for a professional property inspection.

Home Description & Features

Age _____

Size Living Areas _____
Stories _____
Bedrooms _____ Baths _____

Amenities Pool _____ Spa _____
Tennis _____ Views: _____
Rec Room _____ Laundry _____
Other _____

Appliances Washer _____ Dryer _____
Disposal _____ Range _____
Microwave _____ Trash _____
Refrigerator _____ Stove _____

**Detrimental
Conditions** _____

**Easements/
Encroachment** _____
Landscape _____

Garage _____

Home Inspection

Permits _____

Termite Inspection _____

Utilities _____

Asbestos _____

Emergency Shutoff Controls

Electrical Panel _____

Gas Shutoff _____

Sewer Cleanout _____

Water Shut-off _____

Other _____

Energy Conservation

Door
Weather-stripping _____

Window
Weather-stripping _____

Insulation - Floor _____

Insulation - Wall _____

Insulation - Piping _____

Insulation - Ceiling _____

Energy Saving
Devices _____

Low - Flow Toilets _____

Other _____

Home Inspection

HOME INSPECTION CHECKLIST

Repair/Replacement Priority

H = **High Priority** - These items must be repaired immediately and include any issues related to safety or significant non-performance.

M = **Medium Priority** - These items include deferred maintenance items that will require repair or replacement soon.

L = **Low Priority** - These items include cosmetics and upgrades. They are not required for safety but may enhance the appeal of the property.

	Appears Serviceable	Not Applicable	Repair	Repair Priority H M L
FOUNDATION				
Anchor Bolts	☐	☐	☐	☐☐☐
BASEMENT	☐	☐	☐	☐☐☐
Crawl Space	☐	☐	☐	☐☐☐
Grading	☐	☐	☐	☐☐☐
Mudsill	☐	☐	☐	☐☐☐
Sheer Panel	☐	☐	☐	☐☐☐
Soil Conditions	☐	☐	☐	☐☐☐
Slab on Grade	☐	☐	☐	☐☐☐
Other _____	☐	☐	☐	☐☐☐

Home Inspection

	Appears Serviceable	Not Applicable	Repair	Repair Priority
				H M L
GROUNDS				
Exterior Stairs	❏	❏	❏	❏❏❏
Fences & Gates	❏	❏	❏	❏❏❏
Decks	❏	❏	❏	❏❏❏
Driveway	❏	❏	❏	❏❏❏
Patio	❏	❏	❏	❏❏❏
Patio Cover	❏	❏	❏	❏❏❏
Retaining Walls	❏	❏	❏	❏❏❏
Sidewalks	❏	❏	❏	❏❏❏
Trip Hazards	❏	❏	❏	❏❏❏
Other _____	❏	❏	❏	❏❏❏
POOL/SPA				
Blower	❏	❏	❏	❏❏❏
Coping	❏	❏	❏	❏❏❏
Deck	❏	❏	❏	❏❏❏
Electrical	❏	❏	❏	❏❏❏
Heater	❏	❏	❏	❏❏❏
Lights	❏	❏	❏	❏❏❏
Pumps	❏	❏	❏	❏❏❏
Sweep	❏	❏	❏	❏❏❏
Timer	❏	❏	❏	❏❏❏
Water Filter	❏	❏	❏	❏❏❏
Other _____	❏	❏	❏	❏❏❏
EXTERIOR				
Exterior Walls	❏	❏	❏	❏❏❏
Chimney	❏	❏	❏	❏❏❏
Trim	❏	❏	❏	❏❏❏
Other _____	❏	❏	❏	❏❏❏

Home Inspection

	Appears Serviceable	Not Applicable	Repair	Repair Priority H M L
INTERIOR				
Ceilings	❑	❑	❑	❑❑❑
Entry Doors	❑	❑	❑	❑❑❑
Exterior Doors	❑	❑	❑	❑❑❑
Fire Alarms	❑	❑	❑	❑❑❑
Fireplace	❑	❑	❑	❑❑❑
Fireplace Hearth	❑	❑	❑	❑❑❑
Floors	❑	❑	❑	❑❑❑
Interior Doors	❑	❑	❑	❑❑❑
Interior Walls	❑	❑	❑	❑❑❑
Lighting	❑	❑	❑	❑❑❑
Stairs	❑	❑	❑	❑❑❑
Stair Rails	❑	❑	❑	❑❑❑
Wet Bars	❑	❑	❑	❑❑❑
Windows	❑	❑	❑	❑❑❑
Other _____	❑	❑	❑	❑❑❑
HEATING & COOLING				
Air Conditioner	❑	❑	❑	❑❑❑
Air Filters	❑	❑	❑	❑❑❑
Burners	❑	❑	❑	❑❑❑
Controls	❑	❑	❑	❑❑❑
Combustion Air	❑	❑	❑	❑❑❑
Distribution	❑	❑	❑	❑❑❑
Overall System	❑	❑	❑	❑❑❑
Venting	❑	❑	❑	❑❑❑
Other _____	❑	❑	❑	❑❑❑

Home Inspection

	Appears Serviceable	Not Applicable	Repair	Repair Priority H M L
PLUMBING				
Fuel System	❏	❏	❏	❏❏❏
Hose Faucets	❏	❏	❏	❏❏❏
Main Line	❏	❏	❏	❏❏❏
Sprinklers	❏	❏	❏	❏❏❏
Supply Lines	❏	❏	❏	❏❏❏
Waste Lines	❏	❏	❏	❏❏❏
Water Heater	❏	❏	❏	❏❏❏
W/H Brackets (W/H)	❏	❏	❏	❏❏❏
W/H T/P Valve	❏	❏	❏	❏❏❏
Other _____	❏	❏	❏	❏❏❏
ELECTRICAL				
Conductors	❏	❏	❏	❏❏❏
Main Panel	❏	❏	❏	❏❏❏
Outlets	❏	❏	❏	❏❏❏
Sub Panels	❏	❏	❏	❏❏❏
Wiring	❏	❏	❏	❏❏❏
Other _____	❏	❏	❏	❏❏❏
KITCHEN				
Cabinets	❏	❏	❏	❏❏❏
Dishwasher	❏	❏	❏	❏❏❏
Disposal	❏	❏	❏	❏❏❏
Flooring	❏	❏	❏	❏❏❏
Hood/Fan	❏	❏	❏	❏❏❏
Lighting	❏	❏	❏	❏❏❏
Range	❏	❏	❏	❏❏❏
Sink	❏	❏	❏	❏❏❏
Stove/Oven	❏	❏	❏	❏❏❏
Trash Compactor	❏	❏	❏	❏❏❏
Other _____	❏	❏	❏	❏❏❏

	Appears Serviceable	Not Applicable	Repair	Repair Priority
				H M L
BATHROOMS				
Bathtub	☐	☐	☐	☐☐☐
Cabinets	☐	☐	☐	☐☐☐
Electrical	☐	☐	☐	☐☐☐
Heater	☐	☐	☐	☐☐☐
Sink	☐	☐	☐	☐☐☐
Shower	☐	☐	☐	☐☐☐
Toilet	☐	☐	☐	☐☐☐
Ventilation	☐	☐	☐	☐☐☐
Other _____	☐	☐	☐	☐☐☐
LAUNDRY				
240 Volt Capacity	☐	☐	☐	☐☐☐
Cabinets	☐	☐	☐	☐☐☐
Electrical	☐	☐	☐	☐☐☐
Gas Availability	☐	☐	☐	☐☐☐
Plumbing	☐	☐	☐	☐☐☐
Sink & Faucet	☐	☐	☐	☐☐☐
Vents	☐	☐	☐	☐☐☐
Other _____		☐	☐	☐☐☐
GARAGE				
Automatic Opener	☐	☐	☐	☐☐☐
Electrical	☐	☐	☐	☐☐☐
Garage Door(s)	☐	☐	☐	☐☐☐
Door to Exterior	☐	☐	☐	☐☐☐
Fire Wall	☐	☐	☐	☐☐☐
Floor	☐	☐	☐	☐☐☐
Roof	☐	☐	☐	☐☐☐
Ventilation	☐	☐	☐	☐☐☐
Other _____	☐	☐	☐	☐☐☐

Home Inspection

ROOF	Appears Serviceable	Not Applicable	Repair	Repair Priority H M L
Attic	☐	☐	☐	☐☐☐
Exposed Flashing	☐	☐	☐	☐☐☐
Gutters & Downspout	☐	☐	☐	☐☐☐
Main Roof	☐	☐	☐	☐☐☐
Vents	☐	☐	☐	☐☐☐
Other _____	☐	☐	☐	☐☐☐

Home Inspection

CONDOMINIUMS, TOWNHOUSES AND ASSOCIATIONS

Condominiums and townhomes require the same checklists and descriptions as those in the ***Buying a House***, ***Selling a House*** and ***Home Inspections*** chapters. In additions, the following information should be used as a supplement for issues that are unique to these property types.

The distinction between condominiums and townhouses is that townhouses are generally a row of houses with a shared or "party" wall between residences. The land and unit is owned in a *fee simple estate* (i.e. the complete bundle of rights).

On the other hand, the ownership of a condominium unit consists of the "air-rights" within the unit and shared ownership of common areas. Often condominiums have separate units on separate floors while no other units are above or below townhomes.

A prospective buyer of a condominium or townhome unit should be aware that his or her property will be controlled in significant ways by the project's association. There may be stringent regulations as to what improvements may be done to the property, e.g. painting, landscaping, room additions, etc.

There is also the possibility that all property owners may share in the responsibility for costs incurred by the association although the costs may not be related to their own units (such as the repair of damaged units or equipment, etc.). Always carefully review the association's rules and regulations before buying.

Condo/Townhouse

TYPICAL CONDOMINIUM OR
TOWNHOUSE UNIT

Washer,
Dryer &
Water Heater

Patio

Dining
Area

Living
Room

Bedroom

Kitchen

Closets

Bathroom

Entry

Bedroom

Bathroom

CondoTownhouse

TOWNHOUSE & CONDOMINIUM
Supplemental Checklist

*This supplemental checklist should be utilized in conjunction with those in the **Home Inspection** section*

ASSOCIATION FACILITIES	Appears Serviceable	Not Applicable	Repair	Repair Priority H M L
Clubhouse	❑	❑	❑	❑❑❑
Recreation Room	❑	❑	❑	❑❑❑
Front Gates	❑	❑	❑	❑❑❑
Pool	❑	❑	❑	❑❑❑
Spa	❑	❑	❑	❑❑❑
Sauna	❑	❑	❑	❑❑❑
Tennis Courts	❑	❑	❑	❑❑❑
Landscape	❑	❑	❑	❑❑❑
Driveways	❑	❑	❑	❑❑❑
Trash Bins	❑	❑	❑	❑❑❑
Lobby	❑	❑	❑	❑❑❑
Security	❑	❑	❑	❑❑❑

ASSOCIATION MANAGEMENT

Dues	❑	_____
Escalation of Dues	❑	_____
Pending Lawsuits	❑	_____
Minutes of Meetings	❑	_____
Maintenance Schedules	❑	_____
Policies	❑	_____
Rules	❑	_____
Other		_____

Condo|Townhouse

HOME FINANCING

Calculating Home Affordability and Loan Payments

One of the first steps in purchasing a home is determining what is affordable. Lenders use a series of calculations to determine the maximum loan amount, and the following chart utilizes a formula typically used by lenders. It reflects the total affordable sales price of a home based upon the household's monthly gross income. The *Financial Tables* section may be used to determine the actual monthly loan payment.

Together these charts provide a good starting point for determining the affordability of a home and of the monthly payments. Remember that loan parameters vary from lender to lender, so consult with a real estate professional.

Instructions for Using the Charts

Find gross monthly income in the left hand column, and read across to the current interest rate. This is the total sales price of the home that can be afforded with this gross monthly income. This table is based upon a 20% down payment, 30 year loan term, and a 28% front-end ratio. Note that loan requirements vary and that loan programs exist that may greatly increase affordability over a conventional loan. Consult with a real estate professional.

HOME AFFORDABILITY TABLE
Interest Rate

Gross Monthly Income	7.00%	7.50%	8.00%	8.50%
$ 1,000	$ 53,000	$ 48,000	$ 46,000	$ 44,000
$ 1,250	$ 66,000	$ 60,000	$ 57,000	$ 55,000
$ 1,500	$ 79,000	$ 72,000	$ 69,000	$ 66,000
$ 1,750	$ 92,000	$ 84,000	$ 80,000	$ 77,000
$ 2,000	$105,000	$ 97,000	$ 92,000	$ 88,000
$ 2,250	$118,000	$109,000	$103,000	$ 99,000
$ 2,500	$132,000	$121,000	$115,000	$110,000
$ 2,750	$145,000	$133,000	$126,000	$121,000
$ 3,000	$158,000	$145,000	$138,000	$132,000
$ 3,250	$171,000	$157,000	$149,000	$143,000
$ 3,500	$184,000	$169,000	$161,000	$154,000
$ 3,750	$197,000	$181,000	$172,000	$165,000
$ 4,000	$210,000	$193,000	$184,000	$176,000
$ 4,250	$224,000	$205,000	$195,000	$187,000
$ 4,500	$237,000	$217,000	$207,000	$198,000
$ 4,750	$250,000	$229,000	$218,000	$208,000
$ 5,000	$263,000	$241,000	$230,000	$219,000
$ 5,500	$289,000	$265,000	$253,000	$241,000
$ 6,000	$316,000	$290,000	$276,000	$263,000
$ 6,500	$342,000	$314,000	$299,000	$285,000
$ 7,000	$368,000	$338,000	$322,000	$307,000
$ 7,500	$395,000	$375,000	$358,000	$341,000
$ 8,000	$421,000	$400,000	$382,000	$364,000
$ 8,500	$447,000	$425,000	$405,000	$387,000
$ 9,000	$473,000	$451,000	$429,000	$410,000
$ 9,500	$500,000	$476,000	$453,000	$432,000
$10,000	$526,000	$501,000	$477,000	$455,000
$10,500	$552,000	$526,000	$501,000	$478,000

Home Financing

HOME AFFORDABILITY TABLE
Interest Rate

		9.00%	9.50%	10.00%	10.50%
	$ 1,000	$ 42,000	$ 40,000	$ 38,000	$ 37,000
	$ 1,250	$ 52,000	$ 50,000	$ 48,000	$ 46,000
	$ 1,500	$ 63,000	$ 60,000	$ 58,000	$ 55,000
	$ 1,750	$ 73,000	$ 70,000	$ 67,000	$ 65,000
	$ 2,000	$ 84,000	$ 80,000	$ 77,000	$ 74,000
	$ 2,250	$ 94,000	$ 90,000	$ 87,000	$ 83,000
	$ 2,500	$105,000	$100,000	$ 96,000	$ 92,000
	$ 2,750	$115,000	$110,000	$106,000	$101,000
Gross Monthly Income	$ 3,000	$126,000	$120,000	$115,000	$111,000
	$ 3,250	$136,000	$130,000	$125,000	$120,000
	$ 3,500	$147,000	$140,000	$135,000	$129,000
	$ 3,750	$157,000	$151,000	$144,000	$138,000
	$ 4,000	$168,000	$161,000	$154,000	$148,000
	$ 4,250	$178,000	$171,000	$163,000	$157,000
	$ 4,500	$189,000	$181,000	$173,000	$166,000
	$ 4,750	$199,000	$191,000	$183,000	$175,000
	$ 5,000	$210,000	$201,000	$192,000	$184,000
	$ 5,500	$231,000	$221,000	$212,000	$203,000
	$ 6,000	$252,000	$241,000	$231,000	$221,000
	$ 6,500	$273,000	$261,000	$250,000	$240,000
	$ 7,000	$294,000	$281,000	$269,000	$258,000
	$ 7,500	$326,000	$312,000	$299,000	$287,000
	$ 8,000	$348,000	$333,000	$319,000	$306,000
	$ 8,500	$370,000	$354,000	$339,000	$325,000
	$ 9,000	$391,000	$375,000	$359,000	$344,000
	$ 9,500	$413,000	$395,000	$379,000	$363,000
	$10,000	$435,000	$416,000	$399,000	$383,000
	$10,500	$457,000	$437,000	$419,000	$402,000

Home Financing

HOME AFFORDABILITY TABLE
Interest Rate

Gross Monthly Income	11.00%	11.50%	12.00%	12.50%
$ 1,000	$ 35,000	$ 34,000	$ 33,000	$ 32,000
$ 1,250	$ 44,000	$ 43,000	$ 41,000	$ 40,000
$ 1,500	$ 53,000	$ 51,000	$ 49,000	$ 47,000
$ 1,750	$ 62,000	$ 60,000	$ 57,000	$ 55,000
$ 2,000	$ 71,000	$ 68,000	$ 66,000	$ 63,000
$ 2,250	$ 80,000	$ 77,000	$ 74,000	$ 71,000
$ 2,500	$ 89,000	$ 85,000	$ 82,000	$ 79,000
$ 2,750	$ 97,000	$ 94,000	$ 90,000	$ 87,000
$ 3,000	$106,000	$102,000	$ 98,000	$ 95,000
$ 3,250	$115,000	$111,000	$107,000	$103,000
$ 3,500	$124,000	$119,000	$115,000	$111,000
$ 3,750	$133,000	$128,000	$123,000	$119,000
$ 4,000	$142,000	$136,000	$131,000	$126,000
$ 4,250	$151,000	$145,000	$139,000	$134,000
$ 4,500	$159,000	$153,000	$148,000	$142,000
$ 4,750	$168,000	$162,000	$156,000	$150,000
$ 5,000	$177,000	$170,000	$164,000	$158,000
$ 5,500	$195,000	$187,000	$180,000	$174,000
$ 6,000	$213,000	$204,000	$197,000	$190,000
$ 6,500	$230,000	$222,000	$213,000	$206,000
$ 7,000	$248,000	$239,000	$230,000	$221,000
$ 7,500	$276,000	$265,000	$255,000	$246,000
$ 8,000	$294,000	$283,000	$272,000	$262,000
$ 8,500	$312,000	$300,000	$289,000	$279,000
$ 9,000	$331,000	$318,000	$306,000	$295,000
$ 9,500	$349,000	$336,000	$323,000	$312,000
$10,000	$368,000	$353,000	$340,000	$328,000

Home Financing

MOVING

Moving is clearly a very big job and requires thorough organization and preparation. This form is designed to assist with the planning and coordination required for a smooth transition.

MOVING TIPS & CHECKLIST

Do-It-Yourself Move

❑ Reserve a truck, van or trailer well in advance. Remember to order dollies, loading ramps, boxes, tape, padding, etc.

❑ Inquire about one-way vs. local charges. You might save by returning the truck, trailer or van to its point of origin.

❑ Inventory and measure your furniture to be sure you have ordered the correct size truck.

❑ Verify insurance coverage.

Moving

Moving Company

❑ Get competitive bids and be selective in choosing a moving company. Read all policies and contracts carefully.

❑ If applicable, tour your mover's warehouse for interim storage. Note the security, cleanliness, organization, etc.

❑ Consider packing your belongings yourself. This may save considerable cost.

❑ Consider moving during the off-season (October through March) when rates are usually lower.

❑ Consider a weekday move, which is usually less expensive than weekends.

❑ Have a yard sale or discard items you don't want. Many movers charge based on weight.

❑ Keep your shipment registration number in your wallet or purse, in case you need to call your mover with questions about your shipment.

❑ Give the moving foreman a phone number (and an alternate contact) where you can be reached.

Plants

❑ Prune plants at least 2 weeks before moving, to avoid the double shock of moving and pruning.

❑ If moving plants in your car, do not let them rest against the windows, as the leaves may scorch.

Moving

❑ For plants moved in boxes, punch air holes near the top, and cushion with damp newspapers to protect stems and avoid shifting.

❑ When possible, take any plants in your car. The heat inside a van or truck may damage them.

Packing

❑ Use boxes in good condition and that are properly sealed. When possible, keep boxes less than 50 pounds.

❑ Mark all boxes with:

> Name, address and phone
> What room to deliver to
> (Color-code boxes)
> Contents
> Priority of unpacking
> Mark "Fragile" if applicable

❑ Have children write their names and new address on their cartons so that they become familiar with their new address.

❑ Do not combine items from different rooms into one box.

❑ Leave clothes on hangers and pack in a wardrobe box.

❑ Place picture frames between towels, sheets or blankets to give them added protection.

❑ Pad delicate items.

❑ Remove breakable items and liquids from drawers and pack in boxes.

❑ China, plates, CD's and record albums should be packed vertically on-end, rather than stacked flat.

❑ Prior to packing aerosols and bathroom items, be sure that the caps and lids are tightly secured.

❑ Remove light bulbs prior to packing lamps or lighting fixtures.

❑ Disassemble what you can.

❑ Pack your local phone book. You may need to call former neighbors or businesses in your previous hometown area.

❑ Keep any pets calm on moving day by asking a friend or neighbor to watch your pet at their home.

❑ Take valuables or one-of-kind items with you.

❑ Load the items last that you will need first so they will be first to be unloaded. Load heavy furniture first.

Moving

PRIORITY ITEMS
Loaded Last and Unloaded First

Cleaning

Bleach	Broom/Dust Pan
Cleansing Powder	Dish Cloth
Dish Towels	Dusters
Liquid Cleaner	Mop/Bucket
Paper Towels	Scrub Brushes
Sponges	Steel Pads
Vacuum	Window Cleaner

Kitchen

Can Opener	Coffee Maker
Cups	Knives
Napkins	Pitcher
Plates	Pots, Pans, Utensils

Bed & Bathrooms

Comb & Brush	Deodorant
Facial Tissue	First-Aid Kit
Make-Up	Prescriptions
Mattress	Razor
Shampoo	Sheets & Pillows
Soap	Toilet Paper
Toothbrush	Toothpaste
Towels	Washcloth

Food

Bread	Coffee
Cream	Crackers
Dry Cereals	Milk
Sandwich Spreads	Snacks
Soft Drinks	Soup

Family Room

Answering Machine	Games
Phone	Radio/TV

Miscellaneous

Broom	Dust Pan
Flashlight	Garden Hose
Hammer	Light Bulbs
Nail Assortment	Picture Hangers
Pliers	Screw Drivers
Shelf Paper	Small Saw
Tape Measure	Trash Bags

Moving

TAKE-WITH INVENTORY

For the Trip

Baby Supplies, Books & Magazines, Camera and Film, Drinking Water, Keys, Maps, Medications, Paper Towels, Pet Food & Dishes, Pillows & Blanket, Phone for arrival, Phone Answering Machine, Snacks & Gum, Suitcases & Clothing, Sunglasses, Travel Toys, and Wallet & Purses

Valuables

Art, Car Ownership Records, Cameras & Video Cameras, Collections, Currency, Furs, Important Papers & Records, Insurance Policies, Jewelry, Photos, Slides & Videotapes, School Records, Silver, and Medical and Dental Records

Automobile Items

Auto Insurance Papers, Emergency Flares, Fire Extinguisher, First-Aid Kit, Flashlight, Litter Basket, Motor Oil, and Tire Inflator

Moving

COUNTDOWN TO MOVING DAY

Eight to Ten Weeks Prior

☐ Contact truck rental agencies or movers to get bids and make reservations.

☐ Clarify what expenses, if any, are your employer's.

☐ Consider making arrangements for cleaning, painting and remodeling of your new residence prior to moving, while the house is vacant.

☐ Start using up things that can't be moved, such as frozen foods, fuels and cleaning supplies.

☐ Contact the Chamber of Commerce or Visitor's Bureau in your new community for information.

☐ Start clearing out your garage, attic, basement, storage shed, etc.

Six Weeks Prior

☐ Collect all unwanted items and have a yard sale or make donations to charitable organizations.

☐ Notify all friends, creditors, professionals, etc. with change-of-address announcements.

☐ Contact doctors, dentists, lawyers, accountants, vet and schools to obtain copies of personal files and records. Ask for referrals where possible.

☐ Contact the IRS and your accountant for information on what moving expenses are tax-deductible.

Moving

❑ Locate and organize all important papers, such as insurance, auto licensing and registration documents.

Four Weeks Prior

❑ If packing yourself, purchase packing boxes and supplies. Pack items that you won't be needing in the next month.

❑ Obtain a change-of-address kit from the post office and begin filling out cards.

❑ Make any storage arrangements.

❑ Mail change of address cards for subscriptions.

❑ Collect all drapes, rugs, fabrics and clothes that require dry-cleaning and store them for packing.

❑ Subscribe to the local paper in your new community.

❑ Utilize the following checklist to contact utility companies for service disconnect/connect.

❑ Contact insurance companies (auto, homeowner's or renter's, medical, and life) to arrange for coverage at your new residence.

Two to Three Weeks Prior

❑ Collect important papers (insurance, will, deeds, stock, etc.).

❑ Make travel arrangements for your moving trip. Be careful about making plane reservations, because escrow closings are sometimes delayed.

Moving

❑ Arrange to close or transfer accounts in your bank and open accounts in your new community. Arrange to transfer safe deposit boxes.

❑ Have your car serviced for the trip. Consider the weather conditions in which you will be driving.

❑ If you're moving out of or into a building with elevators, reserve the use of freight elevators.

One Week Prior

❑ Withdraw the contents of your safety deposit box.

❑ Pick up any laundry or dry cleaning and return library books, videotapes, etc.

❑ Drain and dispose of gas and oil from power or lawn equipment (lawn mowers, etc.).

❑ Map clear directions to your new home.

Two or Three Days Prior

❑ Clean and dry the inside of your refrigerator. Place baking soda in a sock or nylon stocking inside the refrigerator to help keep the interior odor free. Secure the doors open so they cannot close on children.

❑ Have major appliances disconnected and prepared for the move.

❑ Pack the "take-with-items" and load into your car. Clearly mark these items so that they are not taken by the moving company in error.

Moving Day

❑ Have someone remain at the house until all items are packed by the moving company.

❑ Have drinks and snacks available for all those who assist in the move.

❑ Read your bill of lading and inventory carefully before signing. Keep these in a safe location until all charges and claims, if any, have been settled.

❑ Record utility meter readings (gas, electric, water).

❑ Leave keys, garage door openers, etc. with your agent or broker for your home's new occupant.

❑ Inspect and inventory the contents of all boxes prior to signing any release forms.

Moving

OLD ADDRESS - DISCONTINUE

ELECTRIC CO.
Phone _____
Date Called _____
Person Contacted _____
Date Discontinued _____

TELEPHONE CO.
Phone _____
Date Called _____
Person Contacted _____
Date Discontinued _____

GAS CO.
Phone _____
Date Called _____
Person Contacted _____
Date Discontinued _____

WATER CO.
Phone _____
Date Called _____
Person Contacted _____
Date Discontinued _____

CABLE TV CO.
Phone _____
Date Called _____
Person Contacted _____
Date Discontinued _____

FUEL OIL CO.
Phone _____
Date Called _____
Person Contacted _____
Date Discontinued _____

WATER SOFTENER
Phone _____
Date Called _____
Person Contacted _____
Date Discontinued _____

TRASH PICK-UP
Phone _____
Date Called _____
Person Contacted _____
Date Discontinued _____

Moving

NEW ADDRESS - START-UP

ELECTRIC CO.
Phone
Date Called
Person Contacted
Date Continued

TELEPHONE CO.
Phone
Date Called
Person Contacted
Date Continued

GAS CO.
Phone
Date Called
Person Contacted
Date Continued

WATER CO.
Phone
Date Called
Person Contacted
Date Continued

CABLE TV CO.
Phone
Date Called
Person Contacted
Date Continued

FUEL OIL CO.
Phone
Date Called
Person Contacted
Date Continued

WATER SOFTENER
Phone
Date Called
Person Contacted
Date Continued

TRASH PICK-UP
Phone
Date Called
Person Contacted
Date Continued

Moving

GLOSSARY OF MOVING TERMS

Additional Transportation Charge (ATC)--Additional charges by the carrier for labor rates that are higher than the national average, added transportation time and added travel time caused by traffic congestion

Advanced Charges--Fees or charges for third-party services, at the mover's request, that are added to the Bill of Lading

Accessorial Services--Charges that are in addition to transportation costs, such as packing, unpacking, extra pick-up, appliance servicing, storage-in-transit

Agent--A local moving company that represents a national van line in the capacity of booking, origin, and/or hauling

Annual Carrier's Performance Report--An annual report setting forth a carrier's performance such as estimating, on-time delivery and claims settlement

Appliance Servicing--Service required to disconnect, securing and preparing major appliances for transport

Auxiliary Service (Shuttle)--Shuttle service by a small van or truck between a home and the main moving van, due to narrow roads, bridges or parking constraints

Bill of Lading--Receipt for belongings "released to the carrier" and contract for their transportation

Binding Estimate--An estimate, based upon required services foreseen when the estimate is prepared, of the moving costs

Moving

Booking Agent--The agent who sells and accepts the moving order. A booking agent may or may not be the origin or destination agent

Bulky Article--Items such as cars, trucks, campers, boats, snowmobiles or golf cars that are unusually bulky and require an additional moving charge

Carrier--The moving company providing transportation for the household goods, with ICC operating authority

Change Order--An amendment of the amount indicated on the original estimate, due to added or deleted services requested by the customer

Claim--Statement of loss or damage to household goods while in the care of the carrier or its agent

COD (Cash on Delivery)--Payment at the time of delivery

Consignee--The person to whom the shipment is delivered

Declared Valuation--Shipper's indication of value for the items being shipped, thereby establishing the carrier's maximum liability (If no value is declared, the liability is established by tariff.)

Destination Agent--Agent located at or near the destination who provides necessary assistance, services and information at the end of the move

Estimate--A general calculation of the space requirements, weight, and cost of the move determined by an agent's survey

Moving

Expedited Service-- An agreement, for an additional charge, that sets forth a specific delivery date

Extra Stop--An additional stop, other than the origin or destination

Flight Charge (Stair Carry)--An additional charge for carrying items (such as appliances or pianos) to an upper or lower floor level.

Full-Value Protection--A valuation policy which does not include a deduction for depreciation in a settlement of a claim for loss or damage

Hauling Agent--The agent who owns the van to transport possessions

Interstate Commerce Commission (ICC)--The federal agency governing the interstate transportation industry

Inventory--The itemized list and condition of household furnishings

Long Carry--A set distance, more than a so-many feet, from the rear of the trailer to the entrance of the residence

Moving Counselor--The agent's representative who provides the customer with an estimate of the cost and generally assists with questions and concerns of the customer

Operating Authority--Permission granted by the ICC authorizing a carrier to move goods

Order for Service--Document authorizing the moving company to perform moving services

Moving

Order Number--The number which identifies a specific shipment

Origin Agent--The agent, at the origin, responsible for packing and documentation

Overflow--Additional articles that remain due to insufficient space on a van, to be loaded on a second van

PBO (Packed By Owner)--Items packed by the shipper, not the carrier

Registration Number--The number assigned to identify a shipment

Reweigh--Second weighing of shipment performed at destination, at the shipper's or mover's request

Shipper--The person whose household items are being moved

Storage in Transit (SIT)--The temporary storage of household goods, pending further transportation

Survey--The booking agent's examination of the shipper's goods to estimate moving charges

Tariff--The carrier's provisions and rates, for moving services

Third-Party Services--Services performed by someone other than the carrier at the mover's request or as required by law

Moving

Unpacking--The removal of household goods from their containers including the disposal of the containers and packing materials

Van Line--The moving company that dispatches, routes, monitors, processes paperwork, and settles claims handled by its agents

Van Foreman--The moving representative who has overall responsibility for the loading, transport and unloading of the items being moved

Van Operator--The driver of the van carrying household goods

RENTING vs. BUYING

THE " TALE " OF HOME OWNERSHIP

$$T + A + L = E$$

Tax Advantages	Appreciation	Leverage	Equity
One of the primary features of home ownership is the ability to deduct interest payments for income tax purposes. This is a major benefit of home ownership.	While home ownership can reduce taxes, the home itself may appreciate in value. Over time, appreciation can mean large equity build-up and profits to the home owner.	While homes are expensive, they can be made affordable by borrowing. Even the down payment can be reduced through seller financing, FHA loans, shared equity contracts, lease with option to buy or other means.	The tax advantages, possible appreciation and effects of leveraging can all contribute to building equity and personal financial security.

The following charts and graphs illustrate the various components of the "TALE" of home ownership.

Rent or Buy Comparison

While rental payments may seem attractive on the surface, the effects of tax savings may actually make home ownership more affordable than renting.

This chart illustrates that even when mortgage payments may exceed rental payments, the effective annual payments may in fact be lower than rental payments after the tax advantages. Consult with a licensed real estate professional to determine the specific market conditions in your area.

	Rent vs.	Buy
Property Value	$100,000	$100,000
Down Payment @ 20%	$0	$20,000
Loan Amount	$0	$80,000
Monthly Rent/ Loan Payment @ 10%, 30 Year Term	$600	$ 702
Annual Rent/ Loan Payment	$7,200	$8,425
Real Estate Taxes @ 1% of Value	$0	$1,000
Total Annual Payments	$7,200	$9,425
Less: Tax Savings @ 30% Tax Rate	$0	$2,827
Effective Annual Payments	$7,200	$6,597

Home Affordability Table

Monthly Payment Rate	7.00%	8.00%	9.00%	10.00%	11.00%	12.00%
$ 500	$ 93,000	$ 84,000	$ 77,000	$ 71,000	$ 65,000	$ 60,000
$ 750	$140,000	$127,000	$116,000	$106,000	$ 98,000	$ 91,000
$1,000	$186,000	$169,000	$154,000	$141,000	$130,000	$121,000
$1,250	$233,000	$211,000	$193,000	$177,000	$163,000	$151,000
$1,500	$279,000	$253,000	$231,000	$212,000	$196,000	$181,000
$1,750	$326,000	$296,000	$270,000	$247,000	$228,000	$211,000
$2,000	$372,000	$338,000	$308,000	$283,000	$261,000	$242,000
$2,250	$419,000	$380,000	$347,000	$318,000	$293,000	$272,000
$2,500	$465,000	$422,000	$385,000	$354,000	$326,000	$302,000
$2,750	$512,000	$464,000	$424,000	$389,000	$359,000	$332,000
$3,000	$558,000	$507,000	$462,000	$424,000	$391,000	$362,000

Note that this chart does not include the effects of property taxes, association dues or insurance costs. Consult with a licensed real estate professional to determine your specific situation and current market conditions.

To estimate the affordable price of a home, match the left column with your current rental payment or available monthly income for a loan payment, and read across to the current mortgage interest rate.

This is approximately the value of home that can be purchased with this monthly payment based upon a 20% down payment.

Renting vs. Buying

Equity Build-Up

While renting can be advantageous for short periods of time or while saving for a down payment, the advantages of home ownership go far beyond just the pride of ownership.

This graph depicts the initial equity and the subsequent equity build-up of a home with a 20% down payment and assuming 3% annual appreciation.

Renting vs. Buying

DOWN PAYMENT vs. EQUITY

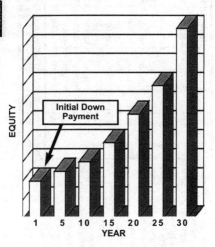

COMMON REPAIRS

Toilet Overflowing

Remove the tank cover (this water is clean). Push the rubber flap (attached to the flush handle) down into the hole. Turn off the water valve at the base of the toilet.

Toilet Unplugging

Do not bother with liquid unclogging agents. Due to the way a toilet is constructed, chemicals usually cannot reach clogs.

Many toilets may be unplugged with a plunger. (A toilet plunger has a cone that extends out of the rubber cup.) Place plunger snugly over the opening to make a tight seal, pump the plunger several times, lift the plunger sharply to snap the seal. Repeat several times if necessary.

If a plunger fails to unplug the toilet, use a toilet or closet auger. This is a thick flexible wire with a hook on one end and crank handle on the other. While cranking the handle, feed the cable slowly into the opening so that it works its way up and over into the toilet trap. If you feel the hook catch something, keep cranking in the same direction and pull out the auger.

If both methods fail, call a plumber.

Common Repairs

Sinks - Unclogging

Fill the sink with water so that at least one-half of the plunger cup is covered. Put a rag into the overfill hole, if any. (This is the hole at the top of the sink, opposite the faucet.) If the sink shares the same drainage with another sink, you need also to place a rag into its drainage and overfill holes as well.

Using a sink plunger (a common small rubber cup, without the extended cone), place the plunger over the opening to create a seal and pump several times. Pull the plunger quickly, and repeat if necessary.

If the plunger doesn't work, check the "trap" (the "J" or "U" shaped pipe under the sink). If the trap has a clean-out plug, and if the blockage is in the trap, it may be removed through the clean-out plug.

If the plunger does not work, and the blockage is located beyond the trap, remove the trap and use an auger as described above.

Sewer Lines

In order to determine whether one toilet or sink is clogged or if the clog is in the main sewer line, flush other toilets in the house several times. (Be prepared for an overflow.) It is necessary to flush the toilets several times because the sewer lines may have the capacity to fill up with considerable water before overflowing. If the other toilets flow correctly, the blockage is limited to the one plugged toilet or sink. If the other toilets overflow, the blockage is in the main sewer line.

Broken Pipes

In the event of a water leak, immediately turn off the main water supply. Locate the main water supply now so that you may react swiftly in the event of a broken pipe. If there is any chance that the water may come in contact with electrical outlets, switches or appliances, turn the electrical main off first; then turn off the water.

Common Repairs

Roof

Roof leaks can be deceptive. The area of the leaking ceiling may be some distance from the roof leak, so the best place to look (and place buckets) is in the attic. Mark the source of the leak so that it can be located in dry weather when making roof repairs.

Property Safety

Fire Protection
Security
Emergency Preparedness
Insurance Inventory

FIRE PROTECTION

This chapter consists of important checklists that are divided into the following six topics:

1. Fire Extinguishers
2. Escape Plan
3. Fire Prevention
4. Procedures for a Small Fire
5. Procedures for a Large Fire
6. What to do if Trapped

FIRE EXTINGUISHERS

 A **Class A: Ordinary combustibles** such as wood, cloth, paper, rubber and many plastics

 B **Class B: Flammable liquids** such as gasoline, oil, grease, tar, oil-based paint, lacquer and flammable gas

C **Class C: Energized electrical equipment** including wiring, fuse boxes, circuit breakers, machinery and appliances

Many household fire extinguishes are "multipurpose" A-B-C models, labeled for use on all three classes of fire.

***WARNING**: It is dangerous to use water or an extinguisher labeled only for Class A fires on a grease of electrical fire. Follow all manufacturer guidelines and maintenance requirements.*

ESCAPE PLAN

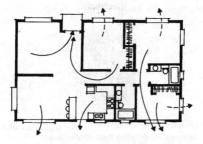

One of the first steps in fire safety is to develop a plan in the event that a fire occurs. All occupants should be involved in practicing the plan.

Plan at least two escape routes from each room. This means that second story windows should be equipped with a rope ladder device to allow for exiting through a second story window.

An exterior meeting place should be established as part of the escape plan. Once all occupants have exited the building, fire fighters should be alerted as to who is missing and the location of their room or likely whereabouts. The escape plan should be practiced to insure that all occupants are aware of both planned escape routes and the meeting place.

FIRE PREVENTION

Electrical

Fire Protection

☐ Un-plug all heat-producing small appliances after use, and never leave them unattended.

☐ Use only appliances that are tested and certified by an independent laboratory for fire safety.

☐ Keep all appliances away from water.

☐ Provide ample space and air around all appliances to avoid over-heating.

☐ Avoid circuit-overloading, and plug each appliance into its own outlet. Avoid using the same plug or circuit for many appliances.

☐ Never run cords under rugs, across traffic patterns, near children or under doors. Never pinch cords between furniture and walls, and keep cords off the appliance.

☐ Never use appliances near combustible items.

☐ Use only heavy-duty extension cords that are properly rated for their use.

❑ Replace any worn cords, and keep all switches professionally repaired.

❑ Keep appliances clean and free of lint and dirt.

❑ Use light bulbs and fuses that are properly rated. Never use a "penny" instead of a fuse. Never reset a circuit breaker or replace a fuse without knowing what caused the problem.

❑ Electric blankets should never be folded or used for over 30 minutes at a time. Set an alarm if required.

❑ Have old wiring updated with three-wired, polarized receptacles. Never cut off the grounding pin or wide prong to fit an old circuit.

❑ If you detect any problem such as recurring blown fuses or tripping circuit breakers, discoloration of outlets, burning smells or odors, flickering lights or tingling when touching a cord or appliance, call a professional electrician or the power company at once.

Fire Protection

SMOKING

❑ Consider a *no smoking* rule in your home.

❑ Check the furniture, floor and rugs after smokers leave.

❑ Never smoke in bed, while reclined, or around any flammable liquid or hair spray.

❑ Use a large, non-tip ashtray.

❑ Never use a waste-basket as an ashtray or for hot ashes.

❑ Make sure an ashtray is cold before disposing of ashes.

Smoke Detectors

❑ Smoke, not flames, causes most fire-related deaths. Select a State-Marshall approved unit that is U.L. approved and follow all manufacturer recommendations. If the unit is electric, a battery-operated system is also recommended as a back-up. Place a smoke detector in every level of the house (including the basement) and outside every bedroom. Install at the high point of ceilings and away from heat ducts. Test detectors monthly and replace batteries as recommended by the manufacturer. Never paint a smoke detector.

Fire Protection

COOKING

❏ Never store children's treats over a stove as their clothing may catch fire while reaching over it.

❏ Do not wear loose clothing while cooking.

❏ Keep any combustible materials away from the stove because grease may spatter and ignite such materials.

❏ Never put foil or metal into a microwave oven.

❏ Keep all pot handles turned so children cannot pull them down.

❏ Never leave a hot stove unattended.

❏ Keep stoves and ovens clean and grease-free.

❏ Remember that animal fat is highly flammable. Trim all meat of excess fat before cooking.

HEATING

❑ Keep all heating units clean with the unit turned off whenever it is being cleaned. Keep chimney clean and professionally inspected.

❑ Keep all matches and lighters out of the reach of children.

❑ Never use flammable liquids to start a fireplace fire.

❑ Never leave a fire unattended.

❑ Open the damper and close the screen or glass doors when the fireplace is in use.

❑ Keep all flammable materials away from any fire or heating unit.

❑ After cooled, dispose of ashes in a metal container with a tight metal lid.

❑ Never use any fuel other than the type specifically approved by the manufacturer of a heating unit.

❑ All heating units must be placed on an approved floor protector or fire resistant floor. Keep all areas properly vented.

❑ Follow all local fire and building codes.

❑ Use an Oxygen Depletion Sensor (ODS), that turns off the unit if carbon monoxide accumulates.

❑ If you smell gas, *turn off the gas supply (if accessible) and get out!* Call the fire department immediately from a neighbor's house.

❑ Never use a flame to test for gas leaks; it could cause an explosion.

OUTSIDE AREAS

❑ Keep all areas cleared in accordance with local fire codes.

❑ Remove all brush near the home.

❑ Prune all branches to a height 15 to 20 feet above the ground, or as instructed by the local fire department.

❑ Dispose of all felled trees, brush and pruned branches.

❑ Build a fire-break at least 6 feet wide surrounding the building site.

❑ Use only outdoor-rated fixtures and outlets.

❑ Never use electric cords in wet weather or near pools or spas.

❑ Never touch a power line. Keep ladders, kites, balloons and other objects away from power lines.

❑ Let gas-powered lawn and garden tool motors cool before refueling.

❑ Install a lightning protection system, and install a fire retardant roof.

❑ Never leave an outdoor barbeque unattended.

STORAGE

❏ Properly dispose of oily rags; they are an extreme fire hazard.

❏ Dry out oily rags outside or in a well-ventilated room and then wash them.

❏ Never store oily rags in a pile.

❏ Remove and dispose of all clutter, old cloths and trash throughout the property.

❏ Flammable liquids should be stored in metal containers away from any sources of heat such as lights, furnaces, water heaters, or pilot lights. Label all such materials.

❏ Store newspapers and magazines in a cool, dry place away from any sources of heat or combustible material. Store coal and barbecue briquettes in a metal can with a metal lid.

HOLIDAYS

☐ Water Christmas trees regularly, and turn off tree lights before going to bed or leaving the home.

☐ Check decorative lights, cords and sockets for damage and for the certification of an independent testing laboratory.

☐ Keep all wrappings cleaned-up.

☐ Avoid candles, and consider the use of flashlights instead. If using candles, extinguish all wicks when not in the room.

☐ Make sure Halloween costumes are fire-retardant.

☐ Keep a list of all household items for insurance reasons. Refer to the section on *Insurance Inventory.*

☐ Keep matches out of the reach of small children.

☐ Always follow the manufacturer's recommendations and warnings on household items.

☐ Consider a home fire-sprinkler system.

Fire Protection

SMALL FIRES

☐ **Precautions:** Before attempting to fight a small fire, make sure that all persons and pets are leaving the building and the fire department has been notified. Do not make the attempt unless the fire is confined to a small area and there is a clear means of exit. Follow the instructions on the fire extinguisher. If these are not the conditions, *get out and stay out!*

☐ **Electrical:** Turn off the appliance and pull out the plug. Extinguish with a "C" or "ABC" rated extinguisher, or smother the fire with a blanket. Never use water because it may cause an electric shock and spread the fire.

☐ **Gas:** Shut off the gas supply. Use a Type "B" or "ABC" rated extinguisher or smother the fire with a blanket. Ventilate the area of gas fumes. Call the fire department and the gas company immediately. Have the gas company check the area and turn the gas back on.

☐ **Heating:** Shut off the heating unit. Use an "ABC" rated fire extinguisher or a blanket to smother the fire. Call the fire department if there is fire up the chimney or if the stove or heating unit pipes are red hot.

❑ **Smoking:** Extinguish all smoking materials. Use an "A" or "ABC" rated fire extinguisher or a blanket to smother flames.

❑ **Cooking:** Turn off the stove or oven immediately and cover the skillet, pan or pot with a lid, or close the oven door. Use a "B"-Type fire extinguisher, or smother with baking soda. Never move a burning pan or turn on a fan while there are flames.

❑ **Outside Areas:** Use a water supply and douse the fire, or smother the fire with dirt. Watch the area for subsequent flair ups.

❑ **Storage:** As the materials on fire may be unknown use an ABC-Rated fire extinguisher, or smother with a blanket.

Fire Protection

LARGE FIRES

❑ **Don't Panic:** Think clearly and avoid heavy breathing of the air. Remember, small children will sometimes become scared and hide under a bed or in a closet if there is a fire. Go to the nearest exit that is not blocked by fire. Do not go back into a burning building. Professional fire fighters are far better trained and prepared to enter a burning building for any rescues.

☐ **Crawl:** Hot air and smoke rises, so crawl along the floor for air. If possible, put a wet cloth over your mouth and nose.

☐ **Feel Doors:** Before opening a door feel the door-knob and door for heat. If it is hot, do not open the door. Close all doors behind you.

☐ **No Elevators:** Never take an elevator during a fire. Use only stairways.

Fire Protection

☐ **Meeting Place:** Once out of the building, go to the pre-designated meeting place.

☐ **Call 911:** Call the fire department immediately from a neighbor's home.

IF TRAPPED IN A FIRE

Fire Protection

❑ Stop where you are and drop immediately to the floor. Cover your face with your hands and roll slowly to smother the flames. Use water to cool off and call 911.

❑ If trapped, stuff rugs, towels, blankets or cloths into any door cracks or vents that are letting in smoke or gases. Turn off all heaters, air-conditioning or fans. Call the fire department, even if they are at the scene, to let them know exactly where you are. Open the top of the windows to let out smoke or gases on the ceiling, but never open windows if there is smoke coming from the floor below you. Breath air close to the floor, and signal to rescuers from a window. Always follow the instructions of a firefighter.

SECURITY

There are more than 6 million residential burglaries every year in the US, or an average of one every 10 seconds. Nearly one-half of these are committed without force and the criminals simply walk in. Remember, home security is like a chain...it is only as good as the weakest link. Thieves are opportunists, and a well-secured house will often send them looking for an easier target. Make a complete security check of your residence using this checklist and any other literature provided by your local law-enforcement officials.

Deadbolts

Doorknob locks offer no real security. All exterior doors should have at least a one-inch dead-bolt, with a hardened steel roller in the center. (The roller rotates and prevents the bolt from being sawed.) The case should be solid brass, steel or bronze. The lock mechanism should have at least a 5-pin tumbler. If a double cylinder deadbolt is used, leave a key in the inside lock when home to allow for escape in case of fire.

Make sure all garage, cellar and storage areas leading to the house are well-locked. It is not of real benefit to have a good lock on the front door and flimsy locks on the side and back doors. The door leading from the garage to the house should be considered an entry and secured accordingly.

The metal plate attached to the door frame is called a "strike". Make sure the strike, and any window or door hardware, are held in place by screws that are at least 2 1/2 inches long.

Doors and Garage Doors

All exterior doors should be solid core and at least 1½

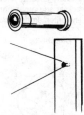

inches thick at any point. If an exterior door is within arms-length (40 inches minimum) of glass, additional security measures are needed to prevent a burglar from breaking the glass and opening the lock. Use a double cylinder deadbolt or replace the glass with polycarbonate plastic. Door-mounted mail shots should have an "intruder hood" to prevent anyone from looking into the house. Install a wide-angle viewer at the front door, and do not open the door to strangers.

Garage doors should be secured with hardened steel hasps and padlocks on both sides. Bikes and motorcycles should be locked (even in a garage). Reset your garage door opener codes periodically. (Refer to the owners manual for details.) Many thieves simply open garage doors by using the standard remote openers.

Hinges

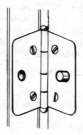

Hinges should never be hung with the pin facing the outside because an intruder could easily remove the pin and open the door. Install "locking pins" which have a nail or screw that protrudes 1/2 inch from one side of the hinge into a hole on the other. With the hinge pins removed, the locking pins will keep the door in place.

Windows and Sliding Doors

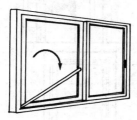

A wood or metal rod may be placed in the track to prevent opening.   (See illustration above.)

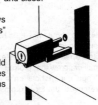

Screw

Track

Door Frame

Glass

To prevent a sliding door from being lifted out of the frame, place three Number 8 or 10 sheet metal screws into the track above the sliding door's closed position. The top of the screw should be placed just high enough to clear the door to allow it to open and close.

Sliding doors and windows should have "ventilation locks" as well as auxiliary locks.

Double sash windows should be secured by drilling two holes at angles and placing steel pins into these holes (see below).

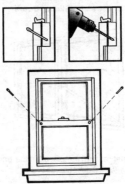

Ventilation openings should not be overlooked. Place grills, screening or bars over any such openings. Strip all nuts, bolts or screws to prevent their removal.

Louvered windows present a security problems as the slats of glass can often be easily removed. Replace these windows completely, or remove each pane of glass and sand the end of each pane where it meets the metal frame. Apply a two-part epoxy resin glue to the sanded area and insert the glass into the frame.

Locks and Chains

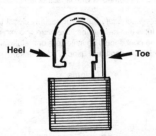

Heel ➤   ◄ Toe

Padlocks minimum standards are a 9/32" shackle, double locking (heel and toe), 5-pin tumbler and a key retaining feature which prevents the key from being removed when the lock is opened. Never leave the key in a padlock, since it may be copied and used later. Combination-type lock cases are easily broken and should not be used as security devices.

Chain minimum standards are 5/16" for household use, and 3/8" for bikes and motorcycles. Use only a hardened steel alloy with continuous welded construction. Secure valuables to a fixed object so that they cannot

Security

be carried away. Hasps should be properly mounted. Make sure that hasp mounting screws are covered when the hasp is locked. Use large washers on the inside. After the nuts are secured, strip any exposed threads to keep the nuts from being removed. Gates and fencing should be solid materials. Equip all gates with good padlocks. Ornamental gates are recommended, because they keep people out, but allow for the observation of someone who is hiding.

Consider a secondary barrier or security closet to store jewelry, furs, cameras, guns silverware and other valuables. The door should be solid core or metal with a single cylinder deadbolt and "pinned" deadbolts.

Lights

Exterior lighting is important and inexpensive. Place lights under eaves to expose a thief next to the house. Place the lights high enough to prevent tampering.

Landscaping

Make sure that shrubbery is trimmed so that intruders do not have a place to hide. All trees should be trimmed to prevent access to a second story.

Going Out

Keep your house completely locked, even if leaving for "just a minute". Never leave a key under the mat, on a ledge, in or under a flower pot or other such "hiding places". These are often the first places a thief will look, and some insurance companies may not honor a claim if there was no forced entrance. Do not put a name tag on your keys.

Have your house address well marked and illuminated all night. Do not place first names on a mail box. To help police helicopters locate your residence, place your house number on a rear roof area. Roof-top numbers should be at least 24 inches high.

Always make the house appear occupied. Leave lights, TV and radios on. Use timers to make these things go "on an off" throughout the house. Never leave notes indicating that the house in unoccupied or when you will return. Close and lock your garage. An empty garage "advertises" that the house is unoccupied.

If leaving for an extended period stop mail, newspaper and milk deliveries, and arrange for lawn and gardening care. Consider a trained guard dog or security system. Whenever you move, have the locks changed at your new address.

Do not announce on your answering machine that you are gone or have left on vacation. Simply say that you "cannot answer the phone right now".

Notify neighbors and police that you will be gone and for how long. Notify the police immediately upon your return.

Consider hiring a "house-sitter". If you return and there are signs of a forced entrance (broken window, broken door, etc) do not enter in case a criminal may still be on the premises. Do not confront a burglar, let him go. Call the police immediately from a car phone or neighbor's house. Do not disturb the scene if a crime has been committed.

Alarm Systems

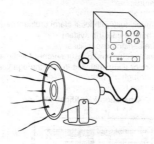

Do not depend on an alarm system only for protection. Be sure to utilize all of the above locking and security measures.

Obtain quotes from several reputable alarm companies, and check references from several local customers who use their services. Do not commit to any company before first investigating information from all the companies you have contacted. Consider utilizing a local alarm company where travel and service-call costs may cost you less than from a company outside your area.

Notify your neighbors of the decision to install an alarm system and make sure the alarms are loud enough to be heard by them.

Consult your local law enforcement authorities directly before installing a system that automatically calls police. Be aware that there may be fines associated with false alarms and some authorities discourage these types of alarm systems.

At a minimum, an alarm system should have all of the following features:

1. Comply fully with local alarm ordinances
2. A battery back-up system
3. Fire sensing capabilities
4. Test mechanism to insure proper functioning
5. Horn or alarm installed in attic through vent

Operation Identification

Despite every preventive measure, a desperate thief may still break in. Make a list of all valuables as detailed in the *Insurance Inventory* section of this book.

Many states have an "operation identification" program. Thieves are less likely to take valuables that have been marked or engraved because they are harder to sell, easier to trace and serve as evidence against them. Some local police departments have engravers to lend. Mark items with your drivers license number and your state abbreviation.

Post an "operation identification" sticker or notice at entrances and windows.

Many police departments provide home inspections as a community service, and provide important information and suggestions for your specific home and area.

Consider a neighborhood watch program. Consult your local law enforcement officials for details. Consult with local law enforcement officials regarding your specific home security issues.

EMERGENCY PREPAREDNESS

FLOOD

Tens of thousands of people are driven from their homes by floods each year. Trained river-watchers often know in advance when flooding will occur and may provide flood warnings via radio, TV, newspaper, sirens or loudspeakers. Know which warning system is used in your community, and when a warning is given, follow all instructions.

Keep a radio on and tuned to local weather stations. If time permits, place necessities in the upper levels of the house. Turn off the electric and gas main. Bring outside furniture and equipment inside. Some experts suggest that water be allowed to enter the basement, rather than being diverted. Consult with local authorities in advance regarding this issue.

During a flood, do not attempt to cross fast moving water. Keep away from low terrain that is subject to sudden flooding. Never attempt to drive on or through a flooded road because the vehicle may stall.

Once the flooding subsides, do not use any water or food that has come in contact with the flood waters. Consult utility companies prior to turning on the gas or electricity.

EARTHQUAKE

Earthquakes are completely unpredictable. If indoors, stay inside and take cover beneath a strong table or desk. Stay away from windows which may shatter.

If you are outdoors, stay outdoors. Stay away from buildings and overhead power lines. Head for a vacant lot or wide open area.

Once the earthquake subsides, check for leaking gas. If you smell gas, open doors and windows and turn off the gas main. It should only be turned back on by the gas company.

Remember, earthquakes are frequently followed by small tremors or after-shocks. Seek a safe place in the interim.

If driving during an earthquake, pull to the side of the road away from overpasses and power lines. When you resume driving watch for fallen trees, power lines and cracked roads.

Never "sightsee" after an earthquake to avoid becoming a hindrance to emergency services.

Emergency Preparedness

TORNADO

Tornado season is considered to be April, May and June, and tornados most often occur between noon and midnight. The National Service Storms Forecast Center in Kansas City, Missouri, keeps watch over the 48 contiguous states. While very destructive, tornados are usually preceded by advance notice: a *tornado watch* (expected to occur) or a *tornado warning* (actually sighted).

If a tornado watch is given, stay tuned to local weather forecasts. If upgraded to a tornado warning, open the windows in the house, and go promptly to a tornado shelter or basement if one exists nearby. If there is no basement, take cover under heavy furniture in the center area of the house. Most schools in tornado areas have a designated tornado shelter. If in a shopping area, go to the designated shelter or store basement. Do not stay in a parked car.

In the open country tornados are often visible. A tornado path averages only about one-quarter mile wide. Move away at a right angle to the tornado. If there is no time to escape, lay down on the ground in the nearest low spot such as a ditch or ravine.

Once a tornado has passed, tune into the local radio station for information.

HURRICANE

Hurricane season is from late summer through late fall. Like tornados, hurricanes are usually preceded with a warning on local TV and radio stations. Follow the advice given in these broadcasts.

Turn off the main gas valve and the main electric switch. Park cars in the garage and move all outside furniture and equipment inside. Board up the windows or close the storm windows. Leave one or two windows open on the side of the house away from the storm's path. (Weather reports will indicate the direction of the hurricane.)

If evacuation is ordered by local authorities, leave immediately. Follow all instructions on which roads to use and proceed where instructed.

Emergency Preparedness

FIRE

Unlike the natural disasters discussed above, fires are often preventable. Fire emergency prevention and procedures are addressed in more detail in the *Fire Protection* section.

Think clearly and avoid inhaling deeply. Remember, small children will sometimes become frightened and hide under a bed or in a closet. Go to the nearest exit that is not blocked by fire. Do not go back into a burning building. Professional fire fighters are far better trained and prepared to enter a burning building for any rescues.

Hot air and smoke rise, so crawl along the floor for air.

If possible, put a wet cloth over your mouth and nose. Before opening a door, feel the doorknob and door for heat. If it is hot, do not open the door. Close all doors behind you. Never take an elevator during a fire. Use only stairways.

Once out of the building, go to the pre-designated meeting place. Call the fire department immediately from a neighbor's home.

EMERGENCY KIT

In the event of an emergency, occupants may be forced to leave their homes or offices for a period of time. Emergency services may be overloaded, so it is a good idea to have an *Emergency Kit* on hand. These kits should contain the basic necessities for at least 72 hours (a week is better) or until assistance can arrive. All items should be placed in a ready-to-carry pack. This kit should be placed next to the primary exit of the building or home, and be ready for instant pick-up. As an emergency may occur while driving, it is also wise to have kits in the trunk of vehicles as well.

Activated Charcoal
Adhesive Bandages
Antiseptic Cream
Aspirin
Bandages
Burn Ointment
Gauze
Gauze Pads
Ice Packs
Ipecac
Mineral Oil
Rubbing Alcohol
Roll Bandages
Scissors
Soap
Sterile Eye Wash
Tape
Thermometer
Triangular Bandage
Tweezers

BATHROOM SUPPLIES

Contact Lens
Glasses
Comb or Brush
Deodorant
Lotion
Mirror
Razor
Shaving Cream
Soap & Shampoo
Toothbrush
Toothpaste
Towels

Emergency Preparedness

Canned/Dry Foods, Baby
Food and Supplies

Notebook, Pencil and
Phone Numbers

Toilet Paper

Trash
Bags

Medicines

Drinking
Water in
Plastic
Bottles

Flashlight and
Extra Batteries

Water
Purification
Tablets

Multi-Purpose Knife

Portable
Stove

Whistle

Cooking and Eating
Utensils

Matches
or Lighter

Portable Radio and Extra
Batteries for Emergency
Broadcasts

Blankets, Sleeping Bag
or Thermal Blanket

Emergency Preparedness

INSURANCE INVENTORY

Record of Contents

This form is designed to organize an inventory of household contents. In the event of a fire or other disaster, a standard insurance claim must be accompanied with a list of household contents. In addition to filling out this form, it is highly recommended that all contents are photographed, videotaped, and this information be updated regularly. Note that this inventory list and any accompanying photographs or videos should <u>not</u> be kept at the property to avoid damage or destruction by a fire or other disaster. It is recommended that this information be kept in a bank safe deposit box.

	Year Purchased	Replacement Cost
Family Room or Den		
Aquarium	_____	_____
Books	_____	_____
Book Cases (Portable)	_____	_____
Cabinets (Portable)	_____	_____
CDs, Records, Tapes	_____	_____
Chairs	_____	_____
Clocks	_____	_____
Computers/Printers	_____	_____
Couches, Sofas	_____	_____
Curtains/Drapes/Blinds	_____	_____
Desk	_____	_____
Drapes	_____	_____
Electric Appliances	_____	_____
Fine Arts*	_____	_____

***Important:** Most fine art items like paintings, etchings, antiques, tapestries, fine rugs or collectables should be listed individually on a Personal Property Schedule.*

	Year Purchased	Replacement Cost
Fireplace Fixtures	_____	_____
Floor Lamps	_____	_____
Game Sets	_____	_____
Lamps	_____	_____
Mirrors (Portable)	_____	_____
Musical Instruments	_____	_____
Piano Bench	_____	_____
Pictures	_____	_____
Planters	_____	_____
Radio	_____	_____
Rugs, Carpets	_____	_____
Sewing Machine, Table	_____	_____
Stereo	_____	_____
Tables	_____	_____
Table Lamps	_____	_____
Television	_____	_____

Kitchen & Pantry

	Year Purchased	Replacement Cost
Brooms, Mops	_____	_____
Cabinets	_____	_____
Canned Goods	_____	_____
Chairs	_____	_____
Clocks	_____	_____
Crockery	_____	_____
Crystal/Glassware	_____	_____
Curtains/Drapes/Blinds	_____	_____
Cutlery	_____	_____
Dishes	_____	_____
Dishwasher	_____	_____
Electric Appliances	_____	_____
Freezer	_____	_____
Glassware	_____	_____
Iron	_____	_____
Kitchen Utensils	_____	_____
Liquor	_____	_____

Insurance Inventory

	Year Purchased	Replacement Cost
Pictures	_____	_____
Pots, Pans	_____	_____
Radio	_____	_____
Refrigerator	_____	_____
Rugs/Carpets	_____	_____
Spices	_____	_____
Stove	_____	_____
Tables	_____	_____
Television	_____	_____
Vacuum Cleaner	_____	_____
Waxer-Buffer	_____	_____

Dining Room & Dinette

	Year Purchased	Replacement Cost
Buffet	_____	_____
Candlesticks	_____	_____
Chairs	_____	_____
China Cabinet	_____	_____
China and Glassware	_____	_____
Clocks	_____	_____
Curtains/Blinds	_____	_____
Drapes	_____	_____
Electric Appliances	_____	_____
Electric Utensils	_____	_____
Fine Arts*	_____	_____
Lamps	_____	_____
Mirrors (Portable)	_____	_____
Pictures	_____	_____
Rugs, Carpets	_____	_____
Serving Tables	_____	_____
Silverware	_____	_____
Table	_____	_____
Table Linens	_____	_____

Important: **Most fine art items like paintings, etchings, antiques, tapestries, fine rugs or collectables should be listed individually on a Personal Property Schedule.**

Insurance Inventory

	Year Purchased	Replacement Cost
Personal Effects - Women		
Belts	_____	_____
Blouses	_____	_____
Coats	_____	_____
Dresses	_____	_____
Formal Wear	_____	_____
Furs	_____	_____
Coats	_____	_____
Jackets	_____	_____
Neck Pieces	_____	_____
Gloves	_____	_____
Handbags	_____	_____
Handkerchiefs	_____	_____
Hats	_____	_____
Hosiery	_____	_____
Lingerie	_____	_____
Shoes	_____	_____
Skirts	_____	_____
Suits	_____	_____
Sweaters	_____	_____
Personal Effects - Men		
Belts/Suspenders	_____	_____
Formal Wear	_____	_____
Handkerchiefs	_____	_____
Hats	_____	_____
Overcoats, Raincoats	_____	_____
Shirts	_____	_____
Shoes	_____	_____
Slacks	_____	_____
Socks	_____	_____
Sport Jackets	_____	_____
Suits	_____	_____
Sweaters	_____	_____
Ties	_____	_____
Underwear	_____	_____

Insurance Inventory

	Year Purchased	Replacement Cost

Special Inventory & Jewelry

Bracelets		
Buckles, Clips		
Cameras		
Collections		
Cuff Links		
Earrings		
Necklaces		
Pins, Broaches		
Rings		
Stick Pins, Studs		
Video Camera		
Watches		

Silverware

Candlesticks		
Pitchers		
Platters		
Silverware		
Butter Knives		
Knives and Forks		
Salad Forks		
Tablespoons		
Teaspoons		
Tea, Coffee Service		

Playroom & Nursery Items

Bassinet		
Bedding		
Blankets		
Books		
Bookcases		
Carriage		
Chairs		
Chests		

Insurance Inventory

	Year Purchased	Replacement Cost
Clock	_____	_____
Clothes	_____	_____
Couches	_____	_____
Crib	_____	_____
Curtains/Drapes/Blinds	_____	_____
Deck	_____	_____
Floor Covering	_____	_____
Lamps	_____	_____
Mattresses, Springs	_____	_____
Mirrors (Portable)	_____	_____
Pictures	_____	_____
Play Pens	_____	_____
Radio	_____	_____
Rugs/Carpets	_____	_____
Scales	_____	_____
Tables	_____	_____
Television	_____	_____
Toys	_____	_____
VCR	_____	_____
Youth Bed	_____	_____

Basement, Laundry, Garage Storage

	Year Purchased	Replacement Cost
Awnings	_____	_____
Barbecue (Portable)	_____	_____
Benches	_____	_____
Bicycles	_____	_____
Camp Equipment	_____	_____
Canned Goods	_____	_____
Dryer	_____	_____
Freezer	_____	_____
Garden Tools	_____	_____
Hand Tools	_____	_____
Hardware	_____	_____
Hose	_____	_____
Irons, Ironing Board	_____	_____

Insurance Inventory

	Year Purchased	Replacement Cost
Ladders		
Luggage		
Mowers		
Patio Furniture		
Pool Floats & Ropes		
Pool Skimmer		
Pool Vacuum		
Power Tools		
Radio		
Roller Skates		
Sports Equipment		
Tables		
Trunks		
Tubs		
Vacuums		
Washing Machine		
Work Benches		

Bedrooms

	Year Purchased	Replacement Cost
Bed Spreads		
Beds		
Blankets		
Books		
Bookcases		
Bureaus		
CD's, Records, Tapes		
Chairs		
Chaise Lounge		
Chests		
Clocks		
Clothing		
Cosmetics		
Curtains/Drapes/Blinds		

	Year Purchased	Replacement Cost
Desk	_____	_____
Dressers	_____	_____
Dressing Tables	_____	_____
Fine Arts*	_____	_____
Jewelry	_____	_____
Lamps	_____	_____
Mattresses, Springs	_____	_____
Mirrors (Portable)	_____	_____
Night Stands	_____	_____
Perfumes	_____	_____
Pictures	_____	_____
Pillows	_____	_____
Pillow Cases	_____	_____
Radios	_____	_____
Rugs, Carpets	_____	_____
Sewing Machines	_____	_____
Sheets	_____	_____
Spreads	_____	_____
Stereo	_____	_____
Television	_____	_____
Toilet Articles	_____	_____

Bathrooms

	Year Purchased	Replacement Cost
Bath Mats	_____	_____
Cabinets	_____	_____
Clothes Hamper	_____	_____
Cosmetics	_____	_____
Curtains	_____	_____
Dressing Tables	_____	_____
Electric Appliances	_____	_____
Linens	_____	_____
Medicines	_____	_____

Insurance Inventory

	Year Purchased	Replacement Cost
Mirrors (Portable)	____	____
Pictures	____	____
Radios	____	____
Rugs/Carpets	____	____
Scales	____	____
Shaving Equipment	____	____
Shower Curtain	____	____
Sun Lamps	____	____
Towels	____	____
Living Room		
Books	____	____
Book Cases (Portable)	____	____
CDs, Records, Tapes	____	____
Chairs	____	____
Clocks	____	____
Coffee and End Tables	____	____
Couches, Sofas	____	____
Curtains/Drapes/Blinds	____	____
Desk	____	____
Drapes	____	____
Fine Arts*	____	____
Fireplace Fixtures	____	____
Lamps	____	____
Mirrors (Portable)	____	____
Musical Instruments	____	____
Piano/Organ, Bench	____	____
Pictures	____	____
Planters	____	____
Radio	____	____
Rugs, Carpets	____	____
Stereos	____	____
Table Lamps	____	____
Tables	____	____
Television	____	____
VCRs	____	____

Insurance Inventory

Detrimental Conditions

Ten Classifications
List of Detrimental Conditions
Environmental Contamination
Geotechnical Issues
Radon
Lead
Formaldehyde
Asbestos
Federal Agencies
Managing the Impact
Detrimental Condition Glossary

THE TEN CLASSIFICATIONS OF
DETRIMENTAL CONDITIONS

Diminution in Value are the legal rules of damage which provide for differences between "before" and "after" values of properties that have been damaged or taken (Black's Law Dictionary). There are over 250 Detrimental Conditions (DCs) that may damage or impact real estate values. These range from construction defects and deferred maintenance to environmental contamination, geotechnical issues and natural disasters. While identifying, categorizing and analyzing these numerous DCs may seem overwhelming, the task becomes manageable when the various common attributes and "groupings" are considered and studied. As the **Bell Chart** sets forth, all DCs may be placed into one of ten standard categories. Each category or group has distinct valuation attributes that correspond with the diminution in value caused by those types of conditions. This classification is important not only to organize a very long list of complex situations but also to avoid the error of measuring the effects of one DC by utilizing data from another category that may have different valuation characteristics altogether.

The basic premise of measuring the value of a property that has been impacted by a DC is to recognize some or all of the basic elements as illustrated in the **Detrimental Condition Model**. Each DC Class has distinct graphic patterns that center upon the inclusion, exclusion, timing and impact of the **_Four Stages of Recovery_**. The first step with any DC is to value the property as if it were a Class I Condition or as if there is no DC. This is reflected as Point A. Upon the discovery of the DC, the value may fall to Point B. Some DCs require **_Assessment Costs_**, such as conducting a soils or engineering study. The value during this period is usually the lowest, as a potential buyer would likely require a very significant discount to entice him or her to purchase a property where the extent of damage is unknown.

10 Classifications

Upon the completion of a study, if one is required, the value will generally increase to Point C. If repairs are required, upon their completion the value will increase to Point D. The **_Repair Process_** includes not only the repair costs themselves but contingencies, carrying costs and a project incentive to entice the buyer to purchase a damaged property. Point E reflects the value of the property after considering the *present value* of any **_Ongoing Costs_** such as absorption costs, loss of utility, continuing oversight or maintenance, additional financing or insurance costs and any other restrictions or costs.

In some conditions a **_Market Resistance_** remains even after the repairs are completed, which is indicated as Point F. This reflects the resistance of buyers to purchase a property that has been damaged or (where there remains a question about the adequacy of the repairs) market perceptions, the fear of future related

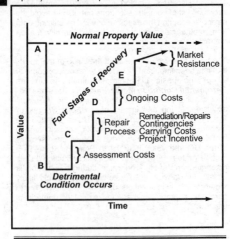

issues arising, or simply the real or perceived trouble of owning a property with a history of being damaged.

As the **Bell Chart** details, the basic classifications reflect the distinct graphic attributes of each class. For example, the value patterns of deferred maintenance are similar to a construction easement, and slope instability is similar to wetlands; however, the value patterns of a construction easement are distinct from slope instability. Both Class IV DCs and Class IX DCs may reflect a loss attributable to market resistance, but these graphic patterns are distinctly different. Class IV DCs do not include special engineering studies or remediation costs, and any related Class IV market resistance virtually always diminishes over time while the perceptions related to a property with soils contamination may worsen over time in the event that governmental standards become more strict.

The chart accommodates the full range of possible situations. For example, one may contend that a DC exists, but upon investigation it may be determined to be a Class I - Benign Condition. This issue may arise when a buyer, acting out of buyer's remorse, cites a benign condition as an excuse for rescinding the sale. On the other hand, some conditions may be so severe, that the cost to repair or remediate is greater than the property's value. This is reflected by the Class X category.

When encountering any DC, the parties involved should first determine its classification and consider all four stages of recovery. This will lay the foundation for a meaningful evaluation of the diminution in value. Once the DC has been properly classified, relevant market data may be researched and applied utilizing the formulas set forth here. The benefit of these formulas is that they itemize each of the components which result in a diminution in value. The categorization of DCs and the accompanying formulas provide thorough, consistent and proven methodologies in the study of conditions that result in a diminution in value.

10 Classifications

			TEN CLASSIFICATIONS OF	
	Class	**Definition**	**Types of Conditions**	
I	**No Detrimental Condition (DC) or Benign Condition**	No DC, or an event occurs, but has no impact on value.	Any DC If No Impact *(If Over: II, If Under: IV)* Sale-Leaseback/Build-to-Suit/Tenant Purchase Condemnation Threat Auction First Right-of-Refusal Double Escrow	
II	**Non-Market Motivation**	Any issue that inflates price over market. Detriment to buyer	Special Buyer Motivation Assemblage/Expansion Redevelopment Zone Feng Shui	
III	**Market Condition**	The increase or decrease of value due to general market	Economy/Supply & Demand/Takedown Recession/Depression Lease or Rolling Option Exercise Option	
IV	**Temporary Condition**	A short-term event or one-time situation	Distress Sale/Tragedy Bulk-Portfolio Sale/RTC Business Inc./Crime Scene Absorption/Deferred Maintenance/Riot/REO Bankruptcy/Probate-Estate-Short Sale/FDIC Accident/Disease	
V	**Imposed Condition**	An act or forced event that affects value. Usually long-term or permanent	Neighboring Nuisance Blight/EMF/Jail Bond or Tax Assessment Downzone/Historical Site Eminent Domain/Ground Lease/Deed Restriction Easement/Sewage-Power-Plant/Traffic-Airport Noise	

10 Classifications

DETRIMENTAL CONDITIONS

Diminution in Value - Key to Graphs

– – – –	Value With No Detrimental Condition
——	Value With Detrimental Condition
A:	Value Prior to Detrimental Condition
B:	Value Upon (Discovery of) Condition
C:	Value Upon Assessment of Condition
D:	Value Upon Repair Process Completed (Repairs, Contingencies, Carrying Costs, Project Incentive)
F:	Market Resistance

No or Benign DC

Non-Market

Increasing Values

Decreasing Values

Temporary Condition

Absorption/Mkt Resist

Imposed Act or Event

Diminish/Leasehold Effect

10 Classifications

10 Classifications

VI	Super-Surface Construction Condition	A construction issue above grade	ADA Non-Compliance Not to Code/Lead Paint/Construction Asbestos/Defect Poor Workmanship Water Intrusion Above Grade
VII	Sub-Surface Construction Condition	A construction issue below grade	Drainage/Tunneling Faulty Foundation Cut-Fill/Grading Retaining Wall or Slope/Soil Compaction Water Intrusion
VIII	Environmental Condition	A man-made environmental or contamination issue	Archeological PCE's/Oil Spill LUST/CERCLA Ground Water Contamination Landfill/PCB's/Soil Contamination Dump/Toxic Waste
IX	Natural Condition	A natural occurrence or natural disaster	Wetlands/Radon Earthquake/Volcano Expansive Soil Geotechnical/Flood Sulfates/Landslide Endangered Species/Infestation Slope Instability
X	Incurable Condition	A condition that cannot be economically or physically remedied	Applicable to many DCs in severe situations

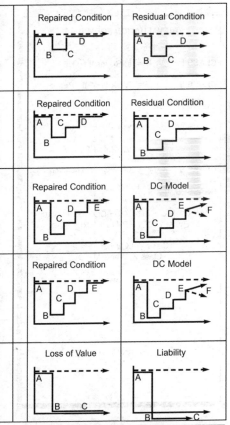

10 Classifications

DC VALUATION FORMULAS

CLASS I $V_I = I_O/R_O$, as if no DC

CLASS II $V_{II} = [V_I \times (1 + P)] - PV_{IR}$

CLASS III $V_{III} = [V_I \times (1 + MT)] + PV_{IR}$

CLASS IV $V_{IV} = V_I - PV_{TC} + PV_{IR}$
                    $= V_I - PV_{AC} + PV_{IR}$
                    $= V_I - MR + PV_{IR}$

CLASS V $V_V = V_I \times (1 + CA) + PV_{IR}$

CLASSES VI-X

$$V = V_I - [AC + RC + CT + CC + PI + PV_{AC} + PV_{OM} + PV_{FI} + PV_{RU} + MR] + PV_{IR}$$

Class VI-IX, Where $V > 0$
Class X, Where $V < 0$

KEY TO FORMULAS

V	=	Value
Io	=	Net Operating Income
Ro	=	Overall Rate, or Capitalization Rate
P	=	Premium Over Market
MT	=	Market Conditions Over Time
PVTC	=	Present Value of Costs or Loss of Utility from Temporary Condition
PVIR	=	Present Value of Insurance and Recoveries
CA	=	Condition Adjustment
AC	=	Assessment Cost i.e. site assessments, Phase I, Phase II, intrusive testing, well monitoring, etc.
RC	=	Remediation or Repair Cost i.e. administrative & general, agency over-sight, back-fill, disposal, engineering excavation, insurance, legal oversight, permits, remediation, repairs sampling & analysis, soil compacting, transport & hauling, treatment, trenching & back-hoe, etc. Includes all demolition and reconstruction costs i.e. structure, landscape, paving, utilities, well site removal, moving, etc.
CT	=	Contingencies for Repair or Remediation
CC	=	Carrying Costs during Repair Process
PI	=	Project Incentive, the financial incentive or discount required to assume risks/effort
PVAC	=	Present Value of Absorption Costs or Loss of Utility i.e. fixed operation costs, lost rents, tenant relocation, leasing commissions
PVOM	=	Present Value of Oversight and Maintenance i.e. operations & management program (O&M), periodic reviews, eventual repairs or remediation, reinstallation of wells, post-remediation monitoring, etc.
PVFI	=	Present Value of Financing and Insurance Cost Premiums
PVRU	=	Present Value of Restrictions on Use
MR	=	Market Resistance, the post-repair taint or negative perception as recognized by the market.

10 Classifications

LIST OF DETRIMENTAL CONDITIONS AND THEIR TYPICAL CLASSIFICATIONS

1. Absorption Loss (IV)
2. ADA Compliance (VI)
3. Access Diminution (V)
4. Accident (IV)
5. Adverse Possession (V)
6. Airport Noise (V)
7. Airport Proximity (V)
8. Air Disaster (IV)
9. Air & Light Diminution (V)
10. Ancient Burial Ground (VIII)
11. Archeological Site (VIII)
12. Asbestos (VI)
13. Ash from Neighboring Incident (IV, V)
14. Assemblage (II)
15. Auction (I)
16. Avalanche (IV)
17. Bankruptcy (IV)
18. Benign Condition (I)
19. Black Carbon from Neighboring Use (IV, V)
20. Blight (V)
21. Bond Assessment (V)
22. Build-to-Suit (I)
23. BTEX's (VIII)
24. Building Not to Code (VI)
25. Business Included (I)
26. Bulk Sale (I)
27. Calamity (IV)
28. Carbonaceous Sediment (IV, V)
29. Catastrophe (IV)
30. Cemetery Proximity (V)
31. CERCLA (VIII)
32. Civil Unrest ((IV)
33. Condemnation (V)
34. Construction Defect (VI, VII)
35. Construction Noise (IV)

36. Construction Not to Code (VI, VII)
37. Contamination (VIII)
38. Contaminated Public Wells (VIII)
39. Cracking (VI, VII, IX)
40. Crime Scene (IV)
41. Crude Oil Spill (VIII)
42. Cut & Fill (VII)
43. Cyclone (IV)
44. Dam Proximity (V)
45. Dam Spillage or Bursting (IV)
46. Death on Property (IV)
47. Deed Restriction (V)
48. Deferred Maintenance (IV)
49. Depression (III)
50. Differential Settlement (VII)
51. Dike Proximity (V)
52. Dike Spillage or Bursting (IV)
53. Direct Condemnation (V)
54. Disaster (IV)
55. Disease (IV)
56. Distress Sale (IV)
57. Double Escrow (I)
58. Downzone (V)
59. Drainage (VI, IX)
60. Drought (IV)
61. Drug Activity (IV)
62. Dump (VIII)
63. Dust from Neighboring Use (V)
64. Earthquake Damage (IX)
65. Earthquake Fault Zone (IX)
66. Earthquake Retrofit (VI, VII)
67. Easement (V)
68. Economy (III)
69. Egress Diminution (V)
70. Electric Plant (V)
71. Electric Lines (V)
72. Electro-Magnetic Fields (EMF) (V)
73. Encroachment (V)

112. Imposed Condition (V)
113. Incurable Condition (X)
114. Infestation (IX)
115. Ingress Diminution (V)
116. Inverse Condemnation (V)
117. Jail Proximity (V)
118. Judicial Foreclosure (IV)
119. Kangaroo Rat (IX)
120. Land Contract (I)
121. Landfill (VIII)
122. Landing Pattern Proximity (V)
123. Landscape Damage (IV)
124. Landslide (IX)
125. Lead Paint (VI)
126. Leaks (VI, VII)
127. Lease Option (I)
128. Legal Issues (IV)
129. Liquefaction, or sinking soils (IX)
130. Lis Pendens, legal dispute as to title (IV)
131. LUST (Leaking Underground Storage Tank) (VIII)
132. Market Conditions (III)
133. Military Base Proximity (V)
134. National Priority List (VIII)
135. Natural Condition (IX)
136. Neighborhood Blight (V)
137. Neighborhood Disturbance (IV, V))
138. Neighboring Construction (IV)
139. Neighboring Nuisance (V)
140. Non-Conforming Use (V)
141. Non-Market Motivation (II)
142. Monsoon (IX)
143. MRI Release (IV)
144. MTBE's (VIII)
145. Nuclear Disaster (V)
146. Nuclear Plant Proximity (V)
147. Nuisance in Area (IV, V)
148. Odors in Area (V)
149. Oil Seepage (VIII, IX)

188. Short Sale (IV)
189. Signage Diminution (V)
190. Sinkhole (VII, IX)
191. Site Grading (VII)
192. Slope Creep (IX)
193. Slope Instability (IX)
194. Soil Compaction (VII)
195. Soil Contamination (VIII)
196. Soils Subsidence (VI, IX)
197. Solid Waste Disposal Proximity (V)
198. Solvent Contamination (VIII)
199. Soot from Neighboring Use (IV, V)
200. Special Buyer Motivation (II)
201. Special Tax Assessment (V)
202. Special Use Permit (II)
203. Spillage (VIII)
204. Storm (IX)
205. Street Noise (V)
206. Sub-Surface Construction Defect (VII)
207. Subsidence (VII, IX)
208. Suicide on Premises (IV)
209. Sulfates (IX)
210. Superfund Site (VIII)
211. Super-Surface Construction Defect (VI)
212. Supply and Demand (III)
213. Takedown (III)
214. Tax Assessment (V)
215. Tax Lien (V)
216. TCE's (VIII)
217. Temporary Condition (IV)
218. Temporary Easement (IV)
219. Tenant Purchase (I)
220. Termites (IX)
221. Threat of Condemnation (IV)
222. Tidal Wave (IX)
223. Title Dispute (IV)
224. Tornado (IX)
225. Toxic Contamination (VIII)

226. Toxic Waste (VIII)
227. TPH's (VIII)
228. Traffic Congestion (IV)
229. Traffic Diminution (V)
230. Traffic Noise (V)
231. Tragedy (IV)
232. Treatment Storage & Disposal Facility (V)
233. Tunnel Collapse (VII)
234. Tunneling (V)
235. Twister (IX)
236. Urban Decay (V)
237. Utility Disruption (IV)
238. Utility Easement (V)
239. US Marshall Sale (IV)
240. Vacancy Problems (IV)
241. Vandalism (IV)
242. View Diminution (V)
243. Volcano (IX)
244. Waste Water Discharge (VIII)
245. War (IV)
246. Water Contamination (VIII)
247. Water Intrusion (VI, VII, IX)
248. Water Leaks (VI, VII)
249. Water Shortage (IV)
250. Wetlands (IX)
251. Woodrot (IX)
252. X-Ray Release (IV)
253. Youth Hostel Proximity (V)
254. Zoning Change (V)
255. Zoning Variance (II)

ENVIRONMENTAL CONTAMINATION

Environmental contamination can result from a variety of pollutants being emitted in a variety of ways. Some contaminates are released into the air through factory or vehicle emissions. Other are discharges or spilled directly into oceans, lakes or rivers.

Real estate values are typically the most directly impacted by soils contamination because the contamination often affects a specific property. The diagram below illustrates some of the typical causes of soils contamination and the danger of these contaminants entering the ground water supply.

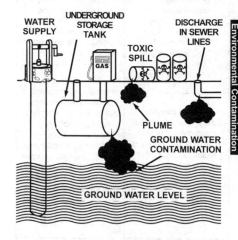

ENVIRONMENTAL MANAGEMENT OVERVIEW

PHASE I Surface Review	PHASE II Sub-Surface Study
An initial review of a site to determine if there is any reason to suspect contamination. It may also address compliance with environmental or OSHA laws and regulations	*The collection of soil or groundwater samples through drilling or excavation and laboratory analysis to determine the nature and extent of any contamination*
A Phase I study may include reviews of: *Aerial Photographs* *Air Quality Department* *Fire/Health Departments* *Government Agency Lists* *Historical Permits* *Historical Uses* *Planning/Building Department* *Surface Inspection* *Tenant Interviews* *Water Quality Control Board*	**A Phase II study may include the following studies or tests:** *Asbestos/Radon Testing* *Ground Water Wells* *Laboratory Analysis* *Lead in Drinking Water/Paint* *Soil Borings & Samples* *Soil Vapor Samples* *Surface Water/Sediment*
Phase I Results *If the Phase I study indicates that no reason exists to suspect contamination, then no other studies may be necessary. However, if evidence indicates that the site may be contaminated, then a Phase II study may be required*	**Phase II Results** *If contamination exists, a feasibility analysis may outline the potential problems and solutions. A Remedial Action Plan (RAP) may then be prepared. Upon the approval of the RAP, Phase III may be instituted. The site may be monitored during or after Phase III to insure the success of contaminant removal*

Environmental Contamination

PHASE III Remediation	
In Situ *Treatment in Place*	**Ex Situ** Soil Excavation-Treatment
Bioremediation- Bioventing *The injection of oxygen or oxygen releasing compounds into the soils or groundwater. This stimulates aerobic biodegration*	**Bioremediation- Biomounding/Land Farming** *The addition of nutrients to mounds of soil to facilitate bioremediation. Or, the soils are spread over a lined treatment area. Nutrients are added and the soils are tilled*
Biodegradation *Microorganisms are added to the soils which break down contaminants within the soils or groundwater*	
Soil Vapor Extraction *The drawing of fresh air into the ground with a vacuum pump. The air mixes with the contaminants and brings them to the surface where they are treated*	**Fixation or Encapsulation** *Fixation materials are mixed with soils which enclose or "encapsulate" contaminants*
	Excavation and Off-Site Landfill Disposal *Contaminated soils are trucked to a landfill*
Passive Biodegradation *The concept of natural attenuation and allowing the natural biodegradation of contaminants*	**Excavation and Off-Site Treatment** *The off site treatment by one of the treatment methods such as incineration*
Ground Water Treatment *The pumping of sub-surface contaminated ground water which is treated on the surface and then pumped back underground or disposed*	**On-Site Low Temperature Thermal Desorption** *Heat treatment which vaporizes the contaminants which are treated by air emission systems*

Environmental Contamination

ENVIRONMENTAL CONTAMINATION
Flow Of Events

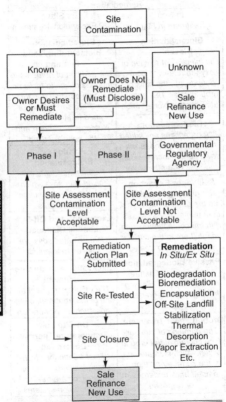

Environmental Contamination

ADDITIONAL ENVIRONMENTAL INFORMATION

A Home Buyer's Guide to Environmental Hazards

Environmental Backgrounder: Hazardous Wastes

Is Your Drinking Water Safe?

This publications are available at no cost from:

> U.S. Environmental Protection Agency
> Public Information Center, 401 M. Street, SW
> Washington, D.C. 20468
> Telephone: (202) 475-7751

Household Hazardous Waste Wheel

This publication is available at a cost of $3.75 from:

> Environmental Hazards Management Institute
> 10 New Market Road
> P.O. Box 932, Lurham, NH 03824
> Telephone: (603) 868-1496

Geotechnical Issues

There are two basic categories of geotechnical problems. First are those that occur naturally such as expansive soils, unstable soils, slope creep, slope instability, etc. Second are those that are construction defects or "man-made" problems such as improperly compacted soils, improper construction, leaking pipes under the foundation, inadequate drainage, retaining walls or slopes, etc. Both situations may result in the foundation cracking, cracks in walls, doors and windows going out-of-joint, and other problems.

The following illustration shows a typical geotechnical construction defect. Also illustrated are three repairs that are often used to correct geotechnical problems. It is important to note that when dealing with geotechnical problems, the problem (and not just the symptoms) must be addressed. If only the symptom is addressed (i.e. cracked foundation), the problem is likely to recur.

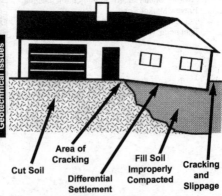

Cut Soil

Area of
Cracking

Differential
Settlement

Fill Soil
Improperly
Compacted

Cracking
and
Slippage

Tell-tale signs of geotechnical problems include cracks in the foundation, walls, driveway, porch or garage. Also, a sinking foundation is a symptom of soil problems. Some problems may be prevented by sloping the yard away from the house or installing rain gutters and spouts to divert water away from the foundation. Any cracks should be promptly patched, and any leaks should be quickly repaired.

There are three primary repairs made to cracked foundations: (1) reinforced repair, (2) underpinning, and (3) caissons or piles:

Reinforced Repair for Cracked Foundation

Small cracks may be filled by injecting epoxy. Larger cracks require this four-step process:

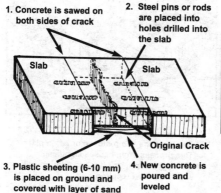

1. **Concrete is sawed on both sides of crack**

2. **Steel pins or rods are placed into holes drilled into the slab**

Slab   Slab

Original Crack

3. **Plastic sheeting (6-10 mm) is placed on ground and covered with layer of sand**

4. **New concrete is poured and leveled**

Geotechnical Issues

Underpinning

In situations where the foundation has settled, it may be lifted back into place through a process called "underpinning". This repair is utilized where the the soils have subsided because of hillside construction, drainage problems, expansive soils or improper soil compaction.

1. Soil excavated

2. Concrete platform constructed

3. Numerous jacks are used to lift the foundation back into place

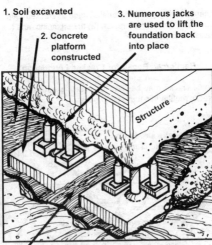

Structure

4. The excavated area is filled with concrete. The jacks may be removed or left in place. This process often causes significant cracking to both exterior and interior walls, which are then repaired.

Geotechnical Issues

Caissons or Piles

With the most serious geotechnical problems, caissons (columns with a widened base) or piles (columns only) may be utilized to set the structure upon firm bedrock or to prevent soil movement in a hillside area. These structures may be over 50 feet in depth and several feet in circumference. Both caissons and piles are constructed of steel reinforced concrete.

1. Soils are excavated, including a deep hole to house the caisson or pile

2. Braces or supports may be put into place, along with supports along the foundation

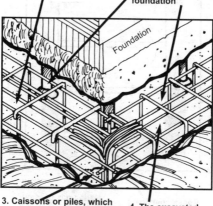

Foundation

3. Caissons or piles, which may be over 50 feet deep, are placed by inserting steel supports into the hole and filling with concrete

4. The excavated area is filled with concrete

Geotechnical Is

Radon

Radon is a naturally forming gas that has been determined by US Environmental Protection Agency (USEPA) to be a carcinogen (cancer-causing) substance. The gas forms when radioactive uranium and radium decays within rocks. The unit of measurement of radon is picocuries per liter of air (pCi/L).

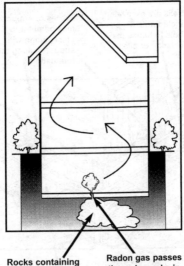

Rocks containing uranium, usually shales and granites, form a radioactive gas - radon

Radon gas passes through cracks in the basement or foundation and circulates within the structure

Radon gas is colorless and odorless and accumulates in the areas closest to the sources, usually at the ground or basement levels. Smokers are impacted most by radon, and the effects may take over 20 years to become apparent. The USEPA recommends that action be taken if radon levels are over 4 pCi/L.

In addition to gases, Radon may also enter the water system, particularly when water comes from wells. Water treatment for radon includes a granular activated carbon unit (GAC) or an aeration unit.

Radon gas is unpredictable and may affect one property and not the one next door. If any reason exists to suspect radon gases may be present, only a special laboratory test will provide conclusive answers.

Additional Information About Radon

USEPA Radon Measurement Proficiency Report
Listing of radon testing laboratories

USEPA Proficiency Report
Listing of mitigation contractors who meet the requirements of the USEPA Radon Contractors' Proficiency Program

Find and Reduce Radon in Your Home

The Inside Story - A Guide to Indoor Air Quality

These publications are available at no cost from:

U.S. Environmental Protection Agency
Public Information Center
401 M. Street, SW
Washington, D.C. 20460
Telephone: (202) 475-7751
Telephone: (800) SOS-RADON

Radon

The Radon Reference Manual
(PB-88196654)

This publication is available for $21.95 from:

National Technical Information Service
5285 Port Royal Road
Springfield, VA 22161.
Telephone: (703) 487-4650

Radon: Problems and Solutions

This publication is available for $6.95 from:

Citizen's Clearinghouse for Hazardous Waste
P.O. Box 926
Arlington, VA 22216
Telephone: (703) 276-7070

LEAD

Lead may be found in paints, dust, pipes and pipe soldering and drinking water. When exposure is excessive, lead can accumulate in the blood, tissues and bones. As a result, there may be damage to the brain, kidneys, male reproductive organs and nervous systems. Lead accumulation can cause learning disabilities, decreased IQ, and behavioral problems.

The two most common sources of lead are paint and water. The Environmental Protection Agency (EPA) estimates that lead-based paints were used in about two-thirds of the homes built before 1940, one-third of the homes built between 1940 and 1960, and in some homes built after 1960.

In 1978, the US Government required that paints for home use contain less than 0.06 percent of lead. Paints for other uses (industrial, military, marine, etc.) may have lead contents much higher than this. For this reason, it is important that paints intended only for home use be used when painting a home.

If home paints contain lead, they may be covered with wallpaper or paneling. Removing the paint in some ways, such as sanding, may actually increase the risk to lead exposure in the form of dust.

Lead may enter the drinking water because of lead pipes or lead solder used on copper pipes. Lead pipes are usually found only in homes built before 1930. Lead soldering materials have been banned since 1988.

The Maximum Contaminant Levels (MCLs) are EPA standards for maximum contaminant levels in drinking water. The MCL for lead is 0.050 parts per million (ppm).

Lead

If lead is found within drinking water, the plumbing system may be renovated, filters may be utilized or only bottled water used.

If any reason exists to suspect that lead is in paint or water, laboratory testing of samples should be conducted. If lead is detected in any samples as a result of laboratory testing, corrective measures should be taken.

Additional Information on Lead

EPA Safe Drinking Water Hotline, Washington, D.C.
Telephone: (800) 426-4791

Lead-Based Paint: *Interim Guidelines for Hazard Identification and Abatement in Public and Indian Housing.*

This publication is available for $3 from:

Department of Housing and Urban Development (HUD) Information Services, HUD User
P.O. Box 6091
Rockville, MO 20850
Telephone: (800) 245-2691

Manual for the Identification and Abatement of Environmental Lead Hazards

This publication is available at no cost from:

The National Maternal and Child Health Clearinghouse
38th and R. Streets, NW
Washington, D.C. 20057
Telephone: (202) 625-8410

Lead

Lead in Your Drinking Water

The Inside Story - A Guide to Indoor Air Quality

These publications are available at no cost from:

U.S. Environmental Protection Agency
Public Information Center
401 M. Street, SW
Washington, D.C. 20460
Telephone: (202) 475-7751

Lead

Formaldehyde

Formaldehyde is a colorless gas emitted from a variety of products, and is categorized as a probable carcinogen by the EPA. Household products that possibly contain formaldehyde include pressed items such as particleboard, urea-formaldehyde foam, insulation, fabrics, paints, plastics, photographic materials and resins. Two main categories of formaldehyde concern are mobile homes and wood-pressed products; however, it may also be produced by improperly vented gas or kerosene heaters. Newer products are more likely to emit formaldehyde gas than older ones.

Formaldehyde exists in the outside air at levels ranging from 0.0002 to 0.050 ppm (parts per million). Many people experience throat or eye irritation at levels of 0.1ppm or above. The only way to determine if formaldehyde levels are excessive (over the outdoor air levels) is through laboratory testing of air samples. Gas levels, if excessive, may be reduced by removing the materials that contain formaldehyde and generally increasing air circulation.

For Additional Information About Formaldehyde

The Inside Story - A Guide to Indoor Air Quality

This publication is available at no cost from:

U.S. Environmental Protection Agency
Public Information Center
401 M. Street, SW.
Washington, D.C. 20460
Telephone: (202) 275-7751

Formaldehyde: *Everything You Wanted to Know But Were Afraid to Ask*

This publication is available at no cost from:

Consumer Federation of America
1424 Sixteenth Street, NW
Washington, D.C. 20036
Telephone: (202) 387-6121
(A stamped, self-addressed envelope is required..)

Formaldehyde

ASBESTOS

Asbestos is a naturally formed fiber that is mined from rock. While asbestos has been used in building construction since the first century by the Romans and Greeks, its days of being considered another staple building material are clearly over.

Asbestos Containing Materials (ACM's) in and of themselves do not pose a health hazard; however, fibers released by disturbance, destruction or decay can cause serious health problems. There are at least six diseases that are attributable to asbestos; the two primary are mesothelioma (a lung cancer) and asbestosis (a chronic lung disease). In the early 1970's, ACM's were declared a health risk by the US Government, and no safe threshold has been established since. Buildings constructed prior to 1979 are likely to have ACM's.

ASBESTOS PRODUCTS IN THE HOME

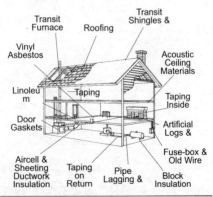

Transit Furnace
Roofing
Transit Shingles &
Vinyl Asbestos
Acoustic Ceiling Materials
Linoleum
Taping
Taping Inside
Door Gaskets
Artificial Logs &
Aircell & Sheeting Ductwork Insulation
Taping on Return
Pipe Lagging &
Fuse-box & Old Wire
Block Insulation

ASBESTOS PRODUCTS IN THE OFFICE

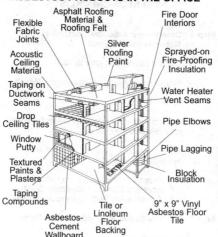

Flexible Fabric Joints

Asphalt Roofing Material & Roofing Felt

Fire Door Interiors

Silver Roofing Paint

Acoustic Ceiling Material

Sprayed-on Fire-Proofing Insulation

Taping on Ductwork Seams

Water Heater Vent Seams

Drop Ceiling Tiles

Pipe Elbows

Window Putty

Pipe Lagging

Textured Paints & Plasters

Block Insulation

Taping Compounds

Asbestos-Cement Wallboard

Tile or Linoleum Floor Backing

9" x 9" Vinyl Asbestos Floor Tile

Asbestos

Asbestos Removal Alternatives

This illustrates the results of a *Discounted Cash Flow Analysis* under four abatement scenarios. The value of a building with no asbestos is compared with immediate removal, staged removal, an O&M program with removal when the building is demolished. Note that results will vary from building to building.

ASBESTOS CHECKLIST

Step 1 Determine if Asbestos Containing Materials (ACMs) Exist

- Likely if constructed prior to 1979

- Friable or sprayed on construction materials

- Review building records

- Air Sampling - OSHA action level of 0.1 fibers per cubic centimeter of air

- Building Material Sampling - ACM if lab analysis indicates >1%

    1. Phase Contrast Microscopy (PCM)
    2. Scanning Electron Microscopy (SEM)
    3. Transmission Electron Microscopy (TEM)

Step 2 Disclose Status to All Appropriate Parties

- Consult attorney

- Follow EPA guidelines

- Post notices as required

- Disclosure to tenants, occupants, lenders, etc.

Step 3 Establish an Operations & Maintenance (O&M) Program

- Hire qualified trainers

- Train management, engineers & custodians

- Instruct building occupants

- Wet cleaning

❑ Routine air sampling

❑ Routine building inspections

❑ Continue until asbestos is removed or the building is demolished

Step 4 Abatement Options

❑ Perform financial analysis

❑ Study abatement timing (Initial, Staged, End)

❑ Select abatement method (encapsulation, enclosure or removal)

Step 5 Abatement

❑ Carefully screen and select contractors (interview, check references, insurance, etc.)

❑ Integrate abatement with tenant relocation

❑ Inspect work-site regularly

❑ Release contractor only after inspections and air sampling

❑ Document all abatement procedures

FEDERAL AGENCIES AND ASSOCIATIONS

Department of Labor Occupational Safety and Health Administration

Region I
(CT, MA, ME, NH, RI, VT)
16-18 North Street
1 Dock Square Building
4th Floor
Boston, MA 02109
(617) 223-6710

Region II
(NJ, NY, Puerto Rico, Virgin Islands)
1 Astor Plaza, Room 3445
1515 Broadway
New York, NY 10036
(212) 944-3432

Region III
(DC, DE, MD, PA, VA, WV)
Gateway Building, Suite 2100
3535 Market Street
Philadelphia, PA 19104
(215) 596-1201

Region IV
(AL, FL, GA, KY, MS, NC, SC,TN)
1375 Peachtree Street, N.E.
Suite 587
Atlanta, GA 30367
(404) 347-3573

Region V
(IL, IN, MI, OH, WI)
230 South Dearborn Street
32nd Floor, Room 3244
Chicago, IL 60604
(312) 353-2220

Region VI
(AR, LA, NM, OK, TX)
525 Griffin Square Building,
Room 602
Dallas, TX 75202
(214) 767-4731

Region VII
(IA, KS, MO, NE)
911 Walnut Street, Room 406
Kansas City, MO 64106
(816) 374-5861

Region VIII
(CO, MT, ND, SD, UT, WY)
Federal Building, Room 1554
1961 Stout Street
Denver, CO 80294
(303) 844-3061

Region IX
(American Samoa, AZ, CA, Guam, HI, NV, Pacific
Trust Territories)
P.O. Box 36017
450 Golden Gate Avenue
San Francisco, CA 94102
(415) 556-7260

Region X
(AK, ID, OR, WA)
Federal Office Building, Room 6003
909 First Avenue
Seattle, WA 98174
(206) 442-5930

Federal Agencies

US Department of Housing and Urban Development (HUD)
Office of Single Family Housing and Mortgage Activities
451 7th Street, Room 9282, SW
Washington, D.C. 20410
Telephone: (202) 708-3175

U.S. Environmental Protection Agency (USEPA)
Public Information Center
401 M. Street, SW
Washington, D.C. 20460
Telephone: (202) 382-2080

Asbestos Information Association
1745 Jefferson Davis Highway
Arlington, VA 22202
(703) 979-1150

Safe Buildings Alliance
655 15th Street, N.W.
Suite 1200
Washington, DC 20005
(202) 879-5120

Asbestos Abatement Council
Association of the Wall and Ceiling
Industries International
25 K Street, N.E.
Washington, DC 20002
(202) 783-2924

National Asbestos Council, Inc.
2786 N. Decatur Road, Suite 240
Decatur, GA 30033
(404) 633-2622

National Insulation Contractors Association
1025 Vermont Avenue, N.W.
Washington, DC 20005
(202) 783-6277

Federal Agencies

MANAGING THE IMPACT
OF DETRIMENTAL CONDITIONS
ON REAL ESTATE

In the event of a detrimental condition occurring, there are a variety of actions a property owner may take to manage the situation. Following are issues to be considered:

1. Address the needs of the victims and families first.

Obviously, if the detrimental condition involves a tragedy such as an earthquake, fire, landslide, other natural disaster or a crime, the best approach is to first forget about the real estate and make a determined attempt to assist the victims and their families. This could take many forms such as organizing a public donations drop-point, financial support, an "information clearinghouse", etc. Of course, full cooperation should be given to police, fire personnel and paramedics.

2. Consult with an Attorney.

There is a wide range in the quality of legal representation available. Select an attorney who is experienced with the condition to provide legal oversight to the situation.

3. Document all activity.

It is important to document activities, damage, comments and the removal of any possessions from the premises. Photographs and videos are helpful. This documentation may assist later in any insurance claims or litigation surrounding the incident.

Managing Detrimental Conditions

4. Secure the property.

Damaged properties may attract tourists and onlookers. While most people will respect the situation, some will attempt to take a "souvenir" or looting may occur. The police will often secure a property during the course of an investigation; however, it becomes the property owner's responsibility when they leave.

5. Deal with the situation. Silence invites negative speculation.

While human nature often resorts to some form of denial in the face of tragedy, a property owner should not attempt to ignore or "cover-up" the incident. Only problems that have been admitted can be dealt with. Demonstrate to the lender, insurance company, public and media that a decisive person has been put in charge to deal with the situation.

6. Deal with the media.

As a general rule, the less media the better; however, some situations are of such public interest that intense media interest is inevitable. Comments to the media should be focused upon the help given to the victims and their family, efforts to assist police, fire personnel, investigators and paramedics. It is important to respond quickly to any inaccurate information.

7. Promptly implement a written action plan with stated goals and objectives.

Within one week after the incident, write a clear action plan that addresses the handling of the situation.

Managing Detrimental Conditions

8. Take the property off the market.

If the property has been listed for sale or lease, consider taking it off the market. It is often difficult to sell a property immediately after a detrimental condition occurs.

9. Be considerate of neighbors or other tenants.

Some detrimental conditions cause difficulty for adjoining property owners. Work to address their concerns.

10. Manage tourists and sight-seekers.

Often tragedies will leave police tape, signs and other "flags" that notify the public of where the incident occurred. These "flags" should be removed as soon as possible to minimize the association of the incident with the property. If a sight-seeker still finds the property despite the removal of the "flags", be polite. Usually these people come and leave quickly. Short-tempered behavior by the property owner towards sight-seers often results in amplifying curiosity and actually prolongs their visit. Instruct any security personnel not to comment to these people.

11. Negotiate with lenders.

As many properties have mortgages, the lender will justifiably have concerns about the situation and the collateral securing their loan. Communicate with the lender promptly to demonstrate you have or will deal with all of the issues. Assure the lender that you have secured the property and are handling the insurance claims. It may be necessary to request that the lender provide some payment relief or moratorium while managing the situation. In such circumstances, reasonable lenders will offer some concessions.

12. File insurance claims.

Many detrimental conditions are covered by insurance policies. The submission of insurance claims is often a new experience for many property owners. Consider utilizing a public claims adjuster in the preparation of the claim. Select an adjuster that is experienced and will submit a reasonable claim that will be taken seriously by the insurance company. Submitting an unreasonable claim will delay payment and may cost additional fees.

13. Keep the situation in perspective.

Detrimental conditions can be traumatic; however, time will tend to ease the tension of the incident.

14. Consider the future uses of the property.

Some detrimental conditions require that other uses of the property be studied. For example, if the improvements are old, it may be best to demolish the building rather than rebuild. If the property is useful to the owner, it may be renovated and operated indefinitely, as opposed to selling them at a loss.

15. Occupy or rent the property.

If stigma is an issue, it can be mitigated by occupying the property even by a tenant at below-market rental rates. Generally a vacant property only serves to prolong or even amplify the effects of stigma.

16. Wait an appropriate amount of time prior to listing the property.

It may take years before a property with stigma may be sold. By recognizing this fact, a property owner may wisely avoid the frustrations of trying to prematurely sell

Managing Detrimental Conditions

the property. If litigation is involved, it is usually best to wait until all trials are over before listing a property for sale.

17. Disclose the incident to potential buyers.

Consult with an attorney about local disclosure laws; however, a good rule is to "disclose, disclose, disclose" to avoid problems in the future.

18. Be prepared to discount the price appropriately.

Even after everything is done to mitigate the damages, market resistance may remain. Usually a buyer may be enticed to purchase the property by offering a modest discount. Generally there is an inverse correlation between the time transpired since the incident and the discount. Also, an "upper-end property" will tend to require a larger discount.

19. Consult with experienced and competent professionals.

Dealing with detrimental conditions may require consulting with a variety of professionals including consultants, engineers, attorneys, public adjusters, contractors, lenders and brokers. Care should be taken to associate with those who are experienced in these situations.

Managing Detrimental Conditions

GLOSSARY OF
DETRIMENTAL CONDITION TERMS

Abatement--Removal of or controlling the release of asbestos fibers. Includes operations and maintenance (O&M), encapsulation, enclosure, and removal

ACM--Asbestos-containing material

Activated Carbon--A substance, often the product of burnt wood, that is used to filter organic solutes. Often used to purify water and remove pesticides and some inorganic solutes such as chlorine (Upon saturation, the carbon filters must be replaced. Activated carbon is ineffective in filtering metals, lead and salts.)

Aeration--The introduction of air into a contaminated liquid which create gases, which is then released

Aerobic--Requiring Oxygen

Air Monitoring--Testing of air samples for asbestos fiber content

Air Sample Clearance Test--Air monitoring at the completion of an asbestos abatement project

Air Stripping--An in situ ground water remediation process (Contaminated ground water is pumped to the surface and processed in an air stripping tower. The water flows over packing materials. The contaminated water comes in contact with air and the contaminants generally volatilize. The contaminated air is released or filtered.)

Amended Water--Mixture of water and surfactant

Aquifer-- Rock or sediment through which ground water moves easily

Asbestos--Natural mineral mined from rock and used in construction; properties include: non-combustibility, corrosion resistance, high tensile strength and both thermal and electrical insulating capability

Asbestosis--A chronic lung disease resulting from the scarring of the lung tissues by asbestos fibers

Backfill--Clean soil replacing excavated contaminated soil

Benzene--2% to 4% of gasoline, known carcinogen

BTXE--Primary toxins of soils and ground water associated with petroleum products

C & D--Construction and Demolition (Landfills)

Carcinogen--A cancer-causing substance

CERCLA--Comprehensive Environmental Response, Compensation and Liability Act of 1980

Certified Laboratory--A laboratory which meets federal and state standards of accuracy and testing

Distillation--A water purification technique which purifies water by heating the water and condensing the steam (The process reduces salt concentration, but is ineffective in removing pesticides and volatile organic contaminants such as benzene or chloroform.)

Encapsulant--Liquid substances that are applied to ACMs to prevent the escape of fibers (Bridging encapsulants form a coating over the ACM surface

Penetrating encapsulants soak into the ACMs to bind its components together. Both types are frequently used together. Removal encapsulants moisten and adhere ACMs being removed.)

Encapsulation--A soil contamination remediation process which encapsulates the soil to prevent leaching and surface seepage of contamination into either the ground water or storm drainage system. Monitoring Facility usually required

Enclosure--Construction of an air-tight structure that surrounds the ACMs

End Removal--The removal of asbestos when the property is eventually demolished

EPA--US Environmental Protection Agency

Equipment Decontamination Enclosure System--A washroom, holding area and un-contaminated area for handling materials and equipment

Exposure--The contact with a contaminant through skin absorption, inhalation or ingestion

Ex-Situ--Off-site, referring to an off-site remediation process

Filtration--Water purification by screening out contaminant through a sediment process, a filter or a sieve

Friable--Materials that may be crumbled by hand pressure

GW--Ground Water

HEPA--High-efficiency particulate air, i.e. HEPA filter or HEPA vacuum, which filters asbestos fibers

Initial Removal--The up-front and immediate removal of ACMs

In-Situ--In place, referring to an on-site remediation process

Leach--Dissolving out by percolating liquid in order to separate the soluble components

Level--The concentration or amount of contaminents in a given volume of gas, liquid or solid

LIA--Local Implementing Agency

Liter--Metric unit of volume equal to 1.057 quarts of liquid. One gallon is equivalent to about 4 liters

LUST--Leaking Underground Storage Tank

Matrix--Hard non-friable material (e.g. concrete) that contains asbestos

MCL--Maximum Contaminant Level, usually mandated by State requirements and references maximum levels of toxins in drinking water

Mesothelioma--A form of chest and abdominal cancer, caused by asbestos exposure

Milligram--A unit of weight. 1,000 milligrams equals one gram and about 28 grams equals one ounce

Monitoring Facility--Equipment usually permanently installed to monitor ground water below or near an encapsulized site; used to test if seepage or leaching is occurring on an encapsulized site

NIOSH--National Institute for Occupational Safety and Health

Non-Friable--Not capable of being crumbled by hand pressure

NPPL--National Priority Pollutants List: a list of common pollutants caused by underground storage tank facilities and related uses

Operations and Maintenance (O&M)--An on-going maintenance program (For example, for asbestos it could include training, HEPA vacuuming, wet cleaning, and air monitoring. This is also termed "end removal" as the ACMs remain until the eventual demolition of the building.)

OSHA--Occupational Safety and Health Administration, a division of the US Department of Labor

OUST--Office of Underground Storage Tanks

Passive Detector--A measurement device which functions without oversight or energy

Parts Per Million (PPM)--A unit of concentration (One part per million can be compared to one cent in ten thousand dollars.)

PCB--Polychlorinated Biphenyls Transformers

PCM--Phased contrast microscopy

Permeability--A measure of a materia'ls ability to transmit water

Picocurie--A unit of measurement of radioactive substances (Five picocuries of radon are five trillionth of a curie, which are equal to 11 radioactive radon atoms decaying every minute.)

PLM--Polarized light microscopy

PPB--Parts per billion

PRG--Non-Official Preliminary Risk Goals set forth by the U.S. EPA, regarding soil contamination; generally not used by State and Local governing authorities

Radioactive--Unstable atoms which decay or break down to another kind of atom (The process emits high energy particles. For example, radium decays to form radon. Radiation includes high energy particles, which include alpha and beta particles, and gamma rays.)

Removal--Physical removal of ACMs

Respirators--Face masks that filter air

Reverse Osmosis--A water purification process used to remove salts, such as sea water (The process yields drinking water and salt residues.)

Risk--The chance of developing a disease after exposure to an environmental hazard, based upon the time period and level of exposure

RP--Responsible Party

SEM--Scanning electron microscopy

Soft Water--Water that contains low levels of dissolved minerals, such as salts, calcium or magnesium

Soil Excavation--A type of remediation process that involves the transfer of contaminated soil from the sub-surface to the surface of the ground, where it is commonly dumped in a pile to be treated and/or disposed of at a later date

Solder--A metal compound used to seal plumbing joints. Solder compounds containing lead are now banned

Staged Removal--The staged removal of ACMs over time (i.e. floor-by-floor, one unit at a time)

Surfactant--Wetting agent that enhances the penetration of water

SVOC--Semivolatile organic compounds

TEM--Transmission electron microscopy

Toxicity--The level to which a substance is toxic

TPE--Total Petroleum Hydro Carbons, typically measured by levels of BTXE

USEPA--United States Environmental Protection Agency

UST-Underground storage tank

Vacuum Extraction--A type of remediation process that removes the majority of contaminants through the use of one or more suction wells or a series of air injection and suction wells (The method is typically less disruptive than soil excavation and is generally less expensive than other techniques.)

VOC--Volatile Organic Compounds

Water Table--The upper level of the saturated zone of groundwater

Worker Decontamination Enclosure System--A series of three temporary rooms for entering or exiting a contaminated work site (Specifically, they are the clean room which is adjacent to the outside or uncontaminated area, the shower room and the equipment room which is also known as the dirty room.)

Finance
&
Lending

Finance & Lending

APPRAISAL

The following chart shows the appraisal process. Checklists and outlines for each category follow the chart.

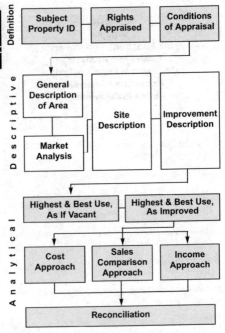

SUBJECT PROPERTY ID

☐ **Assessor's Parcel Number**--The number used for property tax identifying the property

☐ **Street Address**--Number and street

☐ **Legal Description**--The Lot and Tract or Metes and Bounds

RIGHTS APPRAISED

☐ **Fee Simple**--Unencumbered ownership

☐ **Leased Fee**--Lessor's (Landlord's) interest

☐ **Leasehold**--Lessee's (Tenant's) interest

CONDITIONS OF APPRAISAL

☐ **Sandwich Interest**--Interest of one who has leased property and subsequently subleases the property

☐ **Date of Value Estimate**--The date on which the appraised value applies

☐ **Use of Appraisal**--Disclosure of the appraisal

☐ **Definition of Value**--The source and distinct definition of value (i.e. market value, market value as is, prospective market value upon completion, etc.)

☐ **Scope of the Appraisal**--Discussion of work completed in preparing the appraisal report

☐ **Function of the Appraisal**--The role of the appraisal

☐ **Limiting Conditions**--Any conditions that limit the appraisal

GENERAL DESCRIPTION

❏ **Region**--The greater geographical area

❏ **County\City**--The local municipalities

❏ **Neighborhood**--A congruous group of complimentary uses

❏ **Social**--Population, education, culture, employment, crime rate, age, etc.

❏ **Economic**--Rent levels, construction levels, etc.

❏ **Governmental**--Zoning, taxes, police, fire, schools, administration, water/sewage, roads, etc.

❏ **Environmental**--Utilities, over/under improvements, topography, etc.

MARKET ANALYSIS

❑ **Absorption Data**--Rate of filling vacant commercial space or selling homes

❑ **Historical Trends**--Past market activities

❑ **Inventory of Available Properties**--All space available for leasing

❑ **Market Attitudes of Future**--Interviews and research with market participants

❑ **Market Demand**--Occupancy and rental rate trends

❑ **New Competitive Developments**--All proposed properties, or properties under construction

❑ **Sales and Listing Activity**--Historical activity

❑ **Size of Total Market**--e.g. total SqFt, units, and new construction planned

❑ **Vacancy Rates**--Total available SqFt divided by total SqFt.

Appraisal

SITE DESCRIPTION

❏ **Access**--e.g. from street or highways

❏ **Assessor's Parcel**--Number and map to define parcels for property tax

❏ **Adjoining Uses**--(Un)complementary uses

❏ **Assemblage**--Combining 2 or more parcels of land

❏ **Corner/Mid-Street**--Location in block

❏ **Drainage**--Water flow, direction and adequacy

❏ **Easements**--e.g. utilities, roads, railroads

❏ **Elevation**--Measurement above sea level

❏ **Entitlements**--Actual rights granted by local governments to build

❏ **Encroachments**--Improvements of an adjoining property crossing the property line, e.g. fences, walls

❏ **Front Feet**--Frontage on street in terms of feet

❏ **General Plan**--Local government's overall land use plan

❏ **Gross Area**--The total land area (See Net Area)

❏ **Hazardous Conditions**--e.g. flood zone, waste site, earthquake zone, subsidence, intractability

❏ **Legal Description**--e.g. metes/bounds, parcel/tract

Appraisal

- ❑ **Net Area**--The buildable area (See Gross Area)

- ❑ **Offsite Utilities**--Utilities to the site

- ❑ **Onsite Utilities**--Utilities on the site

- ❑ **Plottage**--Incremental value from assemblage of land

- ❑ **Private Restrictions**--Deed restrictions of land use

- ❑ **Riparian Rights**--Water rights, e.g. lake, river

- ❑ **Shape**--e.g. square, rectangular, irregular

- ❑ **Site Improvements**--e.g. roads, gutters, sidewalks

- ❑ **Soil Type**--e.g. silty, sandy, clay

- ❑ **Special Assessments**--e.g. school/utility bonds

- ❑ **Surrounding Influences**--e.g. demographics, infrastructure, climate

- ❑ **Topography**--Land surface: rolling, flat, rough, etc.

- ❑ **Utilities**--Water, electricity, natural gas, telephone, sewer, storm sewer, cable television

- ❑ **Vested**--Foundation in place

- ❑ **View**--e.g. city, ocean, mountain, valley

- ❑ **Zoning**--Local government regulation of land use

Appraisal

IMPROVEMENT DESCRIPTION

❏ **ADA**--Compliance with regulations

❏ **Age**--Actual and effective

❏ **Asbestos**--Highly suspect if built prior to 1979

❏ **Build-Out**--Tenant improvements in place

❏ **Ceilings**--e.g. acoustical tile, sprayed, t-bar

❏ **Deferred Maintenance**--Overdue repairs

❏ **Density**--Number of units allowed, e.g. 5 per acre

❏ **Depreciation**--e.g. physical, economic, external

❏ **Doors**--Interior, exterior, overhead

❏ **Equipment**--e.g. elevators, fire sprinklers, HVAC, security, irrigation, escalators

❏ **Excess Land**--Excess of building/parking needs

❏ **Fenestration**--Design, location of windows

❏ **Flooring**--e.g. marble, carpet, tile, vinyl

❏ **Foundation**--e.g. slab, raised

❏ **Ground-Up Inspection**--Review of all improvements starting from the ground

❏ **Hazards**--e.g. structural, termites, asbestos

❏ **HVAC**--Heating, ventilation, air conditioning

- **Lighting**--e.g. fluorescent or incandescent

- **Parking Ratio**--Spaces/1,000=spaces/(bldg SqFt./1,000)

- **Restrooms**--Count of sinks, water closets, etc

- **Roof**--e.g. flat, gable, gambrel, hip

- **Signs**--e.g. monument, mounted, posted

- **Stories**--Low rise 1-2, mid rise 3-6, high rise 7+

- **Substructure**--Entire foundational structure

- **Superstructure**--Portion above grade

- **Wall**--Bearing (supports building) or demising

- **Walls/Doors/Windows & Roof**-- Type of construction

- **Yard Improvements**--e.g. paving, landscaping

HIGHEST & BEST USE, AS IF VACANT
What should be built if the site were vacant?

1. **Physically Possible**--What are all the uses that are physically possible?

2. **Legal Use**--Of all physically possible uses, which are permitted by zoning, etc.?

3. **Financially Feasible**--Of all legal uses, which are financially feasible?

4. **Maximally Productive**--Of all financially feasible uses, which is maximally productive?

HIGHEST & BEST USE, AS IMPROVED
Do the current improvements contribute to land value?

1. **Physical Description**--Summary of improvements.

2. **Legal Use**--Is the use a legal use?

3. **Financially Feasible**--Is the current use financially feasible?

4.**Maximally Productive**--Is the current use, refurbishment or demolition the best option?

Note: There should be consistency between the "as if vacant analysis" and "as improved analysis".

THREE APPROACHES TO VALUE

The three traditional approaches to value are the Cost Approach, the Income Capitalization Approach and the Sales Comparison Approach. Each approach represents a technique by which market data may be processed into an indication of value. All three approaches to value are, in essence, market data approaches as the data inputs are market derived.

COST APPROACH

This approach in appraisal analysis is based on the proposition that an informed purchaser will pay no more than the cost of producing a substitute property with the same utility as the subject property. The Cost Approach is particularly appropriate when the property being appraised includes relatively new improvements that represent the highest and best use of the land or when relatively unique or specialized improvements are located on the subject site, and when market data of similar properties cannot be obtained.

Replacement Cost New	(e.g. Cost Manual, Contractor's Estimate)
+ Indirect Costs	(e.g. fees, landscape)
+ Developer's Profit	
- Depreciation	(Effective Age/Total Life)
= Depreciated Value of Improvements	
+ Land Value	(From Land Sales Comparables)
= Indicated Value	

SALES COMPARISON APPROACH

The Sales Comparison or Market Data Approach is an appraisal procedure in which the market value estimate is predicated upon prices paid in actual market transactions and is reflected in current listings. The Market Data Approach involves a process of analyzing sales of similar properties with recent sale dates to derive an indication of the most probable sales price of the property being appraised.

**Price per Unit Method
(Commercial or Residential):**

Building Size/Configuration

x Adjusted Price Per Unit (e.g. Square Foot, Room)
_____

= Indicated Value

**Gross Annual Income Multiplier Method
(Income Properties Only):**

Gross Income

x GAIM
_____

= Indicated Value

INCOME CAPITALIZATION APPROACH

This technique converts anticipated income to be derived from the ownership of the property into a value estimate. The Income Approach is widely applied in appraising income-producing properties. Anticipated future income and/or reversions are discounted to a present value through a capitalization process.

Potential Gross Income   (Actual, Market Rents)

+ Other Income   (Parking, Laundry)

+ Tenant Reimbursements

- Vacancy, Collection Losses

= Effective Gross Income

- Expenses   (TIMMUR)Taxes, Insurance, Management, Maintenance, Utilities, Reserves

= Net Operating Income

+ Capitalization Rate

= Indicated Value

RECONCILIATION

A reconciliation process takes into consideration the pros and cons of each approach, with more weight given to the most applicable approach. Generally the income approach is given the most weight, since buyers usually invest for income potential.

PRINCIPLE OF REGRESSION

A property's value is negatively impacted when surrounded by properties of lesser value

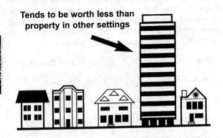

Tends to be worth less than property in other settings

PRINCIPLE OF PROGRESSION

A property of lesser value tends to be enhanced when the adjoining property values are high.

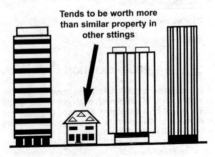

Tends to be worth more than similar property in other sttings

THE PRINCIPLE OF CONFORMITY

Property values are optimal and are maximized when a property generally conforms to the surrounding properties, and are negatively impacted when it does not.

**Value
Negatively
Impacted By
Non-Conformity**

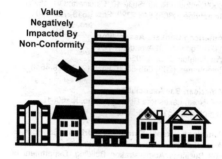

**Optimal
Property
Value**

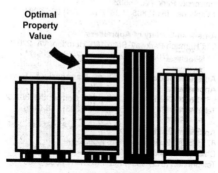

Appraisal

APPRAISAL AND REAL ESTATE RELATED ORGANIZATIONS

American Association of Certified Appraisers
800 Compton Road, Suite 10, Cincinatti, OH 45231
Telephone: (800) 543-2222 Fax: (513) 729-1401

American Bankers Association
1120 Connecticut Avenue, N.W.
Washington, D.C. 20036
Telephone: (202) 663-5000 Fax: (202) 828-4548

American Bar Association
750 North Lakeshore Drive, Chicago, IL 60611
Telephone: (312) 988-5000

American Real Estate & Urban Economics Association
409 Business Administration Building, Department of Insurance & Real Estate, Penn State University, University Park, PA 16802
Telephone: (814) 865-1938 Fax: (814) 865-6284

American Society of Appraisers
535 Herndon Parkway, Suite 150, Herndon, VA 22070
Telephone: (703) 478-2228 Fax: (703) 742-8471

American Society of Farm Managers & Rural Appraisers
950 South Cherry Street, Suite 508, Denver, CO 80222
Telephone: (303) 758-3513 Fax: (303) 758-0190

Appraisal Institute
875 North Michigan Avenue, Floor 2400
Chicago, IL 60611
Telephone: (312) 335-4100 Fax: (312) 335-4400

Black's Office Leasing Guide
818 West Diamond Avenue, 3rd Floor
Gaithersburg, MD 20878
Telephone: (301) 948-0995 (CA: 1-800-500-2450)

Building Owners and Managers Assoc. Inc.
1201 New York Ave, N.W., Suite 300
Washington, D.C. 20005 Telephone: (202) 408-2662

Farm Credit Council
7100 East Belleview, Suite 205, Englewood, CO 80111
Telephone: (303) 740-4264 Fax: (303) 740-4202

Institute of Real Estate Management
430 North Michigan Avenue, Chicago, IL 60611
Telephone: (312) 329-8200

International Association of Assessing Officers
130 East Randolph Street, Suite 850
Chicago, IL 60601-6217
Telephone: (312) 819-6100 Fax: (312) 819-6149

International Council of Shopping Centers
665 Fifth Avenue, New York, NY 10022
Telephone: (212) 421-8181

International Right of Way Association
13650 South Gramercy Place, Suite 100
Gardena, CA 90249
Telephone: (310) 538-0233 Fax: (310) 538-1471

Lender's Service, Inc.
700 Cherrington Avenue, Coraopolis, PA 15108
Telephone: (412) 299-4000

Marshall & Swift Cost Publications
911 Wilshire Boulevard, Los Angeles, CA 90017
Telephone: (213) 250-2222

Appraisal

Mortgage Bankers Association
1125 15th Street, N.W., Suite 700
Washington, D.C. 20005
Telephone: (202) 861-6500 Fax: (202) 785-8357

Mortgage Guaranty Insurance Corporation
MGIC Plaza, P.O. Box 488, Milwaukee, WI 53201
Telephone: (414) 347-6816

Mortgage Insurance Companies of America
727 15th Street, N.W., 12th Floor
Washington, D.C. 20005
Telephone: (202) 393-5566 Fax: (202) 393-5557

National Association of Independent Fee Appraisers
7501 Murdoch Avenue, St. Louis, MO 63119
Telephone: (314) 781-6688 Fax: (314) 781-2872

National Association of Master Appraisers
303 West Cypress Street, San Antonio, TX 78712
Telephone: (210) 271-0781 Fax: (210) 225-8450

National Association of Realtors
430 North Michigan Avenue, Chicago, IL 60611
Telephone: (312) 329-8200 Fax: (312) 329-5960

Real Estate Educators Association
11 S. La Salle Street, Suite 1400, Chicago, IL 60603
Telephone: (312) 201-0101 Fax: (312) 201-0214

Savings & Community Bankers of America
900 19TH Street, N.W., Suite 400
Washington, D.C. 20006
Telephone: (202) 857-3100 Fax: (202) 296-8716

GLOSSARY OF APPRAISAL TERMS

Absorption--Rate of sales/leasing, e.g. 4 units/month

Adjustments--Accounting for differences between the subject property and comparables

Agents of Production--Land, labor, capital and coordination

American Standard--Standards for building measurements established by the *American National Standards Institute*

Analysis--Study beyond appraisal, to determine financing, investment returns, etc.

Appraisal--Estimating the value of a property as of a certain date

Arms-Length--Sale between two disinterested parties

"As Is" Value--Value as property currently stands

Assumptions and Limiting Conditions--Stipulations upon which the appraisal is based

Certification--Statement attesting to an unbiased analysis

Comparable--Similar property for comparative use, e.g. price/square foot, cap rates, lease rates

Creation of Value--Utility, scarcity, desire and effective purchasing power

Date of Value Estimate--The date on which the appraised value applies

Definition of Value--The source and distinct definition of value (i.e., market value, market value as is, prospective market value upon completion, etc.)

Direct Capitalization--A fundamental approach to value in the Income Approach (Net Operating Income/Capitalization Rate = Value)

Discount Rate--The rate utilized as an internal rate of return in the Discounted Cash Flow Analysis

Discounted Cash Flow--A projection of income, vacancy and expenses resulting in a forecasted cash flow that is discounted to a net present value based upon a discount rate

Function of the Appraisal--The role of the appraisal

Gross Annual Income Multiplier--A method of comparison in the Sales Comparison Approach (Gross Income/SqFt)

Highest and Best Use--Physical, legal, economical and maximally productive use

Identification of Real Estate--Assessor's Parcel Number, Legal Description or Street Address to identify the subject property

Influences on Value--Physical, economic, government and social

Land Valuation--Valuation of the land to determine if the improvements in fact contribute to the overall value, and for use in the Cost Approach

MAI--Member of the Appraisal Institute

Market Value--Value as if sold on the open market

Narrative Report--A full narrative report (as opposed to a form or short narrative report) that is a self-contained appraisal

Net Present Value--The indicated value as a result of discounting a stream of projected net cash flow utilizing a discount rate

NOI/SqFt--Measurement of the Net Operating Income of comparable properties to value the subject property

Reversion--The projected value of the subject property upon its hypothetical sale at the term of the Discounted Cash Flow Analysis

Rights Appraised--e.g. fee simple, leased fee

RM--Residential Member of the Appraisal Institute

Scope of the Appraisal--Discussion of work completed in preparing the appraisal report

Stabilized Value--Value as if property is fully leased

Subject Property--The property being appraised

Unit of Comparison--e.g. price per square foot, acre, room, front foot, unit

Use of Appraisal--Disclosure of the intended use of the appraisal

MORTGAGES

CONVENTIONAL FIXED RATE LOAN

DEFINITION

A 30-year term loan where equal loan payments are made monthly. Conventional loans usually require a 20% down payment.

ADVANTAGES

Payments remain fixed over the entire term of the loan, which is a significant advantage if the loan is initiated when the interest rates are low. As with all home loans, the interest payments are tax deductible.

DRAWBACKS

Monthly payments are calculated whereby the interest portion of the payment greatly outweighs the principal pay-down in the earlier years of the loan. This results in slow equity build-up. Conventional loans are not always as affordable as some other alternatives. The fixed interest rate is usually higher than an ARM loan.

COMMENTS

A 30-year term is conventional, but loan terms may be available for longer periods such as 40 years. The longer the term, the lower the monthly payment but the slower the equity build-up.

SHORT-TERM FIXED-RATE MORTGAGE

DEFINITION

Typically a 15-year term loan where equal loan payments are made monthly.

ADVANTAGES

Less interest is paid over the term of the loan and the interest rate is usually lower than a conventional 30-year term loan. This may be a good option for older buyers who wish to pay off the loan prior to retirement.

DRAWBACKS

The monthly loan payments are higher as compared to a 30-year loan. Because loan payments are higher, it may be more difficult to qualify for such a mortgage.

COMMENTS

These shorter term loans may also be available for other terms such as 5, 10 or 20 years. The shorter the term, the higher the payment but the faster the equity build-up.

Mortgages

BALLOON MORTGAGE LOAN

DEFINITION

This is generally a short term mortgage with fixed payments with the loan balance (or balloon payment) due in a lump sum at the term of the loan.

ADVANTAGES

These loans can be beneficial to those who are confident that they will be selling or refinancing the property prior to the balloon payment due date. Interest rates are usually less than a conventional loan.

DRAWBACKS

If the property is not sold, or the property is not refinanced prior to the due date, the full balloon payment is due.

COMMENTS

These loans are often quoted with terms such as "30 years, due in 5", which means a loan with payments as if amortized on a 30 year basis, but with the full loan balance due in 5 years.

Mortgages

ADJUSTABLE MORTGAGE LOAN (AML)

DEFINITION

A loan where the interest rate and monthly payments are variable. The loan rate is indexed to coincide with the prevailing market interest rates. The interest rate may have a "floor" or "ceiling".

ADVANTAGES

The initial interest rate is usually lower than the rate for a fixed loan. If market interest rates drop, so will the monthly payment.

DRAWBACKS

The market is unpredictable, so the monthly payments may actually increase.

COMMENTS

Also called *Adjustable Rate Loans, Adjustable Rate Mortgages* (ARM), and *Variable Rate Loans.*

Mortgages

GRADUATED PAYMENT MORTGAGE LOAN

DEFINITION

A loan offering lower initial payments, which increase at a pre-determined rate and eventually level off.

ADVANTAGES

The payments are lower in the first years of the loan, and unlike AML or ARM loans, the amounts of the future payments are known in advance.

DRAWBACKS

The payments will increase even if market interest rates go down.

COMMENTS

GPM loans may be beneficial when the buyer is confident that his or her income will increase in the future in order to pay for the higher loan payments.

NEGATIVE AMORTIZING MORTGAGE LOAN

DEFINITION

A loan where the monthly payment is not sufficient to pay for the interest charges due, and subsequently the principal amount of the loan increases.

ADVANTAGES

The monthly loan payment is low when compared with a fully amortized loan payment.

DRAWBACKS

The principal amount of the loan is not reduced but actually increases. This erodes equity.

COMMENTS

This type of loan is usually justified only on a very short-term basis.

Mortgages

FHA MORTGAGE LOAN

DEFINITION

An FHA loan is a US Government (Federal Housing Administration) insured first mortgage that facilitates a very low down payment as compared with a conventional loan.

ADVANTAGES

There is little or no down payment required with these types of loans and the interest rate may be below the market interest rates.

DRAWBACKS

FHA loans have a limit on the amount that can be borrowed as compared with conventional loans.

COMMENTS

The type of loan may be a viable option for a first time buyer who has limited funds for a down-payment.

Mortgages

VETERAN ADMINISTRATION (VA) LOAN

DEFINITION

Mortgage loans that are insured by the Veteran's Administration which facilitates a very low down-payment, when compared with a conventional loan.

ADVANTAGES

There is little or no down payment required with these types of loans, and the interest rate may be below the market interest rates.

DRAWBACKS

VA loans have a limit on the amount that can be borrowed. The borrower must be a US military veteran or currently serving in the military.

COMMENTS

This type of loan may be a viable option for a military veteran who has limited funds for a down-payment.

Mortgages

SHARED APPRECIATION MORTGAGE

DEFINITION

This can be any type of loan in which the borrower has a partner (such as a parent) who contributes towards making a portion or all of the down payment. The partner may also co-sign on the loan. Agreements differ, but the borrower often has an option to "buy-out" the partner, or the borrower and the partner share the equity proceeds when the property is sold.

ADVANTAGES

The down payment is small or non-existent for the borrower. The borrower may secure a loan for which he or she may not have otherwise qualified.

DRAWBACKS

The buyer is indebted to both the mortgage lender and the partner. Because the equity is shared, the buyer does not build up equity ownership as with a conventional loan.

COMMENTS

This type of arrangement may be beneficial for partners (often family members) to invest their money at a higher return than savings account rates.

LEASE WITH OPTION TO BUY

DEFINITION

This financial arrangement involves the potential buyer leasing the property with an option to purchase the property at a pre-determined price in the future. All or part of the lease payments may be applied towards the purchase price.

ADVANTAGES

The potential buyer may occupy the property while saving for a down payment. The potential buyer also has the flexibility of actually buying the property or merely leasing it and moving out at the term of the lease.

DRAWBACKS

The potential buyer does not enjoy the tax benefits of a mortgage while leasing the property. If the option is not exercised, there is usually no return of the lease payments.

COMMENTS

This type of financing arrangement may have certain tax benefits for the lessor (potential seller). Also, the buyer maintains flexible options.

Mortgages

INTEREST-ONLY MORTGAGE LOAN

DEFINITION

A loan were only the interest portion of the payment is due monthly. The principal amount of the loan is not amortized.

ADVANTAGES

The monthly loan payment is less than an otherwise similar conventional loan because there is no principal pay-back. This makes the monthly payments more affordable.

DRAWBACKS

The loan is not amortized, so the loan balance is never reduced. There is no equity build-up as a result of making payments. At the term of the loan, the property must be sold, or the loan needs to be refinanced.

COMMENTS

Interest-only loans are generally short term loans, and are commonly associated with balloon mortgages.

SELLER-CARRIED FINANCING

DEFINITION

The actual terms of seller-carried financing can vary and may be similar to conventional or other types of mortgages. The difference is that the seller of the property finances the mortgage rather than an institutional lender.

ADVANTAGES

The seller may receive tax benefits by receiving monthly payments as opposed to receiving a large sum of money upon selling the property. The seller may offer more flexible terms to the buyer as compared to a conventional lender.

DRAWBACKS

Only sellers who have significant equity can consider making such a loan. The seller may be more inclined to "cash out" rather than participate in a seller-carried loan.

COMMENTS

Lending laws and practices are complex. As with all loans, participants in seller-carried financing should always consult with a real estate professional or an attorney.

Mortgages

BI-WEEKLY LOAN PAYMENT

DEFINITION

This type of mortgage can be any of those previously discussed, except that instead of 12 monthly payments, one-half of the monthly loan payment is paid every 2 weeks, or 26 half-payments per year. This is equal to 13 monthly payments, and the extra month's payment is credited towards the loan balance.

ADVANTAGES

If payments are properly credited, the equity build-up is faster and considerable interest is saved over the term of the loan.

DRAWBACKS

The total annual loan payments are higher by the amount of one monthly loan payment which may make them unaffordable. Few banks offer bi-weekly payment plans, and existing loans must usually be refinanced for proper bi-weekly credit.

COMMENTS

Some bi-weekly loan conversion services may not really offer the advantages of a true bi-weekly plan and can have added processing fees. Consult with an independent loan expert or real estate attorney prior to entering such an agreement.

LOAN PRE-PAYMENT

DEFINITION

With many loans, it is possible to make pre-payments in addition to the regular monthly payment.

ADVANTAGES

Loan pre-payments increase the property's equity, and result in substantial interest savings.

DRAWBACKS

The regular monthly payment must always be met, regardless of what pre-payments are or have been made. The loan may have pre-payment penalties that must be considered.

COMMENTS

Pre-payments should only be made with discretionary income to avoid over-extension of personal finances. Refer to the *Bell's Guide* section on *Loan Prepayment*.

Mortgages

FUNCTION 1 Future Value	FUNCTION 2 Future Value of $1 per Period
Definition: The amount to which $1 will grow with compounded interest	**Definition:** The amount to which $1 per period will grow with compounded interest
Other Terms: Future Value of a Lump Sum	**Other Terms:** Future Value of Payments
Example: (Compounded Annually) Land is valued at $100,000 today. At 3% appreciation, what will it be worth in 10 years?	**Example:** (Compounded Annually) A tenant pays $10,000 per year for five years. If the landlord deposits payment in a bank account yielding 8%, what will be the total future value in five years?
Solve For: Future Value	**Solve For:** Future Value
Calculator Key Strokes:	**Calculator Key Strokes:**
n = 10	**n** = 5
I = 3%	**I** = 8%
PV = -100,000	**PV** = Not Used
PMT = Solve $134,392	**PM** = -10,000
FV = Not Used	**FV** = Solve $58,666
Time Line Diagram:	**Time Line Diagram:**
PV -$100,000 FV |—+—+—+—+—+—+—+—+—+—| PMT n = 10 i = 3%	PV FV |—+—+—+—+—| PMT = -10,000 n = 5 i = 8%
Algebraic Formula: $(S = 1 + i)$; $S^n = (1 + i)^n$ Reciprocal of 4	**Algebraic Formula:** $(S = 1 + i)$; $S_n = (S^n - 1)/i$ Reciprocal of 3

Six Functions of a Dollar

FUNCTION 3 Sinking Fund Factor	FUNCTION 4 Present Value of $1
Definition: The amount per period that will grow with compounded interest to $1.	**Definition:** What $1 in the future is worth today.
Other Terms: Annualizor	**Other Terms:** Discounted Cash Flow Reversion
Example: (Compounded Annually) A landlord sets aside payments each year to total $5,000 in five years for a new roof. How much should he set aside each year at a 6% yield on his savings account to save this amount?	**Example:** (Compounded Annually) A building owner feels he can sell his building for $100,000 in five years. At a 12% rate, what is the value of the building today?
Solve For: Payments	**Solve For:** Present Value
Calculator Key Strokes:	**Calculator Key Strokes:**
$\boxed{n}$ = 5	$\boxed{n}$ = 5
$\boxed{I}$ = 6%	$\boxed{I}$ = 12%
$\boxed{PV}$ = Not Used	$\boxed{PV}$ = Solve -$56,743
$\boxed{PM}$ = Solve -$887	$\boxed{PM}$ = Not Used
$\boxed{FV}$ = 5,000	$\boxed{FV}$ = 100,000
Time Line Diagram: PV 5,000 FV	**Time Line Diagram:** PV 100,000 FV
PMT n = 5 i = 6%	PMT n = 5 i = 6%
Algebraic Formula: $(S = 1 + i); 1/S_n = i/(S^n - 1)$ Reciprocal of 2	**Algebraic Formula:** $(S = 1 + i); 1/S^n = 1/(1+i)^n$ Reciprocal of 1

Six Functions of a Dollar

FUNCTION 5 Present Value of $1 per Period	FUNCTION 6 Partial Payment
Definition: What $1 payable periodically is worth today	**Definition:** What $1 payable periodically is worth today
Other Terms: Factor Annuity, Inwood	**Other Terms:** Factor Annual Constant
Example: (Compounded Annually) A tenant pays $10,000 per year for five years at an 11% discount rate. What is the value of the lease today?	**Example:** (Compounded Annually) If $100,000 is borrowed today at 9% interest for 10 years. What is the annual payment required to pay off the loan?
Solve For: Present Value	**Solve For:** Present Value
Calculator Key Strokes:	**Calculator Key Strokes:**
n = 5	n = 10
I = 11%	I = 9%
PV = Solve $36,959	PV = 100,000
PM = -10,000	PM = Solve -15,582
FV = Not Used	FV = Not Used
Time Line Diagram: PV FV PMT = ($10,000) n = 5 i = 11%	**Time Line Diagram:** PV $100,000 FV PMT n = 10 i = 9%
Algebraic Formula: $(S=1+i)$; $a_n = (1-1/S^n)/i$ Reciprocal of 6	**Algebraic Formula:** $(S=1+i)$; $1/a_n = i/(1-1/S^n)$ Reciprocal of 5

TIME LINE DIAGRAM

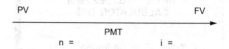

PV   FV

PMT

n =   i =

The *Six Functions of a Dollar* type problem may be diagramed on a time-line such as pictured above. These diagrams are useful in visualizing the timing and sequence of cash flows.

All payments or values received are expressed as a positive number, and all payments or values paid are expressed as a negative number. It is common to put all payments or values received above the time-line and all payments or values paid out below the time line to express this relationship.

For example, the present value of $100,000 received in 5 years with annual payments of $4,000 paid out at an 8% interest rate would by diagrammed as follows:

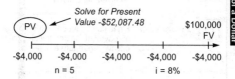

Solve for Present Value -$52,087.48

PV

$100,000
FV

-$4,000   -$4,000   -$4,000   -$4,000   -$4,000

n = 5   i = 8%

The *Six Functions of a Dollar* apply to level periodic payments. Where payments are irregular and/or non-level, refer to the ***Bell's Guide*** section - *Discounted Cash Flow Analysis*.

Six Functions of a Dollar

HP12C, 17B AND 19BII CALCULATOR TIPS

	Term	Definition
n	**Number of Periods**	Months, quarters or years expressed as periods. (For example, monthly payments for 5 years = 60 payments.)
i	**Interest Rate**	Rate required for the use of borrowed money
PV	**Present Value**	Compounded value now of future payments or sums
PMT	**Payments**	The sums paid or received periodically
FV	**Future Value**	Final compounded value of payment and/or initial outlay as of a future date

Six Functions of a Dollar

CALCULATOR REMINDERS

❑ Payments or values paid out are expressed as a negative number.

❑ Payments or values received are expressed as a positive number.

❑ Payments may be made at the beginning or end of a period, such as the beginning or end of the month. Always set the calculator for payments at the beginning or end of each period, as appropriate.

❑ The HP12C requires that the interest rate (i) be divided by the number of payments per year. For example, a 10% interest payment made monthly has an interest rate of 0.83% per month (10%/12). For monthly payments, use the blue 12 and 12 x keys.

❑ Always clear your calculator prior to starting a new calculation. This is a common cause of calculation errors.

HP12C, 17B and 19BII are trademarks of Hewlett-Packard.

Six Functions of a Dollar

1 DISCOUNTED CASH FLOW ANALYSIS
Net Lease - In Thousands *(Reference Numbers in Italics)*

2 INCOME (Year)	1	2	3
3 Base Rent	1,080	1,117	1,156
4 Other Income	25	25	26
5 Total Potential Base Inc.	1,105	1,143	1,183
6 Tenant Reimbursements	508	524	541
7 Total Potential Gross Inc.	1,613	1,668	1,724
8 Less Vacancy	161	166	172
9 EFFECTIVE GROSS INCOME	1,451	1,501	1,552
10 EXPENSES			
11 Reimbursable			
12 Taxes	101	103	105
13 Insurance	16	17	17
14 Management	71	73	76
15 Maintenance	150	155	160
16 Utilities	168	174	180
17 Non-Reimbursable			
18 Reserves	15	15	16
19 NET OPERATING INCOME	928	961	995
20 Tenant Improvements	45	46	48
21 Leasing Commissions	22	22	23
22 Terminal Value			
23 Sales Commissions			
24 CASH FLOW	861	891	923

Note: figures are rounded

4	5	6	7	8	9	10	11
1,197	1,239	1,282	1,327	1,374	1,422	1,471	1,523
27	28	29	30	31	32	34	35
1,225	1,268	1,312	1,358	1,405	1,455	1,506	1,558
558	576	595	614	633	654	675	697
1,783	1,844	1,907	1,972	2,039	2,109	2,181	2,256
178	184	190	197	203	210	218	225
1,605	1,660	1,716	1,775	1,835	1,898	1,963	2,030
107	110	112	114	116	119	121	123
18	18	19	20	20	21	22	23
78	81	84	87	90	93	97	100
166	172	178	184	190	197	204	211
187	193	200	207	214	222	229	238
16	17	17	18	19	19	20	21
1,030	1,066	1,103	1,142	1,182	1,224	1,267	1,311
49	51	53	55	57	59	61	
24	25	26	27	28	29	30	
						12,799	
						383	
955	989	1,024	1,060	1,097	1,136	13,591	

25 Income and Rate Assumptions:

Rentable SqFt	75,000
Market Rate/SqFt/Month	$1.20
Other Income	$25,000
Vacancy & Collections	10.00%
Growth Rate	3.50%
Tax Growth Rate	2.00%
Sales Commissions	3.00%
Terminal Cap Rate	10.25%
Discount Rate	12.50%

26 Expense Assumptions:

Tax Rate	1.10%
Taxable Value	$9,240,000
Insurance	$0.22
Management	$0.95
Maintenance	$2.00
Utilities	$2.25
Reserves	$0.20
Leasing Commissions	2.0%
Tenant Improvements	$3.00

27 Discounted Cash Flow Analysis:

Net Present Value	$9,241,429
Rounded	$9,240,000
Price/SqFt [DCF]	$123.20

28 Direct Capitalization:

Year 1 Income:	$ 928,686
Capitalization Rate:	10.00%
Indicated Value	$9,286,860
Price/SqFt [Dir Cap]	$ 123.87

Cash Flow Analysis

EXPLANATION OF A
DISCOUNTED CASH FLOW

1. **Discounted Cash Flow Analysis (DCF)** — A *Discounted Cash Flow Analysis* projects the cash flow of a property for a period of time (in this example, 10 years) and a reversionary interest (the projected future sales price). These sums are discounted to a *Net Present Value*, based upon a *Discount Rate*. Note that the 11th year's net operating income is calculated and is capitalized for the reversion value in the 10th year.

2. **Income** — The income can be based upon a "lease by lease" analysis or an aggregate sum. In this example, the effective market rental rate is $1.20/SqFt per month, and the income increases at a 3.5% compounded rate annually.

3. **Base Rent** — The base rent is the actual or effective rent actually received from the tenant(s).

4. **Other Income** — Other income may be derived from parking, vending machines or laundry facilities (in the instance of apartments). In this example, other income is estimated to be $25,000 per year.

5. **Total Potential Gross Income** — This is the sum of all base rents and other income collected.

6. **Tenant Reimbursements** — In the case of net leases, such as this example, the tenant reimburses the landlord for their pro-rated share of operating expenses. These reimbursements can vary from lease to lease. In this example, the tenant reimburses the landlord for all taxes, insurance, management, maintenance and utility expenses.

7. **Total Potential Gross Income** — This is the total actual rents and other income received if the building was 100% occupied. In this example, this is the sum of *Total Potential Base Income* and *Tenant Reimbursements*.

8. **Vacancy** — Vacancy accounts for "down time" between leases and can also include the estimated credit losses. In this example, vacancy is estimated to be 10% of the *Total Potential Gross Income*.

9. **Effective Gross Income** — This is the *Total Potential Gross Income* less *Vacancy* and is the <u>actual</u> gross receipts expected.

10. **Expenses** — Management statements vary greatly in terms of the categories of expenses. Virtually all expenses may be put into a "TIMMUR" category which includes Taxes, Insurance, Management, Maintenance, Utilities and Reserves. Organizing expenses using "TIMMUR" is a useful way to categorize expenses into a standard format. In this example, expenses are projected to increase at 3.5% annually.

11. **Reimbursable** — These are the expenses to be reimbursed to the landlord under the terms of a net lease.

12. **Taxes** — This includes all property taxes and any special assessments. In this example, taxes are based upon a 1.1% assessment of market value and increase 2% per year.

13. **Insurance** — This includes fire, property, casualty and any other insurance expenses. In this example, insurance expenses are estimated to be $0.22/SqFt per year.

Cash Flow Analysis

14. **Management** — This includes both the on-site management as well as administrative expenses. In this example, management expenses are estimated to be $0.95/SqFt per year.

15. **Maintenance** — This includes all forms of maintenance such as cleaning, janitorial, security, routine repairs, landscaping, etc. In this example, maintenance expenses average $2.00/SqFt per year.

16. **Utilities** — This includes gas, electric, water, sewer, trash pick-up, etc. In this example, utilities average $2.25/SqFt per year.

17. **Non-Reimbursable** — These are expenses for which the tenant does not reimburse the landlord.

18. **Reserves** — *Reserves for Replacement* accounts for the periodic replacement of short term items such as carpet, parking lot paving, roofing, HVAC, etc. and are estimated to be $0.20/SqFt per year.

19. **Net Operating Income** — This is the *Effective Gross Income* less all expenses.

20. **Tenant Improvements (TI's)** — These are improvements such as carpet, paint, demising walls that suit a particular tenant's needs and configuration requirements. In this example, TI's average $3.00/SqFt per year.

21. **Leasing Commissions** — These are commissions paid to brokers who secure and negotiate tenant leases. In this example, commissions average 4% for 50% of the tenants (or an effective leasing commission of 2% of effective gross income).

Cash Flow Analysis

22. Terminal Value — This is the projected sales price of the subject property at the term of the cash flow analysis. In this example, it is based upon capitalizing the 11th year *Net Operating Income* at 10.25%. Often, the terminal capitalization rate is somewhat higher than the current capitalization rate to reflect the uncertainties of the future market and that the improvements will be significantly older.

23. Sales Commission — This is the sales commission paid to the broker(s) at the termination of the lease. In this example, the sales commission is estimated to be 3% of the terminal value.

24. Cash Flow — This is the actual cash received (both income and terminal value) by the investor before paying debt service and income taxes.

25. Income and Rate Assumptions — In this example, the subject property contains 75,000 rentable SqFt. The *Discount Rate* reflects a typical investor's expected yield, and in this example is 12.5%.

26. Expense Assumptions — These are a summary of the assumptions as previously discussed.

27. Discounted Cash Flow Analysis — This reflects the *Net Present Value* of the subject property based upon the foregoing inputs and assumptions. The *Price per SqFt* is also indicated.

28. Direct Capitalization — The 1st year's income is capitalized as a "test of reasonableness" of the DCF. This is applicable when the building is "stabilized" at market rents. In this example, a 10% capitalization rate was utilized. The final value is within $1.00/SqFt of the value as indicated by the DCF, indicating a reasonable analysis.

Cash Flow Analysis

Seven Common Flaws of
Discounted Cash Flow Analysis

1. DCF's can be dazzling with all the numbers generated. Too often it is taken for granted that the numbers are correct because they are generated by a computer, but many errors can occur due to miscalculations. Always cross-check all calculations for accuracy. These types of errors can result in both unrealisticly high or low conclusions of value.

2. It is a mistake to use contract rents (rents as stated in the lease) in the income category instead of effective rents (the actual rents received after deducting for any concessions i.e. free rents, moving allowances, etc). This error can overstate the actual value of the property.

3. It is a common flaw to exclude management costs because the property is owner-user. This is because a DCF inherently analyzes what an investor, with professional management, would pay for the property. This error understates the expenses and can result in an artificially high value.

4. It is an error to put tenant improvements or leasing commissions under the expense categories. *Tenant Improvements* are generally considered to be a capital improvement, not an operating expense. Leasing commissions are paid only when a broker is involved, and are often paid in lump sum amounts. Again, this is not an operating expense.

Cash Flow Analysis

5. There is a distinct difference between *Net Operating Income* and *Cash Flow*. Confusing these terms may result in mis-stating the value.

6. It is a significant error to not fully calculate expenses in the case of triple net (NNN) or net leases. When this is done, the appraiser or analyst erroneously implies that because all expenses are "passed through" to the tenant, they do not need to be calculated. This is an error because it ignores fixed expenses that the landlord must pay during vacancy. This error may result in an indication of value that is in excess of the actual value.

7. It is a mistake not to calculate the income for one year past the analysis term to generate a terminal value. If this is not done, the resulting terminal value calculation may be below the actual value of the property.

COMMERCIAL LOAN ANALYSIS

Financial Ratios

Break Even Ratio $= \dfrac{\text{Operating Expense + Debt Service}}{\text{Effective Gross Income}}$

Debt Coverage $= \dfrac{\text{Net Operating Income}}{\text{Debt Service}}$

Equity Dividend Rate (Cash on Cash) $= \dfrac{\text{Net Income - Mortgage Payments}}{\text{Value - Loan Balance}}$

Gross Annual Income Multiplier $= \dfrac{\text{Sales Price}}{\text{Gross Annual Income}}$

Loan per Square Foot $= \dfrac{\text{Loan Amount}}{\text{Square Feet of Improvements}}$

Loan to Value	=	Mortgage Debt
		Value of Property

Operating Expense Ratio	=	Operating Expense
		Effective Gross Income

Overall Capitalization Rate (Cap Rate)	=	Net Operating Income
		Sales Price

Sales Price (Value)	=	Net Operating Income
		Overall Capitalization Rate

"TIME VALUE OF MONEY" ALGEBRA

$$PV = FV \times PVF$$
$$FV = PV/PVF$$
$$PVF = 1/(1+i)^n$$
$$NPV = [FV \times (1/(1+IRR)^n)] - CFO$$

PV	=	Present Value
FV	=	Future Value
PVF	=	Present Value Factor
NPV	=	Net Present Value
IRR	=	Internal Rate of Return
CFO	=	Initial Cash Flow
n	=	Number of Years
i	=	Interest Rate

Commercial Loan Analysis

INCOME TAXES

1.   Sales Price
   - Sales Expense

   = **Adjusted Sales Price**

2.   Cost Basis
      (Original Cost less Prior Deferrals)
   + Capital Improvements
   - Depreciation

   = **Adjusted Cost Basis**

3.   Adjusted Sales Price
   - Adjusted Cost Basis

   = **Capital Gain or Loss Realized**

INCOME CAPITALIZATION APPROACH

   Potential Gross Income
   (Actual, Market Rents)
+ Other Income (Parking, Laundry)
+ Tenant Reimbursements
- Vacancy, Collection Losses
= **Effective Gross Income**
- Expenses (TIMMUR)
   Taxes, Insurance, Management,
   Maintenance, Utilities, Reserves
= Net Operating Income
÷ Capitalization Rate
= Indicated Value

Commercial Loan Analysis

TIME VALUE OF MONEY GLOSSARY

❑ **Amortization**--Periodic payments of interest and principal

❑ **Annuity**--Series of periodic payments

❑ **Compound Interest**--Interest paid on principal plus accumulated unpaid interest

❑ **Discounted Cash Flow (DCF)**--Forecasted income, expenses and reversion, with resultant net cash flow discounted by an IRR to yield a NPV

❑ **Discount Rate**--Compound rate to convert future income into a present value

❑ **Future Value (FV)**--Final compounded value of payment(s) on future date

❑ **Interest**--Rate required for the use of money

❑ **Internal Rate of Return (IRR)**--Annual rate of return to compute NPV

❑ **Negative Amortization**--Payment insufficient to pay interest, thus increasing the loan balance

❑ **Net Present Value (NPV)**--Compounded value now, using a set IRR, of future outlays and income

❑ **Payment**--Refer to *Constant Annual Percent Table*

❑ **Present Value (PV)**--Compounded value now of future payment(s)

❑ **Principal**--Loaned funds

❏ **Reversion**--Net proceeds upon sale

❏ **Simple Interest**--Interest paid on principal only

❏ **Sinking Fund**–A series of payments, that compounded, equals a specified sum at a future date

Commercial Loan Analysis

HOME LOAN ANALYSIS

Front-End Debt Ratio

The approval of home loans is generally based upon computations of two ratios; the *front-end debt ratio* and the *back-end debt ratio*. A common rule of thumb for loan approval is 28% or less for the front-end ratio, and 36% or less for the back-end ratio; however, loan policies can vary greatly from lender to lender and these ratios may be significantly higher or lower.

Line 1   Proposed Home
         Purchase Price $_____

Line 2   Less: Down Payment
         (20% Conventional) $_____

Line 3   Principle Loan
         Amount
         (Line 1 - Line 2) $_____

Line 4   Prevalent Interest
         Rate   _____%

Line 5   Loan Factor (See
         Mortgage Constant   _____%
         Table)

Line 6   Monthly Payment
((Line 3 X Line 5)/12)$_____

Line 7   Gross Monthly
Income $_____

Line 8   House Payment
Line 6) $_____

Line 9   Property Taxes $_____

Line 10 Special Assessments $_____

Line 11 Fire Insurance $_____

Line 12 Association Dues $_____

Line 13 Mortgage Insurance $_____

Line 14 Total Front End Debt
(Total Lines 8-13) $_____

Line 15 Front End Ratio   %
Line 14÷ Line 7 (Rule of Thumb, 28% or less)

Home Loan Analysis

Back-End Debt Ratio

Line 16 Automobile Loan
Payments $_____

Line 17 Credit Card
Payments $_____

Line 18 Student Loan
Payments $_____

Line 19 Other Loan or Debt
Payments $_____

Line 20 Total Back End Debt
(Total Lines 16-19 +
Line 14) $_____

Line 21 Back End Ratio   _____%
(Line 20 ÷ Line 7, Rule of Thumb, 36% or less)

LOAN PREPAYMENT
Interest Charges in Perspective

The amount of interest paid on conventional mortgage loans is staggering. For example, at a 10% fixed interest rate, a loan is repaid over three times by the borrower. This chart graphically illustrates the enormous amounts of interest associated with a conventional loan. In fact, most of a loan payment goes towards interest until well after 20 years. Understanding this concept, and knowing the principles of loan prepayments can save many thousands of dollars of interest payments and reduce the term of the loan by several years.

This graph illustrates the interest, principal, and total payment of a $100,000 loan, at 10% interest with a 30-year term.

Interest vs. Principal

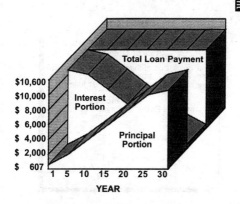

Fixed Increases to Mortgages Payments

A common and effective way to reduce both the interest payments and the term of the loan is to add a fixed amount to the regular monthly payments. This chart illustrates the interest and time savings of various fixed amounts on a conventional loan of $100,000, at a 10%

Excess Payment Per Month		Total Interest Paid	Interest Saved	New Loan Term
$	-	$215,928	$ -	30.0
$	25	$179,259	$ 36,669	25.8
$	50	$155,595	$ 60,333	23.0
$	75	$138,525	$ 77,403	20.9
$	100	$125,417	$ 90,511	19.2
$	200	$ 92,735	$123,193	14.9
$	300	$ 74,514	$141,414	12.4

Loan Prepayment

FIXED LOAN PRE-PAYMENT
"Rule of Thumb"

As a quick rule-of-thumb, to cut a new 30 year loan to approximately 15 years, increase the monthly payment as follows:

Loan Interest Rate	Increase Payments
8%	30%
9%	26%
10%	22%
11%	19%
12%	17%
13%	14%
14%	12%

Stepped Increases to Mortgage Payments

Some people cannot afford or do not desire a fixed increase to their loan payment. They prefer to gradually increase the pre-payment amount. The *3% Rule* states that for a 30% fixed rate loan, when each loan payment is increased 3% annually, the loan will be reduced to 15 years...while saving tens of thousands of dollars in interest.

For example, if the 1st year's payment is $500.00 per month, the 2nd year is increased to $515.00 per month, the 3rd year is increased to $530.15 per month, and so forth on an interest rate of about 12.25%. The chart below more exactly demonstrates the effects of the *3% Rule*, and illustrates the reduced term of an original 30-year loan of $100,000, utilizing various fixed interest rates.

Loan Prepayment

Effects of "The 3% Rule"

Loan Interest Rate	Loan Term
9%	16.8 Years
10%	16.2 Years
11%	15.7 Years
12%	15.2 Years
13%	14.6 Years
14%	14.2 Years

Loan Prepayment
Frequently Asked Questions

Q. Since interest payments are tax deductible, isn't it better to not pre-pay a loan and receive the tax benefits?

A. This is a common misconception regarding tax advantages. Regardless of the tax bracket, tax payers <u>always</u> come out better by avoiding an expense rather than incurring one. Loan pre-payments can save thousands of dollars, which outweighs the tax benefits.

Q. My loan has pre-payment penalties, should I still pre-pay my loan?

A. Many pre-payment penalties are relatively minor, and may not even be enforced by the lender. Often, the advantages of loan pre-payment far outweigh any pre-payment penalties. Consult with a real estate professional for specific details regarding your loan.

Q. Can I skip a payment when I start a pre-payment program?

A. The surplus "pre-payment" portion of the payment may be skipped, but the original loan payment amount <u>cannot</u> be skipped.

Q. I think loan pre-payments may be for me, what is my next step?

A. It is important that pre-payments be made with an attitude of using "spare change" to avoid over-extending finances and jeopardizing timely mortgage payments. Utilize the previous charts to help determine an affordable pre-payment plan, and always consult with your attorney or licensed real estate professional when making significant real estate related decisions.

Q. How do I make the calculations for my specific situation?

A. Utilizing the ***Annual Constant Tables*** that are located in the ***Financial Tables*** section, custom pre-payment schedules can be calculated.

For example, for a $100,000, 30-year loan at 9.50% interest, the factor is 10.0903%. The loan payment is calculated as $100,000 @ 10.0903%, or $10,090 per year ($841 per month). To pay this loan off in only 20 years, find the increased payment factor under "20 Years" of 11.1856.

The increased payment would be $100,000 @ 11.186% per year, or $11,186 per year. ($932 per month). In this example, increasing the monthly payment by about $91 per month reduces the term of the loan by 10 years..

Loan Prepayment

Loan Prepayment

Financial Tables

Year Proration
Loan Payment
Effective Rate with Points
Constant Annual Percent Table

PRORATION OF A YEAR

The following tables are useful in the calculation of a mid-year lease payment or loan payment. For example, if a $10,000 per year lease is terminated on April 16th, the amount owing is $10,000 @ 29.041%, or $2,904.10.

Proration of Year

**PRORATION OF DAYS IN A YEAR
FROM JANUARY 1**

Day	Jan	Feb	Mar	April
1	0.274%	8.767%	16.438%	24.932%
2	0.548%	9.041%	16.712%	25.205%
3	0.822%	9.315%	16.986%	25.479%
4	1.096%	9.589%	17.260%	25.753%
5	1.370%	9.863%	17.534%	26.027%
6	1.644%	10.137%	17.808%	26.301%
7	1.918%	10.411%	18.082%	26.575%
8	2.192%	10.685%	18.356%	26.849%
9	2.466%	10.959%	18.630%	27.123%
10	2.740%	11.233%	18.904%	27.397%
11	3.014%	11.507%	19.178%	27.671%
12	3.288%	11.781%	19.452%	27.945%
13	3.562%	12.055%	19.726%	28.219%
14	3.836%	12.329%	20.000%	28.493%
15	4.110%	12.603%	20.274%	28.767%
16	4.384%	12.877%	20.548%	29.041%
17	4.658%	13.151%	20.822%	29.315%
18	4.932%	13.425%	21.096%	29.589%
19	5.205%	13.699%	21.370%	29.863%
20	5.479%	13.973%	21.644%	30.137%
21	5.753%	14.247%	21.918%	30.411%
22	6.027%	14.521%	22.192%	30.685%
23	6.301%	14.795%	22.466%	30.959%
24	6.575%	15.068%	22.740%	31.233%
25	6.849%	15.342%	23.014%	31.507%
26	7.123%	15.616%	23.288%	31.781%
27	7.397%	15.890%	23.562%	32.055%
28	7.671%	16.164%	23.836%	32.329%
29	7.945%		24.110%	32.603%
30	8.219%		24.384%	32.877%
31	8.493%		24.658%	

PRORATION OF DAYS IN A YEAR
FROM JANUARY 1

Day	May	June	July	Aug
1	33.151%	41.644%	49.863%	58.356%
2	33.425%	41.918%	50.137%	58.630%
3	33.699%	42.192%	50.411%	58.904%
4	33.973%	42.466%	50.685%	59.178%
5	34.247%	42.740%	50.959%	59.452%
6	34.521%	43.014%	51.233%	59.726%
7	34.795%	43.288%	51.507%	60.000%
8	35.068%	43.562%	51.781%	60.274%
9	35.342%	43.836%	52.055%	60.548%
10	35.616%	44.110%	52.329%	60.822%
11	35.890%	44.384%	52.603%	61.096%
12	36.164%	44.658%	52.877%	61.370%
13	36.438%	44.932%	53.151%	61.644%
14	36.712%	45.205%	53.425%	61.918%
15	36.986%	45.479%	53.699%	62.192%
16	37.260%	45.753%	53.973%	62.466%
17	37.534%	46.027%	54.247%	62.740%
18	37.808%	46.301%	54.521%	63.014%
19	38.082%	46.575%	54.795%	63.288%
20	38.356%	46.849%	55.068%	63.562%
21	38.630%	47.123%	55.342%	63.836%
22	38.904%	47.397%	55.616%	64.110%
23	39.178%	47.671%	55.890%	64.384%
24	39.452%	47.945%	56.164%	64.658%
25	39.726%	48.219%	56.438%	64.932%
26	40.000%	48.493%	56.712%	65.205%
27	40.274%	48.767%	56.986%	65.479%
28	40.548%	49.041%	57.260%	65.753%
29	40.822%	49.315%	57.534%	66.027%
30	41.096%	49.589%	57.808%	66.301%
31	41.370%		58.082%	66.575%

PRORATION OF DAYS IN A YEAR
FROM JANUARY 1

Day	Sep	Oct	Nov	Dec
1	66.849%	75.068%	83.562%	91.781%
2	67.123%	75.342%	83.836%	92.055%
3	67.397%	75.616%	84.110%	92.329%
4	67.671%	75.890%	84.384%	92.603%
5	67.945%	76.164%	84.658%	92.877%
6	68.219%	76.438%	84.932%	93.151%
7	68.493%	76.712%	85.205%	93.425%
8	68.767%	76.986%	85.479%	93.699%
9	69.041%	77.260%	85.753%	93.973%
10	69.315%	77.534%	86.027%	94.247%
11	69.589%	77.808%	86.301%	94.521%
12	69.863%	78.082%	86.575%	94.795%
13	70.137%	78.356%	86.849%	95.068%
14	70.411%	78.630%	87.123%	95.342%
15	70.685%	78.904%	87.397%	95.616%
16	70.959%	79.178%	87.671%	95.890%
17	71.233%	79.452%	87.945%	96.164%
18	71.507%	79.726%	88.219%	96.438%
19	71.781%	80.000%	88.493%	96.712%
20	72.055%	80.274%	88.767%	96.986%
21	72.329%	80.548%	89.041%	97.260%
22	72.603%	80.822%	89.315%	97.534%
23	72.877%	81.096%	89.589%	97.808%
24	73.151%	81.370%	89.863%	98.082%
25	73.425%	81.644%	90.137%	98.356%
26	73.699%	81.918%	90.411%	98.630%
27	73.973%	82.192%	90.685%	98.904%
28	74.247%	82.466%	90.959%	99.178%
29	74.521%	82.740%	91.233%	99.452%
30	74.795%	83.014%	91.507%	99.726%
31		83.288%		100.000%

LOAN PAYMENT TABLE
INTEREST RATE: 5.00%
Monthly Payments - Fully Amortized

Loan Amount	5.00%	Term of Loan In Years		
	5	10	15	20
$ 1,000	18.87	10.61	7.91	6.60
5,000	94.36	53.03	39.54	33.00
10,000	188.71	106.07	79.08	66.00
25,000	471.78	265.16	197.70	164.99
40,000	754.85	424.26	316.32	263.98
50,000	943.56	530.33	395.40	329.98
75,000	1,415.34	795.49	593.10	494.97
100,000	1,887.12	1,060.66	790.79	659.96
125,000	2,358.90	1,325.82	988.49	824.94
150,000	2,830.69	1,590.98	1,186.19	989.93
175,000	3,302.47	1,856.15	1,383.89	1,154.92
200,000	3,774.25	2,121.31	1,581.59	1,319.91
225,000	4,246.03	2,386.47	1,779.29	1,484.90
250,000	4,717.81	2,651.64	1,976.98	1,649.89
275,000	5,189.59	2,916.80	2,174.68	1,814.88
300,000	5,661.37	3,181.97	2,372.38	1,979.87
350,000	6,604.93	3,712.29	2,767.78	2,309.85
400,000	7,548.49	4,242.62	3,163.17	2,639.82
450,000	8,492.06	4,772.95	3,558.57	2,969.80
500,000	9,435.62	5,303.28	3,953.97	3,299.78
600,000	11,322.74	6,363.93	4,744.76	3,959.73
700,000	13,209.86	7,424.59	5,535.56	4,619.69
800,000	15,096.99	8,485.24	6,326.35	5,279.65
900,000	16,984.11	9,545.90	7,117.14	5,939.60
1,000,000	18,871.23	10,606.55	7,907.94	6,599.56

Loan Payment

LOAN PAYMENT TABLE
INTEREST RATE: 5.00%
Monthly Payments - Fully Amortized

Loan Amount	5.00%	Term of Loan In Years		
	25	30	35	40
$ 1,000	5.85	5.37	5.05	4.82
5,000	29.23	26.84	25.23	24.11
10,000	58.46	53.68	50.47	48.22
25,000	146.15	134.21	126.17	120.55
40,000	233.84	214.73	201.88	192.88
50,000	292.30	268.41	252.34	241.10
75,000	438.44	402.62	378.52	361.65
100,000	584.59	536.82	504.69	482.20
125,000	730.74	671.03	630.86	602.75
150,000	876.89	805.23	757.03	723.29
175,000	1,023.03	939.44	883.20	843.84
200,000	1,169.18	1,073.64	1,009.38	964.39
225,000	1,315.33	1,207.85	1,135.55	1,084.94
250,000	1,461.48	1,342.05	1,261.72	1,205.49
275,000	1,607.62	1,476.26	1,387.89	1,326.04
300,000	1,753.77	1,610.46	1,514.06	1,446.59
350,000	2,046.07	1,878.88	1,766.41	1,687.69
400,000	2,338.36	2,147.29	2,018.75	1,928.79
450,000	2,630.66	2,415.70	2,271.09	2,169.88
500,000	2,922.95	2,684.11	2,523.44	2,410.98
600,000	3,507.54	3,220.93	3,028.13	2,893.18
700,000	4,092.13	3,757.75	3,532.81	3,375.38
800,000	4,676.72	4,294.57	4,037.50	3,857.57
900,000	5,261.31	4,831.39	4,542.19	4,339.77
1,000,000	5,845.90	5,368.22	5,046.88	4,821.97

Loan Payment

LOAN PAYMENT TABLE
INTEREST RATE: 5.25%
Monthly Payments - Fully Amortized

Loan Amount	5.25%	Term of Loan In Years		
	5	10	15	20
$ 1,000	18.99	10.73	8.04	6.74
5,000	94.93	53.65	40.19	33.69
10,000	189.86	107.29	80.39	67.38
25,000	474.65	268.23	200.97	168.46
40,000	759.44	429.17	321.55	269.54
50,000	949.30	536.46	401.94	336.92
75,000	1,423.95	804.69	602.91	505.38
100,000	1,898.60	1,072.92	803.88	673.84
125,000	2,373.25	1,341.15	1,004.85	842.31
150,000	2,847.90	1,609.38	1,205.82	1,010.77
175,000	3,322.55	1,877.60	1,406.79	1,179.23
200,000	3,797.20	2,145.83	1,607.76	1,347.69
225,000	4,271.85	2,414.06	1,808.72	1,516.15
250,000	4,746.50	2,682.29	2,009.69	1,684.61
275,000	5,221.15	2,950.52	2,210.66	1,853.07
300,000	5,695.80	3,218.75	2,411.63	2,021.53
350,000	6,645.09	3,755.21	2,813.57	2,358.45
400,000	7,594.39	4,291.67	3,215.51	2,695.38
450,000	8,543.69	4,828.13	3,617.45	3,032.30
500,000	9,492.99	5,364.59	4,019.39	3,369.22
600,000	11,391.59	6,437.50	4,823.27	4,043.06
700,000	13,290.19	7,510.42	5,627.14	4,716.91
800,000	15,188.79	8,583.34	6,431.02	5,390.75
900,000	17,087.39	9,656.25	7,234.90	6,064.60
1,000,000	18,985.98	10,729.17	8,038.78	6,738.44

LOAN PAYMENT TABLE
INTEREST RATE: 5.25%
Monthly Payments - Fully Amortized

Loan Amount	5.25%	Term of Loan In Years		
	25	30	35	40
$ 1,000	5.99	5.52	5.21	4.99
5,000	29.96	27.61	26.04	24.94
10,000	59.92	55.22	52.07	49.89
25,000	149.81	138.05	130.19	124.72
40,000	239.70	220.88	208.30	199.55
50,000	299.62	276.10	260.37	249.44
75,000	449.44	414.15	390.56	374.15
100,000	599.25	552.20	520.74	498.87
125,000	749.06	690.25	650.93	623.59
150,000	898.87	828.31	781.11	748.31
175,000	1,048.68	966.36	911.30	873.02
200,000	1,198.50	1,104.41	1,041.49	997.74
225,000	1,348.31	1,242.46	1,171.67	1,122.46
250,000	1,498.12	1,380.51	1,301.86	1,247.18
275,000	1,647.93	1,518.56	1,432.04	1,371.89
300,000	1,797.74	1,656.61	1,562.23	1,496.61
350,000	2,097.37	1,932.71	1,822.60	1,746.05
400,000	2,396.99	2,208.81	2,082.97	1,995.48
450,000	2,696.61	2,484.92	2,343.34	2,244.92
500,000	2,996.24	2,761.02	2,603.72	2,494.35
600,000	3,595.49	3,313.22	3,124.46	2,993.22
700,000	4,194.73	3,865.43	3,645.20	3,492.09
800,000	4,793.98	4,417.63	4,165.94	3,990.96
900,000	5,393.23	4,969.83	4,686.69	4,489.83
1,000,000	5,992.48	5,522.04	5,207.43	4,988.70

Loan Payment

LOAN PAYMENT TABLE
INTEREST RATE: 5.50%
Monthly Payments - Fully Amortized

Loan Amount	5.50%	Term of Loan In Years		
	5	10	15	20
$ 1,000	19.10	10.85	8.17	6.88
5,000	95.51	54.26	40.85	34.39
10,000	191.01	108.53	81.71	68.79
25,000	477.53	271.32	204.27	171.97
40,000	764.05	434.11	326.83	275.15
50,000	955.06	542.63	408.54	343.94
75,000	1,432.59	813.95	612.81	515.92
100,000	1,910.12	1,085.26	817.08	687.89
125,000	2,387.65	1,356.58	1,021.35	859.86
150,000	2,865.17	1,627.89	1,225.63	1,031.83
175,000	3,342.70	1,899.21	1,429.90	1,203.80
200,000	3,820.23	2,170.53	1,634.17	1,375.77
225,000	4,297.76	2,441.84	1,838.44	1,547.75
250,000	4,775.29	2,713.16	2,042.71	1,719.72
275,000	5,252.82	2,984.47	2,246.98	1,891.69
300,000	5,730.35	3,255.79	2,451.25	2,063.66
350,000	6,685.41	3,798.42	2,859.79	2,407.61
400,000	7,640.46	4,341.05	3,268.33	2,751.55
450,000	8,595.52	4,883.68	3,676.88	3,095.49
500,000	9,550.58	5,426.31	4,085.42	3,439.44
600,000	11,460.70	6,511.58	4,902.50	4,127.32
700,000	13,370.81	7,596.84	5,719.58	4,815.21
800,000	15,280.93	8,682.10	6,536.67	5,503.10
900,000	17,191.05	9,767.37	7,353.75	6,190.99
1,000,000	19,101.16	10,852.63	8,170.83	6,878.87

Loan Payment

LOAN PAYMENT TABLE
INTEREST RATE: 5.50%
Monthly Payments - Fully Amortized

Loan Amount	5.50%	Term of Loan In Years		
	25	30	35	40
$ 1,000	6.14	5.68	5.37	5.16
5,000	30.70	28.39	26.85	25.79
10,000	61.41	56.78	53.70	51.58
25,000	153.52	141.95	134.25	128.94
40,000	245.63	227.12	214.81	206.31
50,000	307.04	283.89	268.51	257.89
75,000	460.57	425.84	402.76	386.83
100,000	614.09	567.79	537.02	515.77
125,000	767.61	709.74	671.27	644.71
150,000	921.13	851.68	805.52	773.66
175,000	1,074.65	993.63	939.78	902.60
200,000	1,228.17	1,135.58	1,074.03	1,031.54
225,000	1,381.70	1,277.53	1,208.29	1,160.48
250,000	1,535.22	1,419.47	1,342.54	1,289.43
275,000	1,688.74	1,561.42	1,476.79	1,418.37
300,000	1,842.26	1,703.37	1,611.05	1,547.31
350,000	2,149.31	1,987.26	1,879.56	1,805.20
400,000	2,456.35	2,271.16	2,148.07	2,063.08
450,000	2,763.39	2,555.05	2,416.57	2,320.97
500,000	3,070.44	2,838.95	2,685.08	2,578.85
600,000	3,684.52	3,406.73	3,222.10	3,094.62
700,000	4,298.61	3,974.52	3,759.11	3,610.39
800,000	4,912.70	4,542.31	4,296.13	4,126.16
900,000	5,526.79	5,110.10	4,833.15	4,641.93
1,000,000	6,140.87	5,677.89	5,370.16	5,157.70

LOAN PAYMENT TABLE
INTEREST RATE: 5.75%
Monthly Payments - Fully Amortized

Loan Amount	5.75% 5	Term of Loan In Years 10	15	20
$ 1,000	19.22	10.98	8.30	7.02
5,000	96.08	54.88	41.52	35.10
10,000	192.17	109.77	83.04	70.21
25,000	480.42	274.42	207.60	175.52
40,000	768.67	439.08	332.16	280.83
50,000	960.84	548.85	415.21	351.04
75,000	1,441.26	823.27	622.81	526.56
100,000	1,921.68	1,097.69	830.41	702.08
125,000	2,402.10	1,372.12	1,038.01	877.60
150,000	2,882.52	1,646.54	1,245.62	1,053.13
175,000	3,362.93	1,920.96	1,453.22	1,228.65
200,000	3,843.35	2,195.38	1,660.82	1,404.17
225,000	4,323.77	2,469.81	1,868.42	1,579.69
250,000	4,804.19	2,744.23	2,076.03	1,755.21
275,000	5,284.61	3,018.65	2,283.63	1,930.73
300,000	5,765.03	3,293.08	2,491.23	2,106.25
350,000	6,725.87	3,841.92	2,906.44	2,457.29
400,000	7,686.71	4,390.77	3,321.64	2,808.33
450,000	8,647.55	4,939.61	3,736.85	3,159.38
500,000	9,608.38	5,488.46	4,152.05	3,510.42
600,000	11,530.06	6,586.15	4,982.46	4,212.50
700,000	13,451.74	7,683.85	5,812.87	4,914.58
800,000	15,373.41	8,781.54	6,643.28	5,616.67
900,000	17,295.09	9,879.23	7,473.69	6,318.75
1,000,000	19,216.77	10,976.92	8,304.10	7,020.84

LOAN PAYMENT TABLE
INTEREST RATE: 5.75%
Monthly Payments - Fully Amortized

Loan Amount	5.75%	Term of Loan In Years		
	25	30	35	40
$ 1,000	6.29	5.84	5.54	5.33
5,000	31.46	29.18	27.68	26.64
10,000	62.91	58.36	55.35	53.29
25,000	157.28	145.89	138.38	133.22
40,000	251.64	233.43	221.40	213.16
50,000	314.55	291.79	276.75	266.44
75,000	471.83	437.68	415.13	399.67
100,000	629.11	583.57	553.50	532.89
125,000	786.38	729.47	691.88	666.11
150,000	943.66	875.36	830.25	799.33
175,000	1,100.94	1,021.25	968.63	932.55
200,000	1,258.21	1,167.15	1,107.00	1,065.78
225,000	1,415.49	1,313.04	1,245.38	1,199.00
250,000	1,572.77	1,458.93	1,383.75	1,332.22
275,000	1,730.04	1,604.83	1,522.13	1,465.44
300,000	1,887.32	1,750.72	1,660.50	1,598.66
350,000	2,201.87	2,042.50	1,937.25	1,865.11
400,000	2,516.43	2,334.29	2,214.00	2,131.55
450,000	2,830.98	2,626.08	2,490.75	2,397.99
500,000	3,145.53	2,917.86	2,767.50	2,664.44
600,000	3,774.64	3,501.44	3,321.00	3,197.33
700,000	4,403.74	4,085.01	3,874.51	3,730.21
800,000	5,032.85	4,668.58	4,428.01	4,263.10
900,000	5,661.96	5,252.16	4,981.51	4,795.99
1,000,000	6,291.06	5,835.73	5,535.01	5,328.88

Loan Payment

LOAN PAYMENT TABLE
INTEREST RATE: 6.00%
Monthly Payments - Fully Amortized

Loan Amount	6.00%	Term of Loan In Years		
	5	10	15	20
$ 1,000	19.33	11.10	8.44	7.16
5,000	96.66	55.51	42.19	35.82
10,000	193.33	111.02	84.39	71.64
25,000	483.32	277.55	210.96	179.11
40,000	773.31	444.08	337.54	286.57
50,000	966.64	555.10	421.93	358.22
75,000	1,449.96	832.65	632.89	537.32
100,000	1,933.28	1,110.21	843.86	716.43
125,000	2,416.60	1,387.76	1,054.82	895.54
150,000	2,899.92	1,665.31	1,265.79	1,074.65
175,000	3,383.24	1,942.86	1,476.75	1,253.75
200,000	3,866.56	2,220.41	1,687.71	1,432.86
225,000	4,349.88	2,497.96	1,898.68	1,611.97
250,000	4,833.20	2,775.51	2,109.64	1,791.08
275,000	5,316.52	3,053.06	2,320.61	1,970.19
300,000	5,799.84	3,330.62	2,531.57	2,149.29
350,000	6,766.48	3,885.72	2,953.50	2,507.51
400,000	7,733.12	4,440.82	3,375.43	2,865.72
450,000	8,699.76	4,995.92	3,797.36	3,223.94
500,000	9,666.40	5,551.03	4,219.28	3,582.16
600,000	11,599.68	6,661.23	5,063.14	4,298.59
700,000	13,532.96	7,771.44	5,907.00	5,015.02
800,000	15,466.24	8,881.64	6,750.85	5,731.45
900,000	17,399.52	9,991.85	7,594.71	6,447.88
1,000,000	19,332.80	11,102.05	8,438.57	7,164.31

LOAN PAYMENT TABLE
INTEREST RATE: 6.00%
Monthly Payments - Fully Amortized

Loan Amount	6.00%	Term of Loan In Years		
	25	30	35	40
$ 1,000	6.44	6.00	5.70	5.50
5,000	32.22	29.98	28.51	27.51
10,000	64.43	59.96	57.02	55.02
25,000	161.08	149.89	142.55	137.55
40,000	257.72	239.82	228.08	220.09
50,000	322.15	299.78	285.09	275.11
75,000	483.23	449.66	427.64	412.66
100,000	644.30	599.55	570.19	550.21
125,000	805.38	749.44	712.74	687.77
150,000	966.45	899.33	855.28	825.32
175,000	1,127.53	1,049.21	997.83	962.87
200,000	1,288.60	1,199.10	1,140.38	1,100.43
225,000	1,449.68	1,348.99	1,282.93	1,237.98
250,000	1,610.75	1,498.88	1,425.47	1,375.53
275,000	1,771.83	1,648.76	1,568.02	1,513.09
300,000	1,932.90	1,798.65	1,710.57	1,650.64
350,000	2,255.05	2,098.43	1,995.66	1,925.75
400,000	2,577.21	2,398.20	2,280.76	2,200.85
450,000	2,899.36	2,697.98	2,565.85	2,475.96
500,000	3,221.51	2,997.75	2,850.95	2,751.07
600,000	3,865.81	3,597.30	3,421.14	3,301.28
700,000	4,510.11	4,196.85	3,991.33	3,851.50
800,000	5,154.41	4,796.40	4,561.52	4,401.71
900,000	5,798.71	5,395.95	5,131.71	4,951.92
1,000,000	6,443.01	5,995.51	5,701.90	5,502.14

Loan Payment

LOAN PAYMENT TABLE
INTEREST RATE: 6.25%
Monthly Payments - Fully Amortized

Loan Amount	6.25% 5	Term of Loan In Years 10	15	20
$ 1,000	19.45	11.23	8.57	7.31
5,000	97.25	56.14	42.87	36.55
10,000	194.49	112.28	85.74	73.09
25,000	486.23	280.70	214.36	182.73
40,000	777.97	449.12	342.97	292.37
50,000	972.46	561.40	428.71	365.46
75,000	1,458.69	842.10	643.07	548.20
100,000	1,944.93	1,122.80	857.42	730.93
125,000	2,431.16	1,403.50	1,071.78	913.66
150,000	2,917.39	1,684.20	1,286.13	1,096.39
175,000	3,403.62	1,964.90	1,500.49	1,279.12
200,000	3,889.85	2,245.60	1,714.85	1,461.86
225,000	4,376.08	2,526.30	1,929.20	1,644.59
250,000	4,862.32	2,807.00	2,143.56	1,827.32
275,000	5,348.55	3,087.70	2,357.91	2,010.05
300,000	5,834.78	3,368.40	2,572.27	2,192.78
350,000	6,807.24	3,929.80	3,000.98	2,558.25
400,000	7,779.70	4,491.20	3,429.69	2,923.71
450,000	8,752.17	5,052.60	3,858.40	3,289.18
500,000	9,724.63	5,614.00	4,287.11	3,654.64
600,000	11,669.56	6,736.81	5,144.54	4,385.57
700,000	13,614.48	7,859.61	6,001.96	5,116.50
800,000	15,559.41	8,982.41	6,859.38	5,847.43
900,000	17,504.34	10,105.21	7,716.81	6,578.35
1,000,000	19,449.26	11,228.01	8,574.23	7,309.28

LOAN PAYMENT TABLE
INTEREST RATE: 6.25%
Monthly Payments - Fully Amortized

Loan Amount	6.25%	Term of Loan In Years		
	25	30	35	40
$ 1,000	6.60	6.16	5.87	5.68
5,000	32.98	30.79	29.35	28.39
10,000	65.97	61.57	58.71	56.77
25,000	164.92	153.93	146.77	141.93
40,000	263.87	246.29	234.83	227.10
50,000	329.83	307.86	293.54	283.87
75,000	494.75	461.79	440.31	425.80
100,000	659.67	615.72	587.08	567.74
125,000	824.59	769.65	733.85	709.67
150,000	989.50	923.58	880.61	851.61
175,000	1,154.42	1,077.51	1,027.38	993.54
200,000	1,319.34	1,231.43	1,174.15	1,135.48
225,000	1,484.26	1,385.36	1,320.92	1,277.41
250,000	1,649.17	1,539.29	1,467.69	1,419.35
275,000	1,814.09	1,693.22	1,614.46	1,561.28
300,000	1,979.01	1,847.15	1,761.23	1,703.22
350,000	2,308.84	2,155.01	2,054.77	1,987.09
400,000	2,638.68	2,462.87	2,348.31	2,270.96
450,000	2,968.51	2,770.73	2,641.84	2,554.83
500,000	3,298.35	3,078.59	2,935.38	2,838.70
600,000	3,958.02	3,694.30	3,522.46	3,406.44
700,000	4,617.69	4,310.02	4,109.54	3,974.18
800,000	5,277.36	4,925.74	4,696.61	4,541.92
900,000	5,937.02	5,541.45	5,283.69	5,109.66
1,000,000	6,596.69	6,157.17	5,870.76	5,677.40

Loan Payment

LOAN PAYMENT TABLE
INTEREST RATE: 6.50%
Monthly Payments - Fully Amortized

Loan Amount	6.50%	Term of Loan In Years		
	5	10	15	20
$ 1,000	19.57	11.35	8.71	7.46
5,000	97.83	56.77	43.56	37.28
10,000	195.66	113.55	87.11	74.56
25,000	489.15	283.87	217.78	186.39
40,000	782.65	454.19	348.44	298.23
50,000	978.31	567.74	435.55	372.79
75,000	1,467.46	851.61	653.33	559.18
100,000	1,956.61	1,135.48	871.11	745.57
125,000	2,445.77	1,419.35	1,088.88	931.97
150,000	2,934.92	1,703.22	1,306.66	1,118.36
175,000	3,424.08	1,987.09	1,524.44	1,304.75
200,000	3,913.23	2,270.96	1,742.21	1,491.15
225,000	4,402.38	2,554.83	1,959.99	1,677.54
250,000	4,891.54	2,838.70	2,177.77	1,863.93
275,000	5,380.69	3,122.57	2,395.55	2,050.33
300,000	5,869.84	3,406.44	2,613.32	2,236.72
350,000	6,848.15	3,974.18	3,048.88	2,609.51
400,000	7,826.46	4,541.92	3,484.43	2,982.29
450,000	8,804.77	5,109.66	3,919.98	3,355.08
500,000	9,783.07	5,677.40	4,355.54	3,727.87
600,000	11,739.69	6,812.88	5,226.64	4,473.44
700,000	13,696.30	7,948.36	6,097.75	5,219.01
800,000	15,652.92	9,083.84	6,968.86	5,964.59
900,000	17,609.53	10,219.32	7,839.97	6,710.16
1,000,000	19,566.15	11,354.80	8,711.07	7,455.73

LOAN PAYMENT TABLE
INTEREST RATE: 6.50%
Monthly Payments - Fully Amortized

Loan	6.50%	Term of Loan In Years		
Amount	25	30	35	40
$ 1,000	6.75	6.32	6.04	5.85
5,000	33.76	31.60	30.21	29.27
10,000	67.52	63.21	60.42	58.55
25,000	168.80	158.02	151.04	146.36
40,000	270.08	252.83	241.66	234.18
50,000	337.60	316.03	302.08	292.73
75,000	506.41	474.05	453.12	439.09
100,000	675.21	632.07	604.15	585.46
125,000	844.01	790.09	755.19	731.82
150,000	1,012.81	948.10	906.23	878.19
175,000	1,181.61	1,106.12	1,057.27	1,024.55
200,000	1,350.41	1,264.14	1,208.31	1,170.91
225,000	1,519.22	1,422.15	1,359.35	1,317.28
250,000	1,688.02	1,580.17	1,510.39	1,463.64
275,000	1,856.82	1,738.19	1,661.42	1,610.01
300,000	2,025.62	1,896.20	1,812.46	1,756.37
350,000	2,363.23	2,212.24	2,114.54	2,049.10
400,000	2,700.83	2,528.27	2,416.62	2,341.83
450,000	3,038.43	2,844.31	2,718.69	2,634.56
500,000	3,376.04	3,160.34	3,020.77	2,927.28
600,000	4,051.24	3,792.41	3,624.93	3,512.74
700,000	4,726.45	4,424.48	4,229.08	4,098.20
800,000	5,401.66	5,056.54	4,833.23	4,683.65
900,000	6,076.86	5,688.61	5,437.39	5,269.11
1,000,000	6,752.07	6,320.68	6,041.54	5,854.57

Loan Payment

LOAN PAYMENT TABLE
INTEREST RATE: 6.75%
Monthly Payments - Fully Amortized

Loan Amount	6.75% 5	Term of Loan In Years 10	15	20
$ 1,000	19.68	11.48	8.85	7.60
5,000	98.42	57.41	44.25	38.02
10,000	196.83	114.82	88.49	76.04
25,000	492.09	287.06	221.23	190.09
40,000	787.34	459.30	353.96	304.15
50,000	984.17	574.12	442.45	380.18
75,000	1,476.26	861.18	663.68	570.27
100,000	1,968.35	1,148.24	884.91	760.36
125,000	2,460.43	1,435.30	1,106.14	950.46
150,000	2,952.52	1,722.36	1,327.36	1,140.55
175,000	3,444.61	2,009.42	1,548.59	1,330.64
200,000	3,936.69	2,296.48	1,769.82	1,520.73
225,000	4,428.78	2,583.54	1,991.05	1,710.82
250,000	4,920.87	2,870.60	2,212.27	1,900.91
275,000	5,412.95	3,157.66	2,433.50	2,091.00
300,000	5,905.04	3,444.72	2,654.73	2,281.09
350,000	6,889.21	4,018.84	3,097.18	2,661.27
400,000	7,873.38	4,592.96	3,539.64	3,041.46
450,000	8,857.56	5,167.09	3,982.09	3,421.64
500,000	9,841.73	5,741.21	4,424.55	3,801.82
600,000	11,810.08	6,889.45	5,309.46	4,562.18
700,000	13,778.42	8,037.69	6,194.37	5,322.55
800,000	15,746.77	9,185.93	7,079.28	6,082.91
900,000	17,715.11	10,334.17	7,964.19	6,843.28
1,000,000	19,683.46	11,482.41	8,849.09	7,603.64

LOAN PAYMENT TABLE
INTEREST RATE: 6.75%
Monthly Payments - Fully Amortized

Loan Amount	6.75%	Term of Loan In Years		
	5	10	15	20
$ 1,000	19.68	11.48	8.85	7.60
5,000	98.42	57.41	44.25	38.02
10,000	196.83	114.82	88.49	76.04
25,000	492.09	287.06	221.23	190.09
40,000	787.34	459.30	353.96	304.15
50,000	984.17	574.12	442.45	380.18
75,000	1,476.26	861.18	663.68	570.27
100,000	1,968.35	1,148.24	884.91	760.36
125,000	2,460.43	1,435.30	1,106.14	950.46
150,000	2,952.52	1,722.36	1,327.36	1,140.55
175,000	3,444.61	2,009.42	1,548.59	1,330.64
200,000	3,936.69	2,296.48	1,769.82	1,520.73
225,000	4,428.78	2,583.54	1,991.05	1,710.82
250,000	4,920.87	2,870.60	2,212.27	1,900.91
275,000	5,412.95	3,157.66	2,433.50	2,091.00
300,000	5,905.04	3,444.72	2,654.73	2,281.09
350,000	6,889.21	4,018.84	3,097.18	2,661.27
400,000	7,873.38	4,592.96	3,539.64	3,041.46
450,000	8,857.56	5,167.09	3,982.09	3,421.64
500,000	9,841.73	5,741.21	4,424.55	3,801.82
600,000	11,810.08	6,889.45	5,309.46	4,562.18
700,000	13,778.42	8,037.69	6,194.37	5,322.55
800,000	15,746.77	9,185.93	7,079.28	6,082.91
900,000	17,715.11	10,334.17	7,964.19	6,843.28
1,000,000	19,683.46	11,482.41	8,849.09	7,603.64

Loan Payment

LOAN PAYMENT TABLE
INTEREST RATE: 7.00%
Monthly Payments - Fully Amortized

Loan Amount	7.00%	Term of Loan In Years		
	5	10	15	20
$ 1,000	19.80	11.61	8.99	7.75
5,000	99.01	58.05	44.94	38.76
10,000	198.01	116.11	89.88	77.53
25,000	495.03	290.27	224.71	193.82
40,000	792.05	464.43	359.53	310.12
50,000	990.06	580.54	449.41	387.65
75,000	1,485.09	870.81	674.12	581.47
100,000	1,980.12	1,161.08	898.83	775.30
125,000	2,475.15	1,451.36	1,123.54	969.12
150,000	2,970.18	1,741.63	1,348.24	1,162.95
175,000	3,465.21	2,031.90	1,572.95	1,356.77
200,000	3,960.24	2,322.17	1,797.66	1,550.60
225,000	4,455.27	2,612.44	2,022.36	1,744.42
250,000	4,950.30	2,902.71	2,247.07	1,938.25
275,000	5,445.33	3,192.98	2,471.78	2,132.07
300,000	5,940.36	3,483.25	2,696.48	2,325.90
350,000	6,930.42	4,063.80	3,145.90	2,713.55
400,000	7,920.48	4,644.34	3,595.31	3,101.20
450,000	8,910.54	5,224.88	4,044.73	3,488.85
500,000	9,900.60	5,805.42	4,494.14	3,876.49
600,000	11,880.72	6,966.51	5,392.97	4,651.79
700,000	13,860.84	8,127.59	6,291.80	5,427.09
800,000	15,840.96	9,288.68	7,190.63	6,202.39
900,000	17,821.08	10,449.76	8,089.45	6,977.69
1,000,000	19,801.20	11,610.85	8,988.28	7,752.99

Loan Payment

LOAN PAYMENT TABLE
INTEREST RATE: 7.00%
Monthly Payments - Fully Amortized

Loan Amount	7.00%	Term of Loan In Years		
	25	30	35	40
$ 1,000	7.07	6.65	6.39	6.21
5,000	35.34	33.27	31.94	31.07
10,000	70.68	66.53	63.89	62.14
25,000	176.69	166.33	159.71	155.36
40,000	282.71	266.12	255.54	248.57
50,000	353.39	332.65	319.43	310.72
75,000	530.08	498.98	479.14	466.07
100,000	706.78	665.30	638.86	621.43
125,000	883.47	831.63	798.57	776.79
150,000	1,060.17	997.95	958.28	932.15
175,000	1,236.86	1,164.28	1,118.00	1,087.50
200,000	1,413.56	1,330.60	1,277.71	1,242.86
225,000	1,590.25	1,496.93	1,437.43	1,398.22
250,000	1,766.95	1,663.26	1,597.14	1,553.58
275,000	1,943.64	1,829.58	1,756.85	1,708.94
300,000	2,120.34	1,995.91	1,916.57	1,864.29
350,000	2,473.73	2,328.56	2,236.00	2,175.01
400,000	2,827.12	2,661.21	2,555.43	2,485.73
450,000	3,180.51	2,993.86	2,874.85	2,796.44
500,000	3,533.90	3,326.51	3,194.28	3,107.16
600,000	4,240.68	3,991.81	3,833.14	3,728.59
700,000	4,947.45	4,657.12	4,471.99	4,350.02
800,000	5,654.23	5,322.42	5,110.85	4,971.45
900,000	6,361.01	5,987.72	5,749.71	5,592.88
1,000,000	7,067.79	6,653.02	6,388.56	6,214.31

Loan Payment

LOAN PAYMENT TABLE
INTEREST RATE: 7.25%
Monthly Payments - Fully Amortized

Loan	7.25%	Term of Loan In Years		
Amount	5	10	15	20
$ 1,000	19.92	11.74	9.13	7.90
5,000	99.60	58.70	45.64	39.52
10,000	199.19	117.40	91.29	79.04
25,000	497.98	293.50	228.22	197.59
40,000	796.77	469.60	365.15	316.15
50,000	995.97	587.01	456.43	395.19
75,000	1,493.95	880.51	684.65	592.78
100,000	1,991.94	1,174.01	912.86	790.38
125,000	2,489.92	1,467.51	1,141.08	987.97
150,000	2,987.90	1,761.02	1,369.29	1,185.56
175,000	3,485.89	2,054.52	1,597.51	1,383.16
200,000	3,983.87	2,348.02	1,825.73	1,580.75
225,000	4,481.86	2,641.52	2,053.94	1,778.35
250,000	4,979.84	2,935.03	2,282.16	1,975.94
275,000	5,477.82	3,228.53	2,510.37	2,173.53
300,000	5,975.81	3,522.03	2,738.59	2,371.13
350,000	6,971.78	4,109.04	3,195.02	2,766.32
400,000	7,967.74	4,696.04	3,651.45	3,161.50
450,000	8,963.71	5,283.05	4,107.88	3,556.69
500,000	9,959.68	5,870.05	4,564.31	3,951.88
600,000	11,951.62	7,044.06	5,477.18	4,742.26
700,000	13,943.55	8,218.07	6,390.04	5,532.63
800,000	15,935.49	9,392.08	7,302.90	6,323.01
900,000	17,927.43	10,566.09	8,215.77	7,113.38
1,000,000	19,919.36	11,740.10	9,128.63	7,903.76

Loan Payment

LOAN PAYMENT TABLE
INTEREST RATE: 7.25%
Monthly Payments - Fully Amortized

Loan Amount	7.25% 25	Term of Loan In Years 30	35	40
$ 1,000	7.23	6.82	6.56	6.40
5,000	36.14	34.11	32.82	31.98
10,000	72.28	68.22	65.65	63.97
25,000	180.70	170.54	164.12	159.92
40,000	289.12	272.87	262.59	255.87
50,000	361.40	341.09	328.23	319.84
75,000	542.11	511.63	492.35	479.75
100,000	722.81	682.18	656.47	639.67
125,000	903.51	852.72	820.58	799.59
150,000	1,084.21	1,023.26	984.70	959.51
175,000	1,264.91	1,193.81	1,148.82	1,119.43
200,000	1,445.61	1,364.35	1,312.93	1,279.34
225,000	1,626.32	1,534.90	1,477.05	1,439.26
250,000	1,807.02	1,705.44	1,641.17	1,599.18
275,000	1,987.72	1,875.98	1,805.28	1,759.10
300,000	2,168.42	2,046.53	1,969.40	1,919.02
350,000	2,529.82	2,387.62	2,297.64	2,238.85
400,000	2,891.23	2,728.71	2,625.87	2,558.69
450,000	3,252.63	3,069.79	2,954.10	2,878.52
500,000	3,614.03	3,410.88	3,282.34	3,198.36
600,000	4,336.84	4,093.06	3,938.80	3,838.03
700,000	5,059.65	4,775.23	4,595.27	4,477.70
800,000	5,782.45	5,457.41	5,251.74	5,117.38
900,000	6,505.26	6,139.59	5,908.21	5,757.05
1,000,000	7,228.07	6,821.76	6,564.67	6,396.72

Loan Payment

LOAN PAYMENT TABLE
INTEREST RATE: 7.50%
Monthly Payments - Fully Amortized

| Loan | 7.50% | Term of Loan In Years | | |
Amount	5	10	15	20
$ 1,000	20.04	11.87	9.27	8.06
5,000	100.19	59.35	46.35	40.28
10,000	200.38	118.70	92.70	80.56
25,000	500.95	296.75	231.75	201.40
40,000	801.52	474.81	370.80	322.24
50,000	1,001.90	593.51	463.51	402.80
75,000	1,502.85	890.26	695.26	604.19
100,000	2,003.79	1,187.02	927.01	805.59
125,000	2,504.74	1,483.77	1,158.77	1,006.99
150,000	3,005.69	1,780.53	1,390.52	1,208.39
175,000	3,506.64	2,077.28	1,622.27	1,409.79
200,000	4,007.59	2,374.04	1,854.02	1,611.19
225,000	4,508.54	2,670.79	2,085.78	1,812.58
250,000	5,009.49	2,967.54	2,317.53	2,013.98
275,000	5,510.44	3,264.30	2,549.28	2,215.38
300,000	6,011.38	3,561.05	2,781.04	2,416.78
350,000	7,013.28	4,154.56	3,244.54	2,819.58
400,000	8,015.18	4,748.07	3,708.05	3,222.37
450,000	9,017.08	5,341.58	4,171.56	3,625.17
500,000	10,018.97	5,935.09	4,635.06	4,027.97
600,000	12,022.77	7,122.11	5,562.07	4,833.56
700,000	14,026.56	8,309.12	6,489.09	5,639.15
800,000	16,030.36	9,496.14	7,416.10	6,444.75
900,000	18,034.15	10,683.16	8,343.11	7,250.34
1,000,000	20,037.95	11,870.18	9,270.12	8,055.93

LOAN PAYMENT TABLE
INTEREST RATE: 7.50%
Monthly Payments - Fully Amortized

Loan Amount	7.50%	Term of Loan In Years		
	25	30	35	40
$ 1,000	7.39	6.99	6.74	6.58
5,000	36.95	34.96	33.71	32.90
10,000	73.90	69.92	67.42	65.81
25,000	184.75	174.80	168.56	164.52
40,000	295.60	279.69	269.70	263.23
50,000	369.50	349.61	337.12	329.04
75,000	554.24	524.41	505.68	493.55
100,000	738.99	699.21	674.24	658.07
125,000	923.74	874.02	842.80	822.59
150,000	1,108.49	1,048.82	1,011.36	987.11
175,000	1,293.23	1,223.63	1,179.92	1,151.62
200,000	1,477.98	1,398.43	1,348.49	1,316.14
225,000	1,662.73	1,573.23	1,517.05	1,480.66
250,000	1,847.48	1,748.04	1,685.61	1,645.18
275,000	2,032.23	1,922.84	1,854.17	1,809.69
300,000	2,216.97	2,097.64	2,022.73	1,974.21
350,000	2,586.47	2,447.25	2,359.85	2,303.25
400,000	2,955.96	2,796.86	2,696.97	2,632.28
450,000	3,325.46	3,146.47	3,034.09	2,961.32
500,000	3,694.96	3,496.07	3,371.21	3,290.35
600,000	4,433.95	4,195.29	4,045.46	3,948.42
700,000	5,172.94	4,894.50	4,719.70	4,606.50
800,000	5,911.93	5,593.72	5,393.94	5,264.57
900,000	6,650.92	6,292.93	6,068.18	5,922.64
1,000,000	7,389.91	6,992.15	6,742.43	6,580.71

Loan Payment

LOAN PAYMENT TABLE
INTEREST RATE: 7.75%
Monthly Payments - Fully Amortized

Loan Amount	7.75%	Term of Loan In Years		
	5	10	15	20
$ 1,000	20.16	12.00	9.41	8.21
5,000	100.78	60.01	47.06	41.05
10,000	201.57	120.01	94.13	82.09
25,000	503.92	300.03	235.32	205.24
40,000	806.28	480.04	376.51	328.38
50,000	1,007.85	600.05	470.64	410.47
75,000	1,511.77	900.08	705.96	615.71
100,000	2,015.70	1,200.11	941.28	820.95
125,000	2,519.62	1,500.13	1,176.59	1,026.19
150,000	3,023.54	1,800.16	1,411.91	1,231.42
175,000	3,527.47	2,100.19	1,647.23	1,436.66
200,000	4,031.39	2,400.21	1,882.55	1,641.90
225,000	4,535.32	2,700.24	2,117.87	1,847.13
250,000	5,039.24	3,000.27	2,353.19	2,052.37
275,000	5,543.16	3,300.29	2,588.51	2,257.61
300,000	6,047.09	3,600.32	2,823.83	2,462.85
350,000	7,054.94	4,200.37	3,294.47	2,873.32
400,000	8,062.78	4,800.43	3,765.10	3,283.79
450,000	9,070.63	5,400.48	4,235.74	3,694.27
500,000	10,078.48	6,000.53	4,706.38	4,104.74
600,000	12,094.18	7,200.64	5,647.65	4,925.69
700,000	14,109.87	8,400.74	6,588.93	5,746.64
800,000	16,125.57	9,600.85	7,530.21	6,567.59
900,000	18,141.26	10,800.96	8,471.48	7,388.54
1,000,000	20,156.96	12,001.06	9,412.76	8,209.49

LOAN PAYMENT TABLE
INTEREST RATE: 7.75%
Monthly Payments - Fully Amortized

Loan Amount	7.75%	Term of Loan In Years		
	25	30	35	40
$ 1,000	7.55	7.16	6.92	6.77
5,000	37.77	35.82	34.61	33.83
10,000	75.53	71.64	69.22	67.66
25,000	188.83	179.10	173.04	169.15
40,000	302.13	286.56	276.87	270.65
50,000	377.66	358.21	346.09	338.31
75,000	566.50	537.31	519.13	507.46
100,000	755.33	716.41	692.18	676.62
125,000	944.16	895.52	865.22	845.77
150,000	1,132.99	1,074.62	1,038.26	1,014.93
175,000	1,321.83	1,253.72	1,211.31	1,184.08
200,000	1,510.66	1,432.82	1,384.35	1,353.24
225,000	1,699.49	1,611.93	1,557.40	1,522.39
250,000	1,888.32	1,791.03	1,730.44	1,691.55
275,000	2,077.15	1,970.13	1,903.48	1,860.70
300,000	2,265.99	2,149.24	2,076.53	2,029.86
350,000	2,643.65	2,507.44	2,422.62	2,368.17
400,000	3,021.32	2,865.65	2,768.70	2,706.48
450,000	3,398.98	3,223.86	3,114.79	3,044.79
500,000	3,776.64	3,582.06	3,460.88	3,383.10
600,000	4,531.97	4,298.47	4,153.06	4,059.72
700,000	5,287.30	5,014.89	4,845.23	4,736.34
800,000	6,042.63	5,731.30	5,537.41	5,412.96
900,000	6,797.96	6,447.71	6,229.58	6,089.58
1,000,000	7,553.29	7,164.12	6,921.76	6,766.20

Loan Payment

LOAN PAYMENT TABLE
INTEREST RATE: 8.00%
Monthly Payments - Fully Amortized

Loan Amount	8.00%	Term of Loan In Years		
	5	10	15	20
$ 1,000	20.28	12.13	9.56	8.36
5,000	101.38	60.66	47.78	41.82
10,000	202.76	121.33	95.57	83.64
25,000	506.91	303.32	238.91	209.11
40,000	811.06	485.31	382.26	334.58
50,000	1,013.82	606.64	477.83	418.22
75,000	1,520.73	909.96	716.74	627.33
100,000	2,027.64	1,213.28	955.65	836.44
125,000	2,534.55	1,516.59	1,194.57	1,045.55
150,000	3,041.46	1,819.91	1,433.48	1,254.66
175,000	3,548.37	2,123.23	1,672.39	1,463.77
200,000	4,055.28	2,426.55	1,911.30	1,672.88
225,000	4,562.19	2,729.87	2,150.22	1,881.99
250,000	5,069.10	3,033.19	2,389.13	2,091.10
275,000	5,576.01	3,336.51	2,628.04	2,300.21
300,000	6,082.92	3,639.83	2,866.96	2,509.32
350,000	7,096.74	4,246.47	3,344.78	2,927.54
400,000	8,110.56	4,853.10	3,822.61	3,345.76
450,000	9,124.38	5,459.74	4,300.43	3,763.98
500,000	10,138.20	6,066.38	4,778.26	4,182.20
600,000	12,165.84	7,279.66	5,733.91	5,018.64
700,000	14,193.48	8,492.93	6,689.56	5,855.08
800,000	16,221.12	9,706.21	7,645.22	6,691.52
900,000	18,248.75	10,919.48	8,600.87	7,527.96
1,000,000	20,276.39	12,132.76	9,556.52	8,364.40

LOAN PAYMENT TABLE
INTEREST RATE: 8.00%
Monthly Payments - Fully Amortized

Loan Amount	8.00%	Term of Loan In Years		
		25	30	35	40

Loan Amount	25	30	35	40
$ 1,000	7.72	7.34	7.10	6.95
5,000	38.59	36.69	35.51	34.77
10,000	77.18	73.38	71.03	69.53
25,000	192.95	183.44	177.57	173.83
40,000	308.73	293.51	284.10	278.12
50,000	385.91	366.88	355.13	347.66
75,000	578.86	550.32	532.70	521.48
100,000	771.82	733.76	710.26	695.31
125,000	964.77	917.21	887.83	869.14
150,000	1,157.72	1,100.65	1,065.39	1,042.97
175,000	1,350.68	1,284.09	1,242.96	1,216.80
200,000	1,543.63	1,467.53	1,420.52	1,390.62
225,000	1,736.59	1,650.97	1,598.09	1,564.45
250,000	1,929.54	1,834.41	1,775.65	1,738.28
275,000	2,122.49	2,017.85	1,953.22	1,912.11
300,000	2,315.45	2,201.29	2,130.78	2,085.94
350,000	2,701.36	2,568.18	2,485.91	2,433.59
400,000	3,087.26	2,935.06	2,841.04	2,781.25
450,000	3,473.17	3,301.94	3,196.17	3,128.90
500,000	3,859.08	3,668.82	3,551.30	3,476.56
600,000	4,630.90	4,402.59	4,261.57	4,171.87
700,000	5,402.71	5,136.35	4,971.83	4,867.18
800,000	6,174.53	5,870.12	5,682.09	5,562.49
900,000	6,946.35	6,603.88	6,392.35	6,257.81
1,000,000	7,718.16	7,337.65	7,102.61	6,953.12

Loan Payment

LOAN PAYMENT TABLE
INTEREST RATE: 8.25%
Monthly Payments - Fully Amortized

Loan Amount	8.25% 5	Term of Loan In Years 10	15	20
$ 1,000	20.40	12.27	9.70	8.52
5,000	101.98	61.33	48.51	42.60
10,000	203.96	122.65	97.01	85.21
25,000	509.91	306.63	242.54	213.02
40,000	815.85	490.61	388.06	340.83
50,000	1,019.81	613.26	485.07	426.03
75,000	1,529.72	919.89	727.61	639.05
100,000	2,039.63	1,226.53	970.14	852.07
125,000	2,549.53	1,533.16	1,212.68	1,065.08
150,000	3,059.44	1,839.79	1,455.21	1,278.10
175,000	3,569.34	2,146.42	1,697.75	1,491.11
200,000	4,079.25	2,453.05	1,940.28	1,704.13
225,000	4,589.16	2,759.68	2,182.82	1,917.15
250,000	5,099.06	3,066.32	2,425.35	2,130.16
275,000	5,608.97	3,372.95	2,667.89	2,343.18
300,000	6,118.88	3,679.58	2,910.42	2,556.20
350,000	7,138.69	4,292.84	3,395.49	2,982.23
400,000	8,158.50	4,906.11	3,880.56	3,408.26
450,000	9,178.31	5,519.37	4,365.63	3,834.30
500,000	10,198.13	6,132.63	4,850.70	4,260.33
600,000	12,237.75	7,359.16	5,820.84	5,112.39
700,000	14,277.38	8,585.68	6,790.98	5,964.46
800,000	16,317.00	9,812.21	7,761.12	6,816.53
900,000	18,356.63	11,038.74	8,731.26	7,668.59
1,000,000	20,396.25	12,265.26	9,701.40	8,520.66

LOAN PAYMENT TABLE
INTEREST RATE: 8.25%
Monthly Payments - Fully Amortized

Loan Amount	8.25%	Term of Loan In Years		
	25	30	35	40
$ 1,000	7.88	7.51	7.28	7.14
5,000	39.42	37.56	36.42	35.71
10,000	78.85	75.13	72.85	71.41
25,000	197.11	187.82	182.12	178.53
40,000	315.38	300.51	291.40	285.66
50,000	394.23	375.63	364.25	357.07
75,000	591.34	563.45	546.37	535.60
100,000	788.45	751.27	728.49	714.14
125,000	985.56	939.08	910.61	892.67
150,000	1,182.68	1,126.90	1,092.74	1,071.21
175,000	1,379.79	1,314.72	1,274.86	1,249.74
200,000	1,576.90	1,502.53	1,456.98	1,428.28
225,000	1,774.01	1,690.35	1,639.11	1,606.81
250,000	1,971.13	1,878.17	1,821.23	1,785.35
275,000	2,168.24	2,065.98	2,003.35	1,963.88
300,000	2,365.35	2,253.80	2,185.47	2,142.42
350,000	2,759.58	2,629.43	2,549.72	2,499.49
400,000	3,153.80	3,005.07	2,913.96	2,856.56
450,000	3,548.03	3,380.70	3,278.21	3,213.62
500,000	3,942.25	3,756.33	3,642.46	3,570.69
600,000	4,730.70	4,507.60	4,370.95	4,284.83
700,000	5,519.15	5,258.87	5,099.44	4,998.97
800,000	6,307.60	6,010.13	5,827.93	5,713.11
900,000	7,096.05	6,761.40	6,556.42	6,427.25
1,000,000	7,884.50	7,512.67	7,284.91	7,141.39

Loan Payment

LOAN PAYMENT TABLE
INTEREST RATE: 8.50%
Monthly Payments - Fully Amortized

Loan Amount	8.50% 5	Term of Loan In Years 10	15	20
$ 1,000	20.52	12.40	9.85	8.68
5,000	102.58	61.99	49.24	43.39
10,000	205.17	123.99	98.47	86.78
25,000	512.91	309.96	246.18	216.96
40,000	820.66	495.94	393.90	347.13
50,000	1,025.83	619.93	492.37	433.91
75,000	1,538.74	929.89	738.55	650.87
100,000	2,051.65	1,239.86	984.74	867.82
125,000	2,564.57	1,549.82	1,230.92	1,084.78
150,000	3,077.48	1,859.79	1,477.11	1,301.73
175,000	3,590.39	2,169.75	1,723.29	1,518.69
200,000	4,103.31	2,479.71	1,969.48	1,735.65
225,000	4,616.22	2,789.68	2,215.66	1,952.60
250,000	5,129.13	3,099.64	2,461.85	2,169.56
275,000	5,642.05	3,409.61	2,708.03	2,386.51
300,000	6,154.96	3,719.57	2,954.22	2,603.47
350,000	7,180.79	4,339.50	3,446.59	3,037.38
400,000	8,206.61	4,959.43	3,938.96	3,471.29
450,000	9,232.44	5,579.36	4,431.33	3,905.20
500,000	10,258.27	6,199.28	4,923.70	4,339.12
600,000	12,309.92	7,439.14	5,908.44	5,206.94
700,000	14,361.57	8,679.00	6,893.18	6,074.76
800,000	16,413.23	9,918.86	7,877.92	6,942.59
900,000	18,464.88	11,158.71	8,862.66	7,810.41
1,000,000	20,516.53	12,398.57	9,847.40	8,678.23

LOAN PAYMENT TABLE
INTEREST RATE: 8.50%
Monthly Payments - Fully Amortized

Loan Amount	8.50%	Term of Loan In Years		
	25	30	35	40
$ 1,000	8.05	7.69	7.47	7.33
5,000	40.26	38.45	37.34	36.65
10,000	80.52	76.89	74.69	73.31
25,000	201.31	192.23	186.72	183.27
40,000	322.09	307.57	298.74	293.24
50,000	402.61	384.46	373.43	366.55
75,000	603.92	576.69	560.15	549.82
100,000	805.23	768.91	746.86	733.09
125,000	1,006.53	961.14	933.58	916.37
150,000	1,207.84	1,153.37	1,120.29	1,099.64
175,000	1,409.15	1,345.60	1,307.01	1,282.91
200,000	1,610.45	1,537.83	1,493.72	1,466.19
225,000	1,811.76	1,730.06	1,680.44	1,649.46
250,000	2,013.07	1,922.28	1,867.15	1,832.74
275,000	2,214.37	2,114.51	2,053.87	2,016.01
300,000	2,415.68	2,306.74	2,240.58	2,199.28
350,000	2,818.29	2,691.20	2,614.01	2,565.83
400,000	3,220.91	3,075.65	2,987.44	2,932.38
450,000	3,623.52	3,460.11	3,360.87	3,298.92
500,000	4,026.14	3,844.57	3,734.30	3,665.47
600,000	4,831.36	4,613.48	4,481.16	4,398.56
700,000	5,636.59	5,382.39	5,228.02	5,131.66
800,000	6,441.82	6,151.31	5,974.88	5,864.75
900,000	7,247.04	6,920.22	6,721.75	6,597.85
1,000,000	8,052.27	7,689.13	7,468.61	7,330.94

Loan Payment

LOAN PAYMENT TABLE
INTEREST RATE: 8.75%
Monthly Payments - Fully Amortized

Loan Amount	8.75%	Term of Loan In Years		
	5	10	15	20
$ 1,000	20.64	12.53	9.99	8.84
5,000	103.19	62.66	49.97	44.19
10,000	206.37	125.33	99.94	88.37
25,000	515.93	313.32	249.86	220.93
40,000	825.49	501.31	399.78	353.48
50,000	1,031.86	626.63	499.72	441.86
75,000	1,547.79	939.95	749.59	662.78
100,000	2,063.72	1,253.27	999.45	883.71
125,000	2,579.65	1,566.58	1,249.31	1,104.64
150,000	3,095.58	1,879.90	1,499.17	1,325.57
175,000	3,611.52	2,193.22	1,749.04	1,546.49
200,000	4,127.45	2,506.54	1,998.90	1,767.42
225,000	4,643.38	2,819.85	2,248.76	1,988.35
250,000	5,159.31	3,133.17	2,498.62	2,209.28
275,000	5,675.24	3,446.49	2,748.48	2,430.20
300,000	6,191.17	3,759.80	2,998.35	2,651.13
350,000	7,223.03	4,386.44	3,498.07	3,092.99
400,000	8,254.89	5,013.07	3,997.79	3,534.84
450,000	9,286.75	5,639.70	4,497.52	3,976.70
500,000	10,318.62	6,266.34	4,997.24	4,418.55
600,000	12,382.34	7,519.61	5,996.69	5,302.26
700,000	14,446.06	8,772.87	6,996.14	6,185.97
800,000	16,509.79	10,026.14	7,995.59	7,069.69
900,000	18,573.51	11,279.41	8,995.04	7,953.40
1,000,000	20,637.23	12,532.68	9,994.49	8,837.11

Loan Payment

LOAN PAYMENT TABLE
INTEREST RATE: 8.75%
Monthly Payments - Fully Amortized

Loan Amount	8.75%	Term of Loan In Years		
	25	30	35	40
$ 1,000	8.22	7.87	7.65	7.52
5,000	41.11	39.34	38.27	37.61
10,000	82.21	78.67	76.54	75.22
25,000	205.54	196.68	191.34	188.04
40,000	328.86	314.68	306.15	300.87
50,000	411.07	393.35	382.68	376.09
75,000	616.61	590.03	574.02	564.13
100,000	822.14	786.70	765.36	752.17
125,000	1,027.68	983.38	956.70	940.21
150,000	1,233.22	1,180.05	1,148.04	1,128.26
175,000	1,438.75	1,376.73	1,339.39	1,316.30
200,000	1,644.29	1,573.40	1,530.73	1,504.34
225,000	1,849.82	1,770.08	1,722.07	1,692.38
250,000	2,055.36	1,966.75	1,913.41	1,880.43
275,000	2,260.89	2,163.43	2,104.75	2,068.47
300,000	2,466.43	2,360.10	2,296.09	2,256.51
350,000	2,877.50	2,753.45	2,678.77	2,632.60
400,000	3,288.57	3,146.80	3,061.45	3,008.68
450,000	3,699.65	3,540.15	3,444.13	3,384.77
500,000	4,110.72	3,933.50	3,826.82	3,760.85
600,000	4,932.86	4,720.20	4,592.18	4,513.02
700,000	5,755.01	5,506.90	5,357.54	5,265.19
800,000	6,577.15	6,293.60	6,122.91	6,017.36
900,000	7,399.29	7,080.30	6,888.27	6,769.53
1,000,000	8,221.44	7,867.00	7,653.63	7,521.71

Loan Payment

LOAN PAYMENT TABLE
INTEREST RATE: 9.00%
Monthly Payments - Fully Amortized

Loan Amount	9.00% 5	Term of Loan In Years 10	15	20
$ 1,000	20.76	12.67	10.14	9.00
5,000	103.79	63.34	50.71	44.99
10,000	207.58	126.68	101.43	89.97
25,000	518.96	316.69	253.57	224.93
40,000	830.33	506.70	405.71	359.89
50,000	1,037.92	633.38	507.13	449.86
75,000	1,556.88	950.07	760.70	674.79
100,000	2,075.84	1,266.76	1,014.27	899.73
125,000	2,594.79	1,583.45	1,267.83	1,124.66
150,000	3,113.75	1,900.14	1,521.40	1,349.59
175,000	3,632.71	2,216.83	1,774.97	1,574.52
200,000	4,151.67	2,533.52	2,028.53	1,799.45
225,000	4,670.63	2,850.20	2,282.10	2,024.38
250,000	5,189.59	3,166.89	2,535.67	2,249.31
275,000	5,708.55	3,483.58	2,789.23	2,474.25
300,000	6,227.51	3,800.27	3,042.80	2,699.18
350,000	7,265.42	4,433.65	3,549.93	3,149.04
400,000	8,303.34	5,067.03	4,057.07	3,598.90
450,000	9,341.26	5,700.41	4,564.20	4,048.77
500,000	10,379.18	6,333.79	5,071.33	4,498.63
600,000	12,455.01	7,600.55	6,085.60	5,398.36
700,000	14,530.85	8,867.30	7,099.87	6,298.08
800,000	16,606.68	10,134.06	8,114.13	7,197.81
900,000	18,682.52	11,400.82	9,128.40	8,097.53
1,000,000	20,758.36	12,667.58	10,142.67	8,997.26

Loan Payment

LOAN PAYMENT TABLE
INTEREST RATE: 9.00%
Monthly Payments - Fully Amortized

Loan Amount	9.00%	Term of Loan In Years		
	25	30	35	40
$ 1,000	8.39	8.05	7.84	7.71
5,000	41.96	40.23	39.20	38.57
10,000	83.92	80.46	78.40	77.14
25,000	209.80	201.16	196.00	192.84
40,000	335.68	321.85	313.60	308.54
50,000	419.60	402.31	392.00	385.68
75,000	629.40	603.47	587.99	578.52
100,000	839.20	804.62	783.99	771.36
125,000	1,049.00	1,005.78	979.99	964.20
150,000	1,258.79	1,206.93	1,175.99	1,157.04
175,000	1,468.59	1,408.09	1,371.99	1,349.88
200,000	1,678.39	1,609.25	1,567.99	1,542.72
225,000	1,888.19	1,810.40	1,763.98	1,735.56
250,000	2,097.99	2,011.56	1,959.98	1,928.40
275,000	2,307.79	2,212.71	2,155.98	2,121.24
300,000	2,517.59	2,413.87	2,351.98	2,314.08
350,000	2,937.19	2,816.18	2,743.98	2,699.77
400,000	3,356.79	3,218.49	3,135.97	3,085.45
450,000	3,776.38	3,620.80	3,527.97	3,471.13
500,000	4,195.98	4,023.11	3,919.96	3,856.81
600,000	5,035.18	4,827.74	4,703.96	4,628.17
700,000	5,874.37	5,632.36	5,487.95	5,399.53
800,000	6,713.57	6,436.98	6,271.94	6,170.89
900,000	7,552.77	7,241.60	7,055.94	6,942.25
1,000,000	8,391.96	8,046.23	7,839.93	7,713.61

LOAN PAYMENT TABLE
INTEREST RATE: 9.25%
Monthly Payments - Fully Amortized

Loan Amount	9.25% 5	Term of Loan In Years 10	15	20
$ 1,000	20.88	12.80	10.29	9.16
5,000	104.40	64.02	51.46	45.79
10,000	208.80	128.03	102.92	91.59
25,000	522.00	320.08	257.30	228.97
40,000	835.20	512.13	411.68	366.35
50,000	1,043.99	640.16	514.60	457.93
75,000	1,565.99	960.25	771.89	686.90
100,000	2,087.99	1,280.33	1,029.19	915.87
125,000	2,609.99	1,600.41	1,286.49	1,144.83
150,000	3,131.98	1,920.49	1,543.79	1,373.80
175,000	3,653.98	2,240.57	1,801.09	1,602.77
200,000	4,175.98	2,560.65	2,058.38	1,831.73
225,000	4,697.98	2,880.74	2,315.68	2,060.70
250,000	5,219.97	3,200.82	2,572.98	2,289.67
275,000	5,741.97	3,520.90	2,830.28	2,518.63
300,000	6,263.97	3,840.98	3,087.58	2,747.60
350,000	7,307.96	4,481.15	3,602.17	3,205.53
400,000	8,351.96	5,121.31	4,116.77	3,663.47
450,000	9,395.95	5,761.47	4,631.37	4,121.40
500,000	10,439.95	6,401.64	5,145.96	4,579.33
600,000	12,527.94	7,681.96	6,175.15	5,495.20
700,000	14,615.93	8,962.29	7,204.35	6,411.07
800,000	16,703.92	10,242.62	8,233.54	7,326.93
900,000	18,791.91	11,522.94	9,262.73	8,242.80
1,000,000	20,879.90	12,803.27	10,291.92	9,158.67

Loan Payment

LOAN PAYMENT TABLE
INTEREST RATE: 9.25%
Monthly Payments - Fully Amortized

Loan	9.25%	Term of Loan In Years		
Amount	25	30	35	40
$ 1,000	8.56	8.23	8.03	7.91
5,000	42.82	41.13	40.14	39.53
10,000	85.64	82.27	80.27	79.07
25,000	214.10	205.67	200.69	197.67
40,000	342.55	329.07	321.10	316.26
50,000	428.19	411.34	401.37	395.33
75,000	642.29	617.01	602.06	593.00
100,000	856.38	822.68	802.74	790.66
125,000	1,070.48	1,028.34	1,003.43	988.33
150,000	1,284.57	1,234.01	1,204.12	1,185.99
175,000	1,498.67	1,439.68	1,404.80	1,383.66
200,000	1,712.76	1,645.35	1,605.49	1,581.32
225,000	1,926.86	1,851.02	1,806.17	1,778.99
250,000	2,140.95	2,056.69	2,006.86	1,976.65
275,000	2,355.05	2,262.36	2,207.55	2,174.32
300,000	2,569.15	2,468.03	2,408.23	2,371.98
350,000	2,997.34	2,879.36	2,809.61	2,767.31
400,000	3,425.53	3,290.70	3,210.98	3,162.64
450,000	3,853.72	3,702.04	3,612.35	3,557.97
500,000	4,281.91	4,113.38	4,013.72	3,953.30
600,000	5,138.29	4,936.05	4,816.47	4,743.96
700,000	5,994.67	5,758.73	5,619.21	5,534.62
800,000	6,851.05	6,581.40	6,421.95	6,325.28
900,000	7,707.44	7,404.08	7,224.70	7,115.95
1,000,000	8,563.82	8,226.75	8,027.44	7,906.61

Loan Payment

LOAN PAYMENT TABLE
INTEREST RATE: 9.50%
Monthly Payments - Fully Amortized

Loan Amount	9.50% 5	Term of Loan In Years 10	15	20
$ 1,000	21.00	12.94	10.44	9.32
5,000	105.01	64.70	52.21	46.61
10,000	210.02	129.40	104.42	93.21
25,000	525.05	323.49	261.06	233.03
40,000	840.07	517.59	417.69	372.85
50,000	1,050.09	646.99	522.11	466.07
75,000	1,575.14	970.48	783.17	699.10
100,000	2,100.19	1,293.98	1,044.22	932.13
125,000	2,625.23	1,617.47	1,305.28	1,165.16
150,000	3,150.28	1,940.96	1,566.34	1,398.20
175,000	3,675.33	2,264.46	1,827.39	1,631.23
200,000	4,200.37	2,587.95	2,088.45	1,864.26
225,000	4,725.42	2,911.45	2,349.51	2,097.30
250,000	5,250.47	3,234.94	2,610.56	2,330.33
275,000	5,775.51	3,558.43	2,871.62	2,563.36
300,000	6,300.56	3,881.93	3,132.67	2,796.39
350,000	7,350.65	4,528.91	3,654.79	3,262.46
400,000	8,400.74	5,175.90	4,176.90	3,728.52
450,000	9,450.84	5,822.89	4,699.01	4,194.59
500,000	10,500.93	6,469.88	5,221.12	4,660.66
600,000	12,601.12	7,763.85	6,265.35	5,592.79
700,000	14,701.30	9,057.83	7,309.57	6,524.92
800,000	16,801.49	10,351.80	8,353.80	7,457.05
900,000	18,901.68	11,645.78	9,398.02	8,389.18
1,000,000	21,001.86	12,939.76	10,442.25	9,321.31

Loan Payment

LOAN PAYMENT TABLE
INTEREST RATE: 9.50%
Monthly Payments - Fully Amortized

Loan Amount	9.50% 25	Term of Loan In Years 30	35	40
$ 1,000	8.74	8.41	8.22	8.10
5,000	43.68	42.04	41.08	40.50
10,000	87.37	84.09	82.16	81.01
25,000	218.42	210.21	205.40	202.52
40,000	349.48	336.34	328.64	324.02
50,000	436.85	420.43	410.81	405.03
75,000	655.27	630.64	616.21	607.55
100,000	873.70	840.85	821.61	810.06
125,000	1,092.12	1,051.07	1,027.01	1,012.58
150,000	1,310.54	1,261.28	1,232.42	1,215.09
175,000	1,528.97	1,471.49	1,437.82	1,417.61
200,000	1,747.39	1,681.71	1,643.22	1,620.12
225,000	1,965.82	1,891.92	1,848.63	1,822.64
250,000	2,184.24	2,102.14	2,054.03	2,025.15
275,000	2,402.67	2,312.35	2,259.43	2,227.67
300,000	2,621.09	2,522.56	2,464.83	2,430.18
350,000	3,057.94	2,942.99	2,875.64	2,835.22
400,000	3,494.79	3,363.42	3,286.45	3,240.25
450,000	3,931.63	3,783.84	3,697.25	3,645.28
500,000	4,368.48	4,204.27	4,108.06	4,050.31
600,000	5,242.18	5,045.13	4,929.67	4,860.37
700,000	6,115.88	5,885.98	5,751.28	5,670.43
800,000	6,989.57	6,726.83	6,572.89	6,480.49
900,000	7,863.27	7,567.69	7,394.50	7,290.55
1,000,000	8,736.97	8,408.54	8,216.12	8,100.62

Loan Payment

LOAN PAYMENT TABLE
INTEREST RATE: 9.75%
Monthly Payments - Fully Amortized

Loan Amount	9.75% 5	Term of Loan In Years 10	15	20
$ 1,000	21.12	13.08	10.59	9.49
5,000	105.62	65.39	52.97	47.43
10,000	211.24	130.77	105.94	94.85
25,000	528.11	326.93	264.84	237.13
40,000	844.97	523.08	423.75	379.41
50,000	1,056.21	653.85	529.68	474.26
75,000	1,584.32	980.78	794.52	711.39
100,000	2,112.42	1,307.70	1,059.36	948.52
125,000	2,640.53	1,634.63	1,324.20	1,185.65
150,000	3,168.64	1,961.55	1,589.04	1,422.78
175,000	3,696.74	2,288.48	1,853.88	1,659.90
200,000	4,224.85	2,615.40	2,118.73	1,897.03
225,000	4,752.95	2,942.33	2,383.57	2,134.16
250,000	5,281.06	3,269.26	2,648.41	2,371.29
275,000	5,809.17	3,596.18	2,913.25	2,608.42
300,000	6,337.27	3,923.11	3,178.09	2,845.55
350,000	7,393.49	4,576.96	3,707.77	3,319.81
400,000	8,449.70	5,230.81	4,237.45	3,794.07
450,000	9,505.91	5,884.66	4,767.13	4,268.33
500,000	10,562.12	6,538.51	5,296.81	4,742.58
600,000	12,674.55	7,846.21	6,356.18	5,691.10
700,000	14,786.97	9,153.92	7,415.54	6,639.62
800,000	16,899.39	10,461.62	8,474.90	7,588.13
900,000	19,011.82	11,769.32	9,534.26	8,536.65
1,000,000	21,124.24	13,077.02	10,593.63	9,485.17

Loan Payment

LOAN PAYMENT TABLE
INTEREST RATE: 9.75%
Monthly Payments - Fully Amortized

Loan Amount	9.75% 25	Term of Loan In Years 30	35	40
$ 1,000	8.91	8.59	8.41	8.30
5,000	44.56	42.96	42.03	41.48
10,000	89.11	85.92	84.06	82.96
25,000	222.78	214.79	210.15	207.39
40,000	356.45	343.66	336.24	331.82
50,000	445.57	429.58	420.29	414.78
75,000	668.35	644.37	630.44	622.17
100,000	891.14	859.15	840.59	829.56
125,000	1,113.92	1,073.94	1,050.74	1,036.95
150,000	1,336.71	1,288.73	1,260.88	1,244.34
175,000	1,559.49	1,503.52	1,471.03	1,451.73
200,000	1,782.27	1,718.31	1,681.18	1,659.12
225,000	2,005.06	1,933.10	1,891.33	1,866.51
250,000	2,227.84	2,147.89	2,101.47	2,073.90
275,000	2,450.63	2,362.67	2,311.62	2,281.29
300,000	2,673.41	2,577.46	2,521.77	2,488.68
350,000	3,118.98	3,007.04	2,942.06	2,903.45
400,000	3,564.55	3,436.62	3,362.36	3,318.23
450,000	4,010.12	3,866.19	3,782.65	3,733.01
500,000	4,455.69	4,295.77	4,202.95	4,147.79
600,000	5,346.82	5,154.93	5,043.54	4,977.35
700,000	6,237.96	6,014.08	5,884.13	5,806.91
800,000	7,129.10	6,873.24	6,724.72	6,636.47
900,000	8,020.24	7,732.39	7,565.30	7,466.03
1,000,000	8,911.37	8,591.54	8,405.89	8,295.59

Loan Payment

LOAN PAYMENT TABLE
INTEREST RATE: 10.00%
Monthly Payments - Fully Amortized

Loan Amount	10.00% 5	Term of Loan In Years 10	15	20
$ 1,000	21.25	13.22	10.75	9.65
5,000	106.24	66.08	53.73	48.25
10,000	212.47	132.15	107.46	96.50
25,000	531.18	330.38	268.65	241.26
40,000	849.88	528.60	429.84	386.01
50,000	1,062.35	660.75	537.30	482.51
75,000	1,593.53	991.13	805.95	723.77
100,000	2,124.70	1,321.51	1,074.61	965.02
125,000	2,655.88	1,651.88	1,343.26	1,206.28
150,000	3,187.06	1,982.26	1,611.91	1,447.53
175,000	3,718.23	2,312.64	1,880.56	1,688.79
200,000	4,249.41	2,643.01	2,149.21	1,930.04
225,000	4,780.59	2,973.39	2,417.86	2,171.30
250,000	5,311.76	3,303.77	2,686.51	2,412.55
275,000	5,842.94	3,634.15	2,955.16	2,653.81
300,000	6,374.11	3,964.52	3,223.82	2,895.06
350,000	7,436.47	4,625.28	3,761.12	3,377.58
400,000	8,498.82	5,286.03	4,298.42	3,860.09
450,000	9,561.17	5,946.78	4,835.72	4,342.60
500,000	10,623.52	6,607.54	5,373.03	4,825.11
600,000	12,748.23	7,929.04	6,447.63	5,790.13
700,000	14,872.93	9,250.55	7,522.24	6,755.15
800,000	16,997.64	10,572.06	8,596.84	7,720.17
900,000	19,122.34	11,893.57	9,671.45	8,685.19
1,000,000	21,247.04	13,215.07	10,746.05	9,650.22

Loan Payment

LOAN PAYMENT TABLE
INTEREST RATE: 10.00%
Monthly Payments - Fully Amortized

Loan Amount	10.00% 25	Term of Loan In Years 30	35	40
$ 1,000	9.09	8.78	8.60	8.49
5,000	45.44	43.88	42.98	42.46
10,000	90.87	87.76	85.97	84.91
25,000	227.18	219.39	214.92	212.29
40,000	363.48	351.03	343.87	339.66
50,000	454.35	438.79	429.84	424.57
75,000	681.53	658.18	644.75	636.86
100,000	908.70	877.57	859.67	849.15
125,000	1,135.88	1,096.96	1,074.59	1,061.43
150,000	1,363.05	1,316.36	1,289.51	1,273.72
175,000	1,590.23	1,535.75	1,504.43	1,486.01
200,000	1,817.40	1,755.14	1,719.34	1,698.29
225,000	2,044.58	1,974.54	1,934.26	1,910.58
250,000	2,271.75	2,193.93	2,149.18	2,122.86
275,000	2,498.93	2,413.32	2,364.10	2,335.15
300,000	2,726.10	2,632.71	2,579.02	2,547.44
350,000	3,180.45	3,071.50	3,008.85	2,972.01
400,000	3,634.80	3,510.29	3,438.69	3,396.58
450,000	4,089.15	3,949.07	3,868.53	3,821.16
500,000	4,543.50	4,387.86	4,298.36	4,245.73
600,000	5,452.20	5,265.43	5,158.03	5,094.88
700,000	6,360.91	6,143.00	6,017.71	5,944.02
800,000	7,269.61	7,020.57	6,877.38	6,793.17
900,000	8,178.31	7,898.14	7,737.05	7,642.31
1,000,000	9,087.01	8,775.72	8,596.72	8,491.46

Loan Payment

LOAN PAYMENT TABLE
INTEREST RATE: 10.25%
Monthly Payments - Fully Amortized

Loan Amount	10.25% 5	Term of Loan In Years 10	15	20
$ 1,000	21.37	13.35	10.90	9.82
5,000	106.85	66.77	54.50	49.08
10,000	213.70	133.54	109.00	98.16
25,000	534.26	333.85	272.49	245.41
40,000	854.81	534.16	435.98	392.66
50,000	1,068.51	667.70	544.98	490.82
75,000	1,602.77	1,001.54	817.46	736.23
100,000	2,137.03	1,335.39	1,089.95	981.64
125,000	2,671.28	1,669.24	1,362.44	1,227.05
150,000	3,205.54	2,003.09	1,634.93	1,472.47
175,000	3,739.80	2,336.93	1,907.41	1,717.88
200,000	4,274.05	2,670.78	2,179.90	1,963.29
225,000	4,808.31	3,004.63	2,452.39	2,208.70
250,000	5,342.57	3,338.48	2,724.88	2,454.11
275,000	5,876.82	3,672.32	2,997.37	2,699.52
300,000	6,411.08	4,006.17	3,269.85	2,944.93
350,000	7,479.59	4,673.87	3,814.83	3,435.75
400,000	8,548.11	5,341.56	4,359.80	3,926.57
450,000	9,616.62	6,009.26	4,904.78	4,417.40
500,000	10,685.13	6,676.95	5,449.75	4,908.22
600,000	12,822.16	8,012.34	6,539.71	5,889.86
700,000	14,959.18	9,347.73	7,629.66	6,871.50
800,000	17,096.21	10,683.12	8,719.61	7,853.15
900,000	19,233.24	12,018.51	9,809.56	8,834.79
1,000,000	21,370.26	13,353.90	10,899.51	9,816.43

LOAN PAYMENT TABLE
INTEREST RATE: 10.25%
Monthly Payments - Fully Amortized

Loan	10.25%	Term of Loan In Years		
Amount	25	30	35	40
$ 1,000	9.26	8.96	8.79	8.69
5,000	46.32	44.81	43.94	43.44
10,000	92.64	89.61	87.89	86.88
25,000	231.60	224.03	219.71	217.20
40,000	370.55	358.44	351.54	347.53
50,000	463.19	448.05	439.43	434.41
75,000	694.79	672.08	659.14	651.61
100,000	926.38	896.10	878.86	868.82
125,000	1,157.98	1,120.13	1,098.57	1,086.02
150,000	1,389.57	1,344.15	1,318.28	1,303.23
175,000	1,621.17	1,568.18	1,538.00	1,520.43
200,000	1,852.77	1,792.20	1,757.71	1,737.64
225,000	2,084.36	2,016.23	1,977.43	1,954.84
250,000	2,315.96	2,240.25	2,197.14	2,172.05
275,000	2,547.55	2,464.28	2,416.85	2,389.25
300,000	2,779.15	2,688.30	2,636.57	2,606.45
350,000	3,242.34	3,136.35	3,075.99	3,040.86
400,000	3,705.53	3,584.41	3,515.42	3,475.27
450,000	4,168.72	4,032.46	3,954.85	3,909.68
500,000	4,631.92	4,480.51	4,394.28	4,344.09
600,000	5,558.30	5,376.61	5,273.13	5,212.91
700,000	6,484.68	6,272.71	6,151.99	6,081.73
800,000	7,411.07	7,168.81	7,030.84	6,950.55
900,000	8,337.45	8,064.91	7,909.70	7,819.36
1,000,000	9,263.83	8,961.01	8,788.56	8,688.18

Loan Payment

LOAN PAYMENT TABLE
INTEREST RATE: 10.50%
Monthly Payments - Fully Amortized

Loan Amount	10.50% 5	Term of Loan In Years 10	15	20
$ 1,000	21.49	13.49	11.05	9.98
5,000	107.47	67.47	55.27	49.92
10,000	214.94	134.93	110.54	99.84
25,000	537.35	337.34	276.35	249.59
40,000	859.76	539.74	442.16	399.35
50,000	1,074.70	674.67	552.70	499.19
75,000	1,612.04	1,012.01	829.05	748.78
100,000	2,149.39	1,349.35	1,105.40	998.38
125,000	2,686.74	1,686.69	1,381.75	1,247.97
150,000	3,224.09	2,024.02	1,658.10	1,497.57
175,000	3,761.43	2,361.36	1,934.45	1,747.16
200,000	4,298.78	2,698.70	2,210.80	1,996.76
225,000	4,836.13	3,036.04	2,487.15	2,246.35
250,000	5,373.48	3,373.37	2,763.50	2,495.95
275,000	5,910.82	3,710.71	3,039.85	2,745.54
300,000	6,448.17	4,048.05	3,316.20	2,995.14
350,000	7,522.87	4,722.72	3,868.90	3,494.33
400,000	8,597.56	5,397.40	4,421.60	3,993.52
450,000	9,672.26	6,072.07	4,974.30	4,492.71
500,000	10,746.95	6,746.75	5,526.99	4,991.90
600,000	12,896.34	8,096.10	6,632.39	5,990.28
700,000	15,045.73	9,445.45	7,737.79	6,988.66
800,000	17,195.12	10,794.80	8,843.19	7,987.04
900,000	19,344.51	12,144.15	9,948.59	8,985.42
1,000,000	21,493.90	13,493.50	11,053.99	9,983.80

LOAN PAYMENT TABLE
INTEREST RATE: 10.50%
Monthly Payments - Fully Amortized

Loan Amount	10.50%	Term of Loan In Years		
	25	30	35	40
$ 1,000	9.44	9.15	8.98	8.89
5,000	47.21	45.74	44.91	44.43
10,000	94.42	91.47	89.81	88.86
25,000	236.05	228.68	224.53	222.14
40,000	377.67	365.90	359.25	355.43
50,000	472.09	457.37	449.07	444.29
75,000	708.14	686.05	673.60	666.43
100,000	944.18	914.74	898.13	888.57
125,000	1,180.23	1,143.42	1,122.67	1,110.71
150,000	1,416.27	1,372.11	1,347.20	1,332.86
175,000	1,652.32	1,600.79	1,571.73	1,555.00
200,000	1,888.36	1,829.48	1,796.27	1,777.14
225,000	2,124.41	2,058.16	2,020.80	1,999.28
250,000	2,360.45	2,286.85	2,245.34	2,221.43
275,000	2,596.50	2,515.53	2,469.87	2,443.57
300,000	2,832.55	2,744.22	2,694.40	2,665.71
350,000	3,304.64	3,201.59	3,143.47	3,110.00
400,000	3,776.73	3,658.96	3,592.54	3,554.28
450,000	4,248.82	4,116.33	4,041.60	3,998.57
500,000	4,720.91	4,573.70	4,490.67	4,442.85
600,000	5,665.09	5,488.44	5,388.80	5,331.42
700,000	6,609.27	6,403.18	6,286.94	6,219.99
800,000	7,553.45	7,317.91	7,185.07	7,108.56
900,000	8,497.64	8,232.65	8,083.21	7,997.13
1,000,000	9,441.82	9,147.39	8,981.34	8,885.70

Loan Payment

LOAN PAYMENT TABLE
INTEREST RATE: 10.75%
Monthly Payments - Fully Amortized

Loan Amount	10.75% 5	Term of Loan In Years 10	15	20
$ 1,000	21.62	13.63	11.21	10.15
5,000	108.09	68.17	56.05	50.76
10,000	216.18	136.34	112.09	101.52
25,000	540.45	340.85	280.24	253.81
40,000	864.72	545.35	448.38	406.09
50,000	1,080.90	681.69	560.47	507.61
75,000	1,621.35	1,022.54	840.71	761.42
100,000	2,161.80	1,363.39	1,120.95	1,015.23
125,000	2,702.24	1,704.23	1,401.18	1,269.04
150,000	3,242.69	2,045.08	1,681.42	1,522.84
175,000	3,783.14	2,385.93	1,961.66	1,776.65
200,000	4,323.59	2,726.77	2,241.90	2,030.46
225,000	4,864.04	3,067.62	2,522.13	2,284.27
250,000	5,404.49	3,408.47	2,802.37	2,538.07
275,000	5,944.94	3,749.31	3,082.61	2,791.88
300,000	6,485.39	4,090.16	3,362.84	3,045.69
350,000	7,566.28	4,771.85	3,923.32	3,553.30
400,000	8,647.18	5,453.55	4,483.79	4,060.92
450,000	9,728.08	6,135.24	5,044.27	4,568.53
500,000	10,808.98	6,816.93	5,604.74	5,076.14
600,000	12,970.77	8,180.32	6,725.69	6,091.37
700,000	15,132.57	9,543.71	7,846.64	7,106.60
800,000	17,294.36	10,907.09	8,967.58	8,121.83
900,000	19,456.16	12,270.48	10,088.53	9,137.06
1,000,000	21,617.95	13,633.87	11,209.48	10,152.29

LOAN PAYMENT TABLE
INTEREST RATE: 10.75%
Monthly Payments - Fully Amortized

Loan Amount	10.75% 25	Term of Loan In Years 30	35	40
$ 1,000	9.62	9.33	9.18	9.08
5,000	48.10	46.67	45.88	45.42
10,000	96.21	93.35	91.75	90.84
25,000	240.52	233.37	229.38	227.10
40,000	384.84	373.39	367.00	363.36
50,000	481.05	466.74	458.75	454.20
75,000	721.57	700.11	688.13	681.30
100,000	962.09	933.48	917.50	908.40
125,000	1,202.62	1,166.85	1,146.88	1,135.50
150,000	1,443.14	1,400.22	1,376.25	1,362.60
175,000	1,683.66	1,633.59	1,605.63	1,589.70
200,000	1,924.19	1,866.96	1,835.01	1,816.79
225,000	2,164.71	2,100.33	2,064.38	2,043.89
250,000	2,405.23	2,333.70	2,293.76	2,270.99
275,000	2,645.75	2,567.07	2,523.13	2,498.09
300,000	2,886.28	2,800.44	2,752.51	2,725.19
350,000	3,367.32	3,267.18	3,211.26	3,179.39
400,000	3,848.37	3,733.93	3,670.01	3,633.59
450,000	4,329.42	4,200.67	4,128.76	4,087.79
500,000	4,810.46	4,667.41	4,587.51	4,541.99
600,000	5,772.56	5,600.89	5,505.02	5,450.38
700,000	6,734.65	6,534.37	6,422.52	6,358.78
800,000	7,696.74	7,467.85	7,340.02	7,267.18
900,000	8,658.83	8,401.33	8,257.53	8,175.58
1,000,000	9,620.93	9,334.81	9,175.03	9,083.97

Loan Payment

LOAN PAYMENT TABLE
INTEREST RATE: 11.00%
Monthly Payments - Fully Amortized

Loan Amount	11.00% 5	Term of Loan In Years 10	15	20
$ 1,000	21.74	13.78	11.37	10.32
5,000	108.71	68.88	56.83	51.61
10,000	217.42	137.75	113.66	103.22
25,000	543.56	344.38	284.15	258.05
40,000	869.70	551.00	454.64	412.88
50,000	1,087.12	688.75	568.30	516.09
75,000	1,630.68	1,033.13	852.45	774.14
100,000	2,174.24	1,377.50	1,136.60	1,032.19
125,000	2,717.80	1,721.88	1,420.75	1,290.24
150,000	3,261.36	2,066.25	1,704.90	1,548.28
175,000	3,804.92	2,410.63	1,989.04	1,806.33
200,000	4,348.48	2,755.00	2,273.19	2,064.38
225,000	4,892.05	3,099.38	2,557.34	2,322.42
250,000	5,435.61	3,443.75	2,841.49	2,580.47
275,000	5,979.17	3,788.13	3,125.64	2,838.52
300,000	6,522.73	4,132.50	3,409.79	3,096.57
350,000	7,609.85	4,821.25	3,978.09	3,612.66
400,000	8,696.97	5,510.00	4,546.39	4,128.75
450,000	9,784.09	6,198.75	5,114.69	4,644.85
500,000	10,871.21	6,887.50	5,682.98	5,160.94
600,000	13,045.45	8,265.00	6,819.58	6,193.13
700,000	15,219.70	9,642.50	7,956.18	7,225.32
800,000	17,393.94	11,020.00	9,092.78	8,257.51
900,000	19,568.18	12,397.50	10,229.37	9,289.70
1,000,000	21,742.42	13,775.00	11,365.97	10,321.88

Loan Payment

LOAN PAYMENT TABLE
INTEREST RATE: 11.00%
Monthly Payments - Fully Amortized

Loan Amount	11.00%	Term of Loan In Years		
	25	30	35	40
$ 1,000	9.80	9.52	9.37	9.28
5,000	49.01	47.62	46.85	46.41
10,000	98.01	95.23	93.70	92.83
25,000	245.03	238.08	234.24	232.07
40,000	392.05	380.93	374.78	371.32
50,000	490.06	476.16	468.48	464.15
75,000	735.08	714.24	702.72	696.22
100,000	980.11	952.32	936.96	928.29
125,000	1,225.14	1,190.40	1,171.20	1,160.37
150,000	1,470.17	1,428.49	1,405.44	1,392.44
175,000	1,715.20	1,666.57	1,639.68	1,624.52
200,000	1,960.23	1,904.65	1,873.92	1,856.59
225,000	2,205.25	2,142.73	2,108.15	2,088.66
250,000	2,450.28	2,380.81	2,342.39	2,320.74
275,000	2,695.31	2,618.89	2,576.63	2,552.81
300,000	2,940.34	2,856.97	2,810.87	2,784.88
350,000	3,430.40	3,333.13	3,279.35	3,249.03
400,000	3,920.45	3,809.29	3,747.83	3,713.18
450,000	4,410.51	4,285.46	4,216.31	4,177.32
500,000	4,900.57	4,761.62	4,684.79	4,641.47
600,000	5,880.68	5,713.94	5,621.75	5,569.77
700,000	6,860.79	6,666.26	6,558.70	6,498.06
800,000	7,840.90	7,618.59	7,495.66	7,426.36
900,000	8,821.02	8,570.91	8,432.62	8,354.65
1,000,000	9,801.13	9,523.23	9,369.58	9,282.94

Loan Payment

LOAN PAYMENT TABLE
INTEREST RATE: 11.25%
Monthly Payments - Fully Amortized

Loan Amount	11.25% 5	Term of Loan In Years 10	15	20
$ 1,000	21.87	13.92	11.52	10.49
5,000	109.34	69.58	57.62	52.46
10,000	218.67	139.17	115.23	104.93
25,000	546.68	347.92	288.09	262.31
40,000	874.69	556.68	460.94	419.70
50,000	1,093.37	695.84	576.17	524.63
75,000	1,640.05	1,043.77	864.26	786.94
100,000	2,186.73	1,391.69	1,152.34	1,049.26
125,000	2,733.41	1,739.61	1,440.43	1,311.57
150,000	3,280.10	2,087.53	1,728.52	1,573.88
175,000	3,826.78	2,435.46	2,016.60	1,836.20
200,000	4,373.46	2,783.38	2,304.69	2,098.51
225,000	4,920.14	3,131.30	2,592.78	2,360.83
250,000	5,466.83	3,479.22	2,880.86	2,623.14
275,000	6,013.51	3,827.15	3,168.95	2,885.45
300,000	6,560.19	4,175.07	3,457.03	3,147.77
350,000	7,653.56	4,870.91	4,033.21	3,672.40
400,000	8,746.92	5,566.76	4,609.38	4,197.02
450,000	9,840.29	6,262.60	5,185.55	4,721.65
500,000	10,933.65	6,958.45	5,761.72	5,246.28
600,000	13,120.38	8,350.14	6,914.07	6,295.54
700,000	15,307.12	9,741.83	8,066.41	7,344.79
800,000	17,493.85	11,133.52	9,218.76	8,394.05
900,000	19,680.58	12,525.21	10,371.10	9,443.30
1,000,000	21,867.31	13,916.89	11,523.45	10,492.56

LOAN PAYMENT TABLE
INTEREST RATE: 11.25%
Monthly Payments - Fully Amortized

Loan Amount	11.25%	Term of Loan In Years		
	25	30	35	40
$ 1,000	9.98	9.71	9.56	9.48
5,000	49.91	48.56	47.82	47.41
10,000	99.82	97.13	95.65	94.83
25,000	249.56	242.82	239.12	237.06
40,000	399.30	388.50	382.60	379.30
50,000	499.12	485.63	478.25	474.13
75,000	748.68	728.45	717.37	711.19
100,000	998.24	971.26	956.49	948.26
125,000	1,247.80	1,214.08	1,195.62	1,185.32
150,000	1,497.36	1,456.89	1,434.74	1,422.39
175,000	1,746.92	1,699.71	1,673.86	1,659.45
200,000	1,996.48	1,942.52	1,912.99	1,896.51
225,000	2,246.04	2,185.34	2,152.11	2,133.58
250,000	2,495.60	2,428.15	2,391.23	2,370.64
275,000	2,745.16	2,670.97	2,630.36	2,607.71
300,000	2,994.72	2,913.78	2,869.48	2,844.77
350,000	3,493.84	3,399.41	3,347.73	3,318.90
400,000	3,992.96	3,885.05	3,825.98	3,793.03
450,000	4,492.08	4,370.68	4,304.22	4,267.16
500,000	4,991.20	4,856.31	4,782.47	4,741.29
600,000	5,989.44	5,827.57	5,738.96	5,689.54
700,000	6,987.68	6,798.83	6,695.46	6,637.80
800,000	7,985.92	7,770.09	7,651.95	7,586.06
900,000	8,984.16	8,741.35	8,608.44	8,534.32
1,000,000	9,982.40	9,712.61	9,564.94	9,482.57

Loan Payment

LOAN PAYMENT TABLE
INTEREST RATE: 11.50%
Monthly Payments - Fully Amortized

Loan Amount	11.50%	Term of Loan In Years		
	5	10	15	20
$ 1,000	21.99	14.06	11.68	10.66
5,000	109.96	70.30	58.41	53.32
10,000	219.93	140.60	116.82	106.64
25,000	549.82	351.49	292.05	266.61
40,000	879.70	562.38	467.28	426.57
50,000	1,099.63	702.98	584.09	533.21
75,000	1,649.45	1,054.47	876.14	799.82
100,000	2,199.26	1,405.95	1,168.19	1,066.43
125,000	2,749.08	1,757.44	1,460.24	1,333.04
150,000	3,298.89	2,108.93	1,752.28	1,599.64
175,000	3,848.71	2,460.42	2,044.33	1,866.25
200,000	4,398.52	2,811.91	2,336.38	2,132.86
225,000	4,948.34	3,163.40	2,628.43	2,399.47
250,000	5,498.15	3,514.89	2,920.47	2,666.07
275,000	6,047.97	3,866.37	3,212.52	2,932.68
300,000	6,597.78	4,217.86	3,504.57	3,199.29
350,000	7,697.41	4,920.84	4,088.66	3,732.50
400,000	8,797.04	5,623.82	4,672.76	4,265.72
450,000	9,896.67	6,326.79	5,256.85	4,798.93
500,000	10,996.30	7,029.77	5,840.95	5,332.15
600,000	13,195.56	8,435.73	7,009.14	6,398.58
700,000	15,394.83	9,841.68	8,177.33	7,465.01
800,000	17,594.09	11,247.64	9,345.52	8,531.44
900,000	19,793.35	12,653.59	10,513.71	9,597.87
1,000,000	21,992.61	14,059.54	11,681.90	10,664.30

Loan Payment

LOAN PAYMENT TABLE
INTEREST RATE: 11.50%
Monthly Payments - Fully Amortized

Loan Amount	11.50% 25	Term of Loan In Years 30	35	40
$ 1,000	10.16	9.90	9.76	9.68
5,000	50.82	49.51	48.81	48.41
10,000	101.65	99.03	97.61	96.83
25,000	254.12	247.57	244.03	242.07
40,000	406.59	396.12	390.44	387.31
50,000	508.23	495.15	488.05	484.14
75,000	762.35	742.72	732.08	726.21
100,000	1,016.47	990.29	976.11	968.28
125,000	1,270.59	1,237.86	1,220.13	1,210.35
150,000	1,524.70	1,485.44	1,464.16	1,452.42
175,000	1,778.82	1,733.01	1,708.19	1,694.49
200,000	2,032.94	1,980.58	1,952.21	1,936.56
225,000	2,287.06	2,228.16	2,196.24	2,178.63
250,000	2,541.17	2,475.73	2,440.27	2,420.70
275,000	2,795.29	2,723.30	2,684.30	2,662.78
300,000	3,049.41	2,970.87	2,928.32	2,904.85
350,000	3,557.64	3,466.02	3,416.38	3,388.99
400,000	4,065.88	3,961.17	3,904.43	3,873.13
450,000	4,574.11	4,456.31	4,392.48	4,357.27
500,000	5,082.34	4,951.46	4,880.54	4,841.41
600,000	6,098.81	5,941.75	5,856.64	5,809.69
700,000	7,115.28	6,932.04	6,832.75	6,777.97
800,000	8,131.75	7,922.33	7,808.86	7,746.25
900,000	9,148.22	8,912.62	8,784.97	8,714.54
1,000,000	10,164.69	9,902.91	9,761.07	9,682.82

Loan Payment

LOAN PAYMENT TABLE
INTEREST RATE: 11.75%
Monthly Payments - Fully Amortized

Loan Amount	11.75% 5	Term of Loan In Years 10	15	20
$ 1,000	22.12	14.20	11.84	10.84
5,000	110.59	71.01	59.21	54.19
10,000	221.18	142.03	118.41	108.37
25,000	552.96	355.07	296.03	270.93
40,000	884.73	568.12	473.65	433.48
50,000	1,105.92	710.15	592.07	541.85
75,000	1,658.87	1,065.22	888.10	812.78
100,000	2,211.83	1,420.29	1,184.13	1,083.71
125,000	2,764.79	1,775.37	1,480.16	1,354.63
150,000	3,317.75	2,130.44	1,776.20	1,625.56
175,000	3,870.71	2,485.52	2,072.23	1,896.49
200,000	4,423.66	2,840.59	2,368.26	2,167.41
225,000	4,976.62	3,195.66	2,664.30	2,438.34
250,000	5,529.58	3,550.74	2,960.33	2,709.27
275,000	6,082.54	3,905.81	3,256.36	2,980.19
300,000	6,635.50	4,260.88	3,552.39	3,251.12
350,000	7,741.41	4,971.03	4,144.46	3,792.97
400,000	8,847.33	5,681.18	4,736.53	4,334.83
450,000	9,953.24	6,391.33	5,328.59	4,876.68
500,000	11,059.16	7,101.47	5,920.66	5,418.54
600,000	13,270.99	8,521.77	7,104.79	6,502.24
700,000	15,482.82	9,942.06	8,288.92	7,585.95
800,000	17,694.66	11,362.36	9,473.05	8,669.66
900,000	19,906.49	12,782.65	10,657.18	9,753.36
1,000,000	22,118.32	14,202.95	11,841.31	10,837.07

LOAN PAYMENT TABLE
INTEREST RATE: 11.75%
Monthly Payments - Fully Amortized

Loan Amount	11.75%	Term of Loan In Years		
	25	30	35	40
$ 1,000	10.35	10.09	9.96	9.88
5,000	51.74	50.47	49.79	49.42
10,000	103.48	100.94	99.58	98.84
25,000	258.70	252.35	248.95	247.09
40,000	413.92	403.76	398.32	395.35
50,000	517.40	504.70	497.90	494.18
75,000	776.10	757.06	746.85	741.27
100,000	1,034.80	1,009.41	995.79	988.36
125,000	1,293.50	1,261.76	1,244.74	1,235.45
150,000	1,552.20	1,514.11	1,493.69	1,482.55
175,000	1,810.90	1,766.47	1,742.64	1,729.64
200,000	2,069.60	2,018.82	1,991.59	1,976.73
225,000	2,328.30	2,271.17	2,240.54	2,223.82
250,000	2,587.00	2,523.52	2,489.48	2,470.91
275,000	2,845.70	2,775.88	2,738.43	2,718.00
300,000	3,104.39	3,028.23	2,987.38	2,965.09
350,000	3,621.79	3,532.93	3,485.28	3,459.27
400,000	4,139.19	4,037.64	3,983.18	3,953.46
450,000	4,656.59	4,542.34	4,481.07	4,447.64
500,000	5,173.99	5,047.05	4,978.97	4,941.82
600,000	6,208.79	6,056.46	5,974.76	5,930.18
700,000	7,243.59	7,065.87	6,970.56	6,918.55
800,000	8,278.39	8,075.28	7,966.35	7,906.91
900,000	9,313.18	9,084.69	8,962.15	8,895.28
1,000,000	10,347.98	10,094.10	9,957.94	9,883.64

LOAN PAYMENT TABLE
INTEREST RATE: 12.00%
Monthly Payments - Fully Amortized

Loan Amount	12.00%	Term of Loan In Years		
	5	10	15	20
$ 1,000	22.24	14.35	12.00	11.01
5,000	111.22	71.74	60.01	55.05
10,000	222.44	143.47	120.02	110.11
25,000	556.11	358.68	300.04	275.27
40,000	889.78	573.88	480.07	440.43
50,000	1,112.22	717.35	600.08	550.54
75,000	1,668.33	1,076.03	900.13	825.81
100,000	2,224.44	1,434.71	1,200.17	1,101.09
125,000	2,780.56	1,793.39	1,500.21	1,376.36
150,000	3,336.67	2,152.06	1,800.25	1,651.63
175,000	3,892.78	2,510.74	2,100.29	1,926.90
200,000	4,448.89	2,869.42	2,400.34	2,202.17
225,000	5,005.00	3,228.10	2,700.38	2,477.44
250,000	5,561.11	3,586.77	3,000.42	2,752.72
275,000	6,117.22	3,945.45	3,300.46	3,027.99
300,000	6,673.33	4,304.13	3,600.50	3,303.26
350,000	7,785.56	5,021.48	4,200.59	3,853.80
400,000	8,897.78	5,738.84	4,800.67	4,404.34
450,000	10,010.00	6,456.19	5,400.76	4,954.89
500,000	11,122.22	7,173.55	6,000.84	5,505.43
600,000	13,346.67	8,608.26	7,201.01	6,606.52
700,000	15,571.11	10,042.97	8,401.18	7,707.60
800,000	17,795.56	11,477.68	9,601.34	8,808.69
900,000	20,020.00	12,912.39	10,801.51	9,909.78
1,000,000	22,244.45	14,347.09	12,001.68	11,010.86

Loan Payment

LOAN PAYMENT TABLE
INTEREST RATE: 12.00%
Monthly Payments - Fully Amortized

Loan Amount	12.00% 25	Term of Loan In Years 30	35	40
$ 1,000	10.53	10.29	10.16	10.08
5,000	52.66	51.43	50.78	50.42
10,000	105.32	102.86	101.55	100.85
25,000	263.31	257.15	253.89	252.12
40,000	421.29	411.45	406.22	403.40
50,000	526.61	514.31	507.77	504.25
75,000	789.92	771.46	761.66	756.37
100,000	1,053.22	1,028.61	1,015.55	1,008.50
125,000	1,316.53	1,285.77	1,269.44	1,260.62
150,000	1,579.84	1,542.92	1,523.32	1,512.75
175,000	1,843.14	1,800.07	1,777.21	1,764.87
200,000	2,106.45	2,057.23	2,031.10	2,017.00
225,000	2,369.75	2,314.38	2,284.99	2,269.12
250,000	2,633.06	2,571.53	2,538.87	2,521.25
275,000	2,896.37	2,828.68	2,792.76	2,773.37
300,000	3,159.67	3,085.84	3,046.65	3,025.50
350,000	3,686.28	3,600.14	3,554.42	3,529.75
400,000	4,212.90	4,114.45	4,062.20	4,034.00
450,000	4,739.51	4,628.76	4,569.97	4,538.25
500,000	5,266.12	5,143.06	5,077.75	5,042.50
600,000	6,319.34	6,171.68	6,093.30	6,051.00
700,000	7,372.57	7,200.29	7,108.85	7,059.50
800,000	8,425.79	8,228.90	8,124.40	8,068.00
900,000	9,479.02	9,257.51	9,139.95	9,076.50
1,000,000	10,532.24	10,286.13	10,155.50	10,085.00

Loan Payment

LOAN PAYMENT TABLE
INTEREST RATE: 12.25%
Monthly Payments - Fully Amortized

Loan Amount	12.25% 5	Term of Loan In Years 10	15	20
$ 1,000	22.37	14.49	12.16	11.19
5,000	111.85	72.46	60.81	55.93
10,000	223.71	144.92	121.63	111.86
25,000	559.27	362.30	304.07	279.64
40,000	894.84	579.68	486.52	447.43
50,000	1,118.55	724.60	608.15	559.28
75,000	1,677.82	1,086.90	912.22	838.92
100,000	2,237.10	1,449.20	1,216.30	1,118.56
125,000	2,796.37	1,811.50	1,520.37	1,398.21
150,000	3,355.65	2,173.80	1,824.45	1,677.85
175,000	3,914.92	2,536.10	2,128.52	1,957.49
200,000	4,474.20	2,898.40	2,432.60	2,237.13
225,000	5,033.47	3,260.70	2,736.67	2,516.77
250,000	5,592.75	3,623.00	3,040.75	2,796.41
275,000	6,152.02	3,985.30	3,344.82	3,076.05
300,000	6,711.30	4,347.60	3,648.90	3,355.69
350,000	7,829.85	5,072.20	4,257.05	3,914.98
400,000	8,948.39	5,796.79	4,865.19	4,474.26
450,000	10,066.94	6,521.39	5,473.34	5,033.54
500,000	11,185.49	7,245.99	6,081.49	5,592.82
600,000	13,422.59	8,695.19	7,297.79	6,711.39
700,000	15,659.69	10,144.39	8,514.09	7,829.95
800,000	17,896.79	11,593.59	9,730.39	8,948.52
900,000	20,133.89	13,042.79	10,946.69	10,067.08
1,000,000	22,370.99	14,491.99	12,162.99	11,185.65

LOAN PAYMENT TABLE
INTEREST RATE: 12.25%
Monthly Payments - Fully Amortized

Loan Amount	12.25%	Term of Loan In Years		
	25	30	35	40
$ 1,000	10.72	10.48	10.35	10.29
5,000	53.59	52.39	51.77	51.43
10,000	107.17	104.79	103.54	102.87
25,000	267.94	261.97	258.84	257.17
40,000	428.70	419.16	414.15	411.47
50,000	535.87	523.95	517.69	514.34
75,000	803.81	785.92	776.53	771.51
100,000	1,071.74	1,047.90	1,035.37	1,028.69
125,000	1,339.68	1,309.87	1,294.21	1,285.86
150,000	1,607.62	1,571.84	1,553.06	1,543.03
175,000	1,875.55	1,833.82	1,811.90	1,800.20
200,000	2,143.49	2,095.79	2,070.74	2,057.37
225,000	2,411.42	2,357.77	2,329.59	2,314.54
250,000	2,679.36	2,619.74	2,588.43	2,571.72
275,000	2,947.30	2,881.72	2,847.27	2,828.89
300,000	3,215.23	3,143.69	3,106.11	3,086.06
350,000	3,751.10	3,667.64	3,623.80	3,600.40
400,000	4,286.98	4,191.59	4,141.48	4,114.74
450,000	4,822.85	4,715.53	4,659.17	4,629.09
500,000	5,358.72	5,239.48	5,176.86	5,143.43
600,000	6,430.46	6,287.38	6,212.23	6,172.12
700,000	7,502.21	7,335.28	7,247.60	7,200.80
800,000	8,573.95	8,383.17	8,282.97	8,229.49
900,000	9,645.69	9,431.07	9,318.34	9,258.18
1,000,000	10,717.44	10,478.96	10,353.71	10,286.86

Loan Payment

LOAN PAYMENT TABLE
INTEREST RATE: 12.50%
Monthly Payments - Fully Amortized

Loan Amount	12.50% 5	Term of Loan In Years 10	15	20
$ 1,000	22.50	14.64	12.33	11.36
5,000	112.49	73.19	61.63	56.81
10,000	224.98	146.38	123.25	113.61
25,000	562.45	365.94	308.13	284.04
40,000	899.92	585.50	493.01	454.46
50,000	1,124.90	731.88	616.26	568.07
75,000	1,687.35	1,097.82	924.39	852.11
100,000	2,249.79	1,463.76	1,232.52	1,136.14
125,000	2,812.24	1,829.70	1,540.65	1,420.18
150,000	3,374.69	2,195.64	1,848.78	1,704.21
175,000	3,937.14	2,561.58	2,156.91	1,988.25
200,000	4,499.59	2,927.52	2,465.04	2,272.28
225,000	5,062.04	3,293.46	2,773.17	2,556.32
250,000	5,624.48	3,659.40	3,081.31	2,840.35
275,000	6,186.93	4,025.34	3,389.44	3,124.39
300,000	6,749.38	4,391.29	3,697.57	3,408.42
350,000	7,874.28	5,123.17	4,313.83	3,976.49
400,000	8,999.18	5,855.05	4,930.09	4,544.56
450,000	10,124.07	6,586.93	5,546.35	5,112.63
500,000	11,248.97	7,318.81	6,162.61	5,680.70
600,000	13,498.76	8,782.57	7,395.13	6,816.84
700,000	15,748.56	10,246.33	8,627.65	7,952.98
800,000	17,998.35	11,710.09	9,860.18	9,089.12
900,000	20,248.14	13,173.86	11,092.70	10,225.26
1,000,000	22,497.94	14,637.62	12,325.22	11,361.41

Loan Payment

LOAN PAYMENT TABLE
INTEREST RATE: 12.50%
Monthly Payments - Fully Amortized

Loan	12.50%	Term of Loan In Years		
Amount	25	30	35	40
$ 1,000	10.90	10.67	10.55	10.49
5,000	54.52	53.36	52.76	52.45
10,000	109.04	106.73	105.53	104.89
25,000	272.59	266.81	263.81	262.23
40,000	436.14	426.90	422.10	419.57
50,000	545.18	533.63	527.63	524.46
75,000	817.77	800.44	791.44	786.69
100,000	1,090.35	1,067.26	1,055.25	1,048.92
125,000	1,362.94	1,334.07	1,319.07	1,311.15
150,000	1,635.53	1,600.89	1,582.88	1,573.38
175,000	1,908.12	1,867.70	1,846.70	1,835.61
200,000	2,180.71	2,134.52	2,110.51	2,097.84
225,000	2,453.30	2,401.33	2,374.32	2,360.07
250,000	2,725.89	2,668.14	2,638.14	2,622.30
275,000	2,998.47	2,934.96	2,901.95	2,884.53
300,000	3,271.06	3,201.77	3,165.76	3,146.76
350,000	3,816.24	3,735.40	3,693.39	3,671.22
400,000	4,361.42	4,269.03	4,221.02	4,195.68
450,000	4,906.59	4,802.66	4,748.64	4,720.14
500,000	5,451.77	5,336.29	5,276.27	5,244.60
600,000	6,542.12	6,403.55	6,331.53	6,293.52
700,000	7,632.48	7,470.80	7,386.78	7,342.44
800,000	8,722.83	8,538.06	8,442.04	8,391.36
900,000	9,813.19	9,605.32	9,497.29	9,440.27
1,000,000	10,903.54	10,672.58	10,552.54	10,489.19

Loan Payment

LOAN PAYMENT TABLE
INTEREST RATE: 12.75%
Monthly Payments - Fully Amortized

Loan Amount	12.75%	Term of Loan In Years		
	5	10	15	20
$ 1,000	22.63	14.78	12.49	11.54
5,000	113.13	73.92	62.44	57.69
10,000	226.25	147.84	124.88	115.38
25,000	565.63	369.60	312.21	288.45
40,000	905.01	591.36	499.53	461.52
50,000	1,131.27	739.20	624.42	576.91
75,000	1,696.90	1,108.80	936.63	865.36
100,000	2,262.53	1,478.40	1,248.84	1,153.81
125,000	2,828.16	1,848.00	1,561.05	1,442.26
150,000	3,393.80	2,217.60	1,873.26	1,730.72
175,000	3,959.43	2,587.20	2,185.46	2,019.17
200,000	4,525.06	2,956.80	2,497.67	2,307.62
225,000	5,090.69	3,326.40	2,809.88	2,596.08
250,000	5,656.33	3,696.00	3,122.09	2,884.53
275,000	6,221.96	4,065.59	3,434.30	3,172.98
300,000	6,787.59	4,435.19	3,746.51	3,461.43
350,000	7,918.86	5,174.39	4,370.93	4,038.34
400,000	9,050.12	5,913.59	4,995.35	4,615.25
450,000	10,181.39	6,652.79	5,619.77	5,192.15
500,000	11,312.65	7,391.99	6,244.18	5,769.06
600,000	13,575.18	8,870.39	7,493.02	6,922.87
700,000	15,837.71	10,348.79	8,741.86	8,076.68
800,000	18,100.24	11,827.18	9,990.70	9,230.49
900,000	20,362.77	13,305.58	11,239.53	10,384.30
1,000,000	22,625.30	14,783.98	12,488.37	11,538.12

LOAN PAYMENT TABLE
INTEREST RATE: 12.75%
Monthly Payments - Fully Amortized

Loan Amount	12.75%	Term of Loan In Years		
	25	30	35	40
$ 1,000	11.09	10.87	10.75	10.69
5,000	55.45	54.33	53.76	53.46
10,000	110.91	108.67	107.52	106.92
25,000	277.26	271.67	268.80	267.30
40,000	443.62	434.68	430.08	427.68
50,000	554.53	543.35	537.60	534.60
75,000	831.79	815.02	806.40	801.90
100,000	1,109.05	1,086.69	1,075.20	1,069.20
125,000	1,386.32	1,358.37	1,344.00	1,336.50
150,000	1,663.58	1,630.04	1,612.79	1,603.79
175,000	1,940.84	1,901.71	1,881.59	1,871.09
200,000	2,218.10	2,173.39	2,150.39	2,138.39
225,000	2,495.37	2,445.06	2,419.19	2,405.69
250,000	2,772.63	2,716.73	2,687.99	2,672.99
275,000	3,049.89	2,988.41	2,956.79	2,940.29
300,000	3,327.16	3,260.08	3,225.59	3,207.59
350,000	3,881.68	3,803.43	3,763.19	3,742.19
400,000	4,436.21	4,346.77	4,300.78	4,276.79
450,000	4,990.74	4,890.12	4,838.38	4,811.38
500,000	5,545.26	5,433.47	5,375.98	5,345.98
600,000	6,654.31	6,520.16	6,451.18	6,415.18
700,000	7,763.37	7,606.85	7,526.37	7,484.37
800,000	8,872.42	8,693.55	8,601.57	8,553.57
900,000	9,981.47	9,780.24	9,676.77	9,622.77
1,000,000	11,090.52	10,866.93	10,751.96	10,691.96

LOAN PAYMENT TABLE
INTEREST RATE: 13.00%
Monthly Payments - Fully Amortized

Loan Amount	13.00%	Term of Loan In Years		
	5	10	15	20
$ 1,000	22.75	14.93	12.65	11.72
5,000	113.77	74.66	63.26	58.58
10,000	227.53	149.31	126.52	117.16
25,000	568.83	373.28	316.31	292.89
40,000	910.12	597.24	506.10	468.63
50,000	1,137.65	746.55	632.62	585.79
75,000	1,706.48	1,119.83	948.93	878.68
100,000	2,275.31	1,493.11	1,265.24	1,171.58
125,000	2,844.13	1,866.38	1,581.55	1,464.47
150,000	3,412.96	2,239.66	1,897.86	1,757.36
175,000	3,981.79	2,612.94	2,214.17	2,050.26
200,000	4,550.61	2,986.21	2,530.48	2,343.15
225,000	5,119.44	3,359.49	2,846.79	2,636.05
250,000	5,688.27	3,732.77	3,163.11	2,928.94
275,000	6,257.10	4,106.05	3,479.42	3,221.83
300,000	6,825.92	4,479.32	3,795.73	3,514.73
350,000	7,963.58	5,225.88	4,428.35	4,100.51
400,000	9,101.23	5,972.43	5,060.97	4,686.30
450,000	10,238.88	6,718.98	5,693.59	5,272.09
500,000	11,376.54	7,465.54	6,326.21	5,857.88
600,000	13,651.84	8,958.64	7,591.45	7,029.45
700,000	15,927.15	10,451.75	8,856.70	8,201.03
800,000	18,202.46	11,944.86	10,121.94	9,372.61
900,000	20,477.77	13,437.97	11,387.18	10,544.18
1,000,000	22,753.07	14,931.07	12,652.42	11,715.76

Loan Payment

LOAN PAYMENT TABLE
INTEREST RATE: 13.00%
Monthly Payments - Fully Amortized

Loan Amount	13.00%	Term of Loan In Years		
	25	30	35	40
$ 1,000	11.28	11.06	10.95	10.90
5,000	56.39	55.31	54.76	54.48
10,000	112.78	110.62	109.52	108.95
25,000	281.96	276.55	273.80	272.38
40,000	451.13	442.48	438.08	435.81
50,000	563.92	553.10	547.60	544.76
75,000	845.88	829.65	821.39	817.14
100,000	1,127.84	1,106.20	1,095.19	1,089.51
125,000	1,409.79	1,382.75	1,368.99	1,361.89
150,000	1,691.75	1,659.30	1,642.79	1,634.27
175,000	1,973.71	1,935.85	1,916.59	1,906.65
200,000	2,255.67	2,212.40	2,190.39	2,179.03
225,000	2,537.63	2,488.95	2,464.18	2,451.41
250,000	2,819.59	2,765.50	2,737.98	2,723.79
275,000	3,101.55	3,042.05	3,011.78	2,996.16
300,000	3,383.51	3,318.60	3,285.58	3,268.54
350,000	3,947.42	3,871.70	3,833.18	3,813.30
400,000	4,511.34	4,424.80	4,380.77	4,358.06
450,000	5,075.26	4,977.90	4,928.37	4,902.81
500,000	5,639.18	5,531.00	5,475.97	5,447.57
600,000	6,767.01	6,637.20	6,571.16	6,537.08
700,000	7,894.85	7,743.40	7,666.35	7,626.60
800,000	9,022.68	8,849.60	8,761.55	8,716.11
900,000	10,150.52	9,955.80	9,856.74	9,805.63
1,000,000	11,278.35	11,062.00	10,951.93	10,895.14

Loan Payment

LOAN PAYMENT TABLE
INTEREST RATE: 13.25%
Monthly Payments - Fully Amortized

Loan Amount	13.25%	Term of Loan In Years		
	5	10	15	20
$ 1,000	22.88	15.08	12.82	11.89
5,000	114.41	75.39	64.09	59.47
10,000	228.81	150.79	128.17	118.94
25,000	572.03	376.97	320.43	297.36
40,000	915.25	603.16	512.69	475.77
50,000	1,144.06	753.94	640.87	594.72
75,000	1,716.09	1,130.92	961.30	892.07
100,000	2,288.13	1,507.89	1,281.74	1,189.43
125,000	2,860.16	1,884.86	1,602.17	1,486.79
150,000	3,432.19	2,261.83	1,922.60	1,784.15
175,000	4,004.22	2,638.81	2,243.04	2,081.50
200,000	4,576.25	3,015.78	2,563.47	2,378.86
225,000	5,148.28	3,392.75	2,883.91	2,676.22
250,000	5,720.31	3,769.72	3,204.34	2,973.58
275,000	6,292.35	4,146.70	3,524.78	3,270.93
300,000	6,864.38	4,523.67	3,845.21	3,568.29
350,000	8,008.44	5,277.61	4,486.08	4,163.01
400,000	9,152.50	6,031.56	5,126.95	4,757.72
450,000	10,296.56	6,785.50	5,767.81	5,352.44
500,000	11,440.63	7,539.45	6,408.68	5,947.15
600,000	13,728.75	9,047.33	7,690.42	7,136.58
700,000	16,016.88	10,555.22	8,972.16	8,326.02
800,000	18,305.00	12,063.11	10,253.89	9,515.45
900,000	20,593.13	13,571.00	11,535.63	10,704.88
1,000,000	22,881.26	15,078.89	12,817.36	11,894.31

Loan Payment

LOAN PAYMENT TABLE
INTEREST RATE: 13.25%
Monthly Payments - Fully Amortized

Loan Amount	13.25%	Term of Loan In Years		
	25	30	35	40
$ 1,000	11.47	11.26	11.15	11.10
5,000	57.34	56.29	55.76	55.49
10,000	114.67	112.58	111.52	110.99
25,000	286.68	281.44	278.81	277.47
40,000	458.68	450.31	446.10	443.95
50,000	573.35	562.89	557.62	554.93
75,000	860.03	844.33	836.43	832.40
100,000	1,146.70	1,125.77	1,115.24	1,109.87
125,000	1,433.38	1,407.22	1,394.05	1,387.34
150,000	1,720.05	1,688.66	1,672.86	1,664.80
175,000	2,006.73	1,970.10	1,951.67	1,942.27
200,000	2,293.40	2,251.55	2,230.48	2,219.74
225,000	2,580.08	2,532.99	2,509.30	2,497.21
250,000	2,866.75	2,814.43	2,788.11	2,774.67
275,000	3,153.43	3,095.88	3,066.92	3,052.14
300,000	3,440.10	3,377.32	3,345.73	3,329.61
350,000	4,013.45	3,940.21	3,903.35	3,884.54
400,000	4,586.80	4,503.09	4,460.97	4,439.48
450,000	5,160.15	5,065.98	5,018.59	4,994.41
500,000	5,733.50	5,628.87	5,576.21	5,549.35
600,000	6,880.20	6,754.64	6,691.45	6,659.22
700,000	8,026.90	7,880.41	7,806.70	7,769.09
800,000	9,173.60	9,006.19	8,921.94	8,878.96
900,000	10,320.30	10,131.96	10,037.18	9,988.83
1,000,000	11,467.00	11,257.74	11,152.42	11,098.70

Loan Payment

LOAN PAYMENT TABLE
INTEREST RATE: 13.50%
Monthly Payments - Fully Amortized

Loan Amount	13.50%	Term of Loan In Years		
	5	10	15	20
$ 1,000	23.01	15.23	12.98	12.07
5,000	115.05	76.14	64.92	60.37
10,000	230.10	152.27	129.83	120.74
25,000	575.25	380.69	324.58	301.84
40,000	920.39	609.10	519.33	482.95
50,000	1,150.49	761.37	649.16	603.69
75,000	1,725.74	1,142.06	973.74	905.53
100,000	2,300.98	1,522.74	1,298.32	1,207.37
125,000	2,876.23	1,903.43	1,622.90	1,509.22
150,000	3,451.48	2,284.11	1,947.48	1,811.06
175,000	4,026.72	2,664.80	2,272.06	2,112.91
200,000	4,601.97	3,045.49	2,596.64	2,414.75
225,000	5,177.22	3,426.17	2,921.22	2,716.59
250,000	5,752.46	3,806.86	3,245.80	3,018.44
275,000	6,327.71	4,187.54	3,570.38	3,320.28
300,000	6,902.95	4,568.23	3,894.96	3,622.12
350,000	8,053.45	5,329.60	4,544.11	4,225.81
400,000	9,203.94	6,090.97	5,193.27	4,829.50
450,000	10,354.43	6,852.34	5,842.43	5,433.19
500,000	11,504.92	7,613.71	6,491.59	6,036.87
600,000	13,805.91	9,136.46	7,789.91	7,244.25
700,000	16,106.89	10,659.20	9,088.23	8,451.62
800,000	18,407.88	12,181.94	10,386.55	9,659.00
900,000	20,708.86	13,704.69	11,684.87	10,866.37
1,000,000	23,009.85	15,227.43	12,983.19	12,073.75

LOAN PAYMENT TABLE
INTEREST RATE: 13.50%
Monthly Payments - Fully Amortized

Loan Amount	13.50%	Term of Loan In Years		
	25	30	35	40
$ 1,000	11.66	11.45	11.35	11.30
5,000	58.28	57.27	56.77	56.51
10,000	116.56	114.54	113.53	113.03
25,000	291.41	286.35	283.84	282.57
40,000	466.26	458.16	454.14	452.10
50,000	582.82	572.71	567.67	565.13
75,000	874.23	859.06	851.51	847.70
100,000	1,165.64	1,145.41	1,135.34	1,130.26
125,000	1,457.06	1,431.77	1,419.18	1,412.83
150,000	1,748.47	1,718.12	1,703.01	1,695.39
175,000	2,039.88	2,004.47	1,986.85	1,977.96
200,000	2,331.29	2,290.82	2,270.68	2,260.52
225,000	2,622.70	2,577.18	2,554.52	2,543.09
250,000	2,914.11	2,863.53	2,838.35	2,825.65
275,000	3,205.52	3,149.88	3,122.19	3,108.22
300,000	3,496.93	3,436.24	3,406.02	3,390.78
350,000	4,079.76	4,008.94	3,973.69	3,955.91
400,000	4,662.58	4,581.65	4,541.36	4,521.04
450,000	5,245.40	5,154.35	5,109.03	5,086.18
500,000	5,828.22	5,727.06	5,676.70	5,651.31
600,000	6,993.87	6,872.47	6,812.04	6,781.57
700,000	8,159.51	8,017.89	7,947.38	7,911.83
800,000	9,325.16	9,163.30	9,082.72	9,042.09
900,000	10,490.80	10,308.71	10,218.06	10,172.35
1,000,000	11,656.45	11,454.12	11,353.41	11,302.61

Loan Payment

LOAN PAYMENT TABLE
INTEREST RATE: 13.75%
Monthly Payments - Fully Amortized

Loan Amount	13.75% 5	Term of Loan In Years 10	15	20
$ 1,000	23.14	15.38	13.15	12.25
5,000	115.69	76.88	65.75	61.27
10,000	231.39	153.77	131.50	122.54
25,000	578.47	384.42	328.75	306.35
40,000	925.55	615.07	525.99	490.16
50,000	1,156.94	768.83	657.49	612.70
75,000	1,735.41	1,153.25	986.24	919.05
100,000	2,313.88	1,537.67	1,314.99	1,225.41
125,000	2,892.36	1,922.09	1,643.73	1,531.76
150,000	3,470.83	2,306.50	1,972.48	1,838.11
175,000	4,049.30	2,690.92	2,301.23	2,144.46
200,000	4,627.77	3,075.34	2,629.97	2,450.81
225,000	5,206.24	3,459.75	2,958.72	2,757.16
250,000	5,784.71	3,844.17	3,287.47	3,063.51
275,000	6,363.18	4,228.59	3,616.21	3,369.86
300,000	6,941.65	4,613.00	3,944.96	3,676.22
350,000	8,098.60	5,381.84	4,602.46	4,288.92
400,000	9,255.54	6,150.67	5,259.95	4,901.62
450,000	10,412.48	6,919.51	5,917.44	5,514.32
500,000	11,569.42	7,688.34	6,574.94	6,127.03
600,000	13,883.31	9,226.01	7,889.92	7,352.43
700,000	16,197.19	10,763.68	9,204.91	8,577.84
800,000	18,511.08	12,301.34	10,519.90	9,803.24
900,000	20,824.96	13,839.01	11,834.89	11,028.65
1,000,000	23,138.84	15,376.68	13,149.87	12,254.05

LOAN PAYMENT TABLE
INTEREST RATE: 13.75%
Monthly Payments - Fully Amortized

Loan Amount	13.75%	Term of Loan In Years		
	25	30	35	40
$ 1,000	11.85	11.65	11.55	11.51
5,000	59.23	58.26	57.77	57.53
10,000	118.47	116.51	115.55	115.07
25,000	296.17	291.28	288.87	287.67
40,000	473.87	466.05	462.19	460.27
50,000	592.33	582.56	577.74	575.34
75,000	888.50	873.83	866.61	863.01
100,000	1,184.67	1,165.11	1,155.49	1,150.69
125,000	1,480.83	1,456.39	1,444.36	1,438.36
150,000	1,777.00	1,747.67	1,733.23	1,726.03
175,000	2,073.17	2,038.95	2,022.10	2,013.70
200,000	2,369.33	2,330.23	2,310.97	2,301.37
225,000	2,665.50	2,621.50	2,599.84	2,589.04
250,000	2,961.66	2,912.78	2,888.71	2,876.71
275,000	3,257.83	3,204.06	3,177.58	3,164.38
300,000	3,554.00	3,495.34	3,466.46	3,452.06
350,000	4,146.33	4,077.89	4,044.20	4,027.40
400,000	4,738.66	4,660.45	4,621.94	4,602.74
450,000	5,331.00	5,243.01	5,199.68	5,178.08
500,000	5,923.33	5,825.56	5,777.43	5,753.43
600,000	7,108.00	6,990.68	6,932.91	6,904.11
700,000	8,292.66	8,155.79	8,088.40	8,054.80
800,000	9,477.33	9,320.90	9,243.88	9,205.48
900,000	10,661.99	10,486.01	10,399.37	10,356.17
1,000,000	11,846.66	11,651.13	11,554.85	11,506.85

Loan Payment

LOAN PAYMENT TABLE
INTEREST RATE: 14.00%
Monthly Payments - Fully Amortized

Loan Amount	14.00% 5	Term of Loan In Years 10	15	20
$ 1,000	23.27	15.53	13.32	12.44
5,000	116.34	77.63	66.59	62.18
10,000	232.68	155.27	133.17	124.35
25,000	581.71	388.17	332.94	310.88
40,000	930.73	621.07	532.70	497.41
50,000	1,163.41	776.33	665.87	621.76
75,000	1,745.12	1,164.50	998.81	932.64
100,000	2,326.83	1,552.66	1,331.74	1,243.52
125,000	2,908.53	1,940.83	1,664.68	1,554.40
150,000	3,490.24	2,329.00	1,997.61	1,865.28
175,000	4,071.94	2,717.16	2,330.55	2,176.16
200,000	4,653.65	3,105.33	2,663.48	2,487.04
225,000	5,235.36	3,493.49	2,996.42	2,797.92
250,000	5,817.06	3,881.66	3,329.35	3,108.80
275,000	6,398.77	4,269.83	3,662.29	3,419.68
300,000	6,980.48	4,657.99	3,995.22	3,730.56
350,000	8,143.89	5,434.33	4,661.09	4,352.32
400,000	9,307.30	6,210.66	5,326.97	4,974.08
450,000	10,470.71	6,986.99	5,992.84	5,595.84
500,000	11,634.13	7,763.32	6,658.71	6,217.60
600,000	13,960.95	9,315.99	7,990.45	7,461.12
700,000	16,287.78	10,868.65	9,322.19	8,704.65
800,000	18,614.60	12,421.31	10,653.93	9,948.17
900,000	20,941.43	13,973.98	11,985.67	11,191.69
1,000,000	23,268.25	15,526.64	13,317.41	12,435.21

LOAN PAYMENT TABLE
INTEREST RATE: 14.00%
Monthly Payments - Fully Amortized

Loan	14.00%	Term of Loan In Years		
Amount	25	30	35	40
$ 1,000	12.04	11.85	11.76	11.71
5,000	60.19	59.24	58.78	58.56
10,000	120.38	118.49	117.57	117.11
25,000	300.94	296.22	293.92	292.79
40,000	481.50	473.95	470.27	468.46
50,000	601.88	592.44	587.84	585.57
75,000	902.82	888.65	881.75	878.36
100,000	1,203.76	1,184.87	1,175.67	1,171.14
125,000	1,504.70	1,481.09	1,469.59	1,463.93
150,000	1,805.64	1,777.31	1,763.51	1,756.71
175,000	2,106.58	2,073.53	2,057.43	2,049.50
200,000	2,407.52	2,369.74	2,351.35	2,342.28
225,000	2,708.46	2,665.96	2,645.26	2,635.07
250,000	3,009.40	2,962.18	2,939.18	2,927.85
275,000	3,310.34	3,258.40	3,233.10	3,220.64
300,000	3,611.28	3,554.62	3,527.02	3,513.42
350,000	4,213.16	4,147.05	4,114.86	4,098.99
400,000	4,815.04	4,739.49	4,702.69	4,684.56
450,000	5,416.92	5,331.92	5,290.53	5,270.13
500,000	6,018.81	5,924.36	5,878.37	5,855.70
600,000	7,222.57	7,109.23	7,054.04	7,026.84
700,000	8,426.33	8,294.10	8,229.71	8,197.98
800,000	9,630.09	9,478.97	9,405.39	9,369.12
900,000	10,833.85	10,663.85	10,581.06	10,540.26
1,000,000	12,037.61	11,848.72	11,756.73	11,711.40

Loan Payment

LOAN PAYMENT TABLE
INTEREST RATE: 14.25%
Monthly Payments - Fully Amortized

Loan Amount	14.25% 5	Term of Loan In Years 10	15	20
$ 1,000	23.40	15.68	13.49	12.62
5,000	116.99	78.39	67.43	63.09
10,000	233.98	156.77	134.86	126.17
25,000	584.95	391.93	337.14	315.43
40,000	935.92	627.09	539.43	504.69
50,000	1,169.90	783.87	674.29	630.86
75,000	1,754.85	1,175.80	1,011.43	946.29
100,000	2,339.81	1,567.73	1,348.58	1,261.72
125,000	2,924.76	1,959.66	1,685.72	1,577.15
150,000	3,509.71	2,351.60	2,022.87	1,892.58
175,000	4,094.66	2,743.53	2,360.01	2,208.01
200,000	4,679.61	3,135.46	2,697.16	2,523.44
225,000	5,264.56	3,527.39	3,034.30	2,838.87
250,000	5,849.52	3,919.33	3,371.45	3,154.30
275,000	6,434.47	4,311.26	3,708.59	3,469.73
300,000	7,019.42	4,703.19	4,045.74	3,785.16
350,000	8,189.32	5,487.06	4,720.03	4,416.02
400,000	9,359.23	6,270.92	5,394.32	5,046.88
450,000	10,529.13	7,054.79	6,068.61	5,677.74
500,000	11,699.03	7,838.66	6,742.90	6,308.59
600,000	14,038.84	9,406.39	8,091.48	7,570.31
700,000	16,378.64	10,974.12	9,440.06	8,832.03
800,000	18,718.45	12,541.85	10,788.64	10,093.75
900,000	21,058.26	14,109.58	12,137.22	11,355.47
1,000,000	23,398.06	15,677.31	13,485.80	12,617.19

LOAN PAYMENT TABLE
INTEREST RATE: 14.25%
Monthly Payments - Fully Amortized

Loan Amount	14.25%	Term of Loan In Years		
	25	30	35	40
$ 1,000	12.23	12.05	11.96	11.92
5,000	61.15	60.23	59.80	59.58
10,000	122.29	120.47	119.59	119.16
25,000	305.73	301.17	298.98	297.91
40,000	489.17	481.87	478.36	476.65
50,000	611.46	602.34	597.95	595.81
75,000	917.20	903.52	896.93	893.72
100,000	1,222.93	1,204.69	1,195.90	1,191.62
125,000	1,528.66	1,505.86	1,494.88	1,489.53
150,000	1,834.39	1,807.03	1,793.85	1,787.43
175,000	2,140.12	2,108.20	2,092.83	2,085.34
200,000	2,445.86	2,409.37	2,391.81	2,383.25
225,000	2,751.59	2,710.55	2,690.78	2,681.15
250,000	3,057.32	3,011.72	2,989.76	2,979.06
275,000	3,363.05	3,312.89	3,288.73	3,276.96
300,000	3,668.78	3,614.06	3,587.71	3,574.87
350,000	4,280.25	4,216.40	4,185.66	4,170.68
400,000	4,891.71	4,818.75	4,783.61	4,766.49
450,000	5,503.17	5,421.09	5,381.56	5,362.30
500,000	6,114.64	6,023.44	5,979.51	5,958.12
600,000	7,337.57	7,228.12	7,175.42	7,149.74
700,000	8,560.49	8,432.81	8,371.32	8,341.36
800,000	9,783.42	9,637.50	9,567.22	9,532.99
900,000	11,006.35	10,842.18	10,763.12	10,724.61
1,000,000	12,229.28	12,046.87	11,959.03	11,916.23

Loan Payment

LOAN PAYMENT TABLE
INTEREST RATE: 14.50%
Monthly Payments - Fully Amortized

Loan Amount	14.50%	Term of Loan In Years		
	5	10	15	20
$ 1,000	23.53	15.83	13.66	12.80
5,000	117.64	79.14	68.28	64.00
10,000	235.28	158.29	136.55	128.00
25,000	588.21	395.72	341.38	320.00
40,000	941.13	633.15	546.20	512.00
50,000	1,176.41	791.43	682.75	640.00
75,000	1,764.62	1,187.15	1,024.13	960.00
100,000	2,352.83	1,582.87	1,365.50	1,280.00
125,000	2,941.04	1,978.58	1,706.88	1,600.00
150,000	3,529.24	2,374.30	2,048.25	1,920.00
175,000	4,117.45	2,770.02	2,389.63	2,240.00
200,000	4,705.66	3,165.74	2,731.00	2,560.00
225,000	5,293.86	3,561.45	3,072.38	2,879.99
250,000	5,882.07	3,957.17	3,413.75	3,199.99
275,000	6,470.28	4,352.89	3,755.13	3,519.99
300,000	7,058.48	4,748.60	4,096.50	3,839.99
350,000	8,234.90	5,540.04	4,779.25	4,479.99
400,000	9,411.31	6,331.47	5,462.00	5,119.99
450,000	10,587.73	7,122.91	6,144.75	5,759.99
500,000	11,764.14	7,914.34	6,827.50	6,399.99
600,000	14,116.97	9,497.21	8,193.01	7,679.99
700,000	16,469.80	11,080.08	9,558.51	8,959.98
800,000	18,822.62	12,662.94	10,924.01	10,239.98
900,000	21,175.45	14,245.81	12,289.51	11,519.98
1,000,000	23,528.28	15,828.68	13,655.01	12,799.98

LOAN PAYMENT TABLE
INTEREST RATE: 14.50%
Monthly Payments - Fully Amortized

Loan Amount	14.50%	Term of Loan In Years		
	25	30	35	40
$ 1,000	12.42	12.25	12.16	12.12
5,000	62.11	61.23	60.81	60.61
10,000	124.22	122.46	121.62	121.21
25,000	310.54	306.14	304.04	303.03
40,000	496.87	489.82	486.47	484.85
50,000	621.08	612.28	608.09	606.07
75,000	931.62	918.42	912.13	909.10
100,000	1,242.16	1,224.56	1,216.17	1,212.13
125,000	1,552.70	1,530.69	1,520.21	1,515.17
150,000	1,863.24	1,836.83	1,824.26	1,818.20
175,000	2,173.79	2,142.97	2,128.30	2,121.23
200,000	2,484.33	2,449.11	2,432.34	2,424.27
225,000	2,794.87	2,755.25	2,736.38	2,727.30
250,000	3,105.41	3,061.39	3,040.43	3,030.33
275,000	3,415.95	3,367.53	3,344.47	3,333.37
300,000	3,726.49	3,673.67	3,648.51	3,636.40
350,000	4,347.57	4,285.95	4,256.60	4,242.47
400,000	4,968.65	4,898.22	4,864.68	4,848.53
450,000	5,589.73	5,510.50	5,472.77	5,454.60
500,000	6,210.81	6,122.78	6,080.85	6,060.66
600,000	7,452.98	7,347.34	7,297.02	7,272.80
700,000	8,695.14	8,571.89	8,513.19	8,484.93
800,000	9,937.30	9,796.45	9,729.36	9,697.06
900,000	11,179.47	11,021.00	10,945.53	10,909.20
1,000,000	12,421.63	12,245.56	12,161.71	12,121.33

Loan Payment

LOAN PAYMENT TABLE
INTEREST RATE: 14.75%
Monthly Payments - Fully Amortized

Loan Amount	14.75% 5	Term of Loan In Years 10	15	20
$ 1,000	23.66	15.98	13.83	12.98
5,000	118.29	79.90	69.13	64.92
10,000	236.59	159.81	138.25	129.84
25,000	591.47	399.52	345.63	324.59
40,000	946.36	639.23	553.00	519.34
50,000	1,182.95	799.04	691.25	649.18
75,000	1,774.42	1,198.56	1,036.88	973.77
100,000	2,365.89	1,598.07	1,382.50	1,298.36
125,000	2,957.36	1,997.59	1,728.13	1,622.94
150,000	3,548.84	2,397.11	2,073.76	1,947.53
175,000	4,140.31	2,796.63	2,419.38	2,272.12
200,000	4,731.78	3,196.15	2,765.01	2,596.71
225,000	5,323.25	3,595.67	3,110.63	2,921.30
250,000	5,914.73	3,995.19	3,456.26	3,245.89
275,000	6,506.20	4,394.70	3,801.89	3,570.48
300,000	7,097.67	4,794.22	4,147.51	3,895.07
350,000	8,280.62	5,593.26	4,838.76	4,544.24
400,000	9,463.56	6,392.30	5,530.02	5,193.42
450,000	10,646.51	7,191.33	6,221.27	5,842.60
500,000	11,829.45	7,990.37	6,912.52	6,491.78
600,000	14,195.34	9,588.45	8,295.02	7,790.13
700,000	16,561.23	11,186.52	9,677.53	9,088.49
800,000	18,927.12	12,784.59	11,060.03	10,386.84
900,000	21,293.01	14,382.67	12,442.53	11,685.20
1,000,000	23,658.90	15,980.74	13,825.04	12,983.55

Loan Payment

LOAN PAYMENT TABLE
INTEREST RATE: 14.75%
Monthly Payments - Fully Amortized

Loan Amount	14.75% 25	Term of Loan In Years 30	35	40
$ 1,000	12.61	12.44	12.36	12.33
5,000	63.07	62.22	61.82	61.63
10,000	126.15	124.45	123.65	123.27
25,000	315.37	311.12	309.12	308.17
40,000	504.59	497.79	494.59	493.07
50,000	630.73	622.24	618.24	616.33
75,000	946.10	933.36	927.36	924.50
100,000	1,261.46	1,244.48	1,236.47	1,232.67
125,000	1,576.83	1,555.59	1,545.59	1,540.83
150,000	1,892.20	1,866.71	1,854.71	1,849.00
175,000	2,207.56	2,177.83	2,163.83	2,157.17
200,000	2,522.93	2,488.95	2,472.95	2,465.33
225,000	2,838.30	2,800.07	2,782.07	2,773.50
250,000	3,153.66	3,111.19	3,091.19	3,081.67
275,000	3,469.03	3,422.31	3,400.31	3,389.83
300,000	3,784.39	3,733.43	3,709.42	3,698.00
350,000	4,415.13	4,355.67	4,327.66	4,314.34
400,000	5,045.86	4,977.90	4,945.90	4,930.67
450,000	5,676.59	5,600.14	5,564.14	5,547.00
500,000	6,307.32	6,222.38	6,182.37	6,163.34
600,000	7,568.79	7,466.85	7,418.85	7,396.00
700,000	8,830.25	8,711.33	8,655.32	8,628.67
800,000	10,091.72	9,955.81	9,891.80	9,861.34
900,000	11,353.18	11,200.28	11,128.27	11,094.00
1,000,000	12,614.65	12,444.76	12,364.75	12,326.67

Loan Payment

LOAN PAYMENT TABLE
INTEREST RATE: 15.00%
Monthly Payments - Fully Amortized

Loan Amount	15.00% 5	Term of Loan In Years 10	15	20
$ 1,000	23.79	16.13	14.00	13.17
5,000	118.95	80.67	69.98	65.84
10,000	237.90	161.33	139.96	131.68
25,000	594.75	403.34	349.90	329.20
40,000	951.60	645.34	559.83	526.72
50,000	1,189.50	806.67	699.79	658.39
75,000	1,784.24	1,210.01	1,049.69	987.59
100,000	2,378.99	1,613.35	1,399.59	1,316.79
125,000	2,973.74	2,016.69	1,749.48	1,645.99
150,000	3,568.49	2,420.02	2,099.38	1,975.18
175,000	4,163.24	2,823.36	2,449.28	2,304.38
200,000	4,757.99	3,226.70	2,799.17	2,633.58
225,000	5,352.73	3,630.04	3,149.07	2,962.78
250,000	5,947.48	4,033.37	3,498.97	3,291.97
275,000	6,542.23	4,436.71	3,848.86	3,621.17
300,000	7,136.98	4,840.05	4,198.76	3,950.37
350,000	8,326.48	5,646.72	4,898.55	4,608.76
400,000	9,515.97	6,453.40	5,598.35	5,267.16
450,000	10,705.47	7,260.07	6,298.14	5,925.55
500,000	11,894.97	8,066.75	6,997.94	6,583.95
600,000	14,273.96	9,680.10	8,397.52	7,900.74
700,000	16,652.95	11,293.45	9,797.11	9,217.53
800,000	19,031.94	12,906.80	11,196.70	10,534.32
900,000	21,410.94	14,520.15	12,596.28	11,851.11
1,000,000	23,789.93	16,133.50	13,995.87	13,167.90

LOAN PAYMENT TABLE
INTEREST RATE: 15.00%
Monthly Payments - Fully Amortized

Loan Amount	15.00%	Term of Loan In Years		
	25	30	35	40
$ 1,000	12.81	12.64	12.57	12.53
5,000	64.04	63.22	62.84	62.66
10,000	128.08	126.44	125.68	125.32
25,000	320.21	316.11	314.20	313.31
40,000	512.33	505.78	502.73	501.29
50,000	640.42	632.22	628.41	626.61
75,000	960.62	948.33	942.61	939.92
100,000	1,280.83	1,264.44	1,256.81	1,253.22
125,000	1,601.04	1,580.56	1,571.02	1,566.53
150,000	1,921.25	1,896.67	1,885.22	1,879.84
175,000	2,241.45	2,212.78	2,199.42	2,193.14
200,000	2,561.66	2,528.89	2,513.63	2,506.45
225,000	2,881.87	2,845.00	2,827.83	2,819.75
250,000	3,202.08	3,161.11	3,142.03	3,133.06
275,000	3,522.28	3,477.22	3,456.24	3,446.37
300,000	3,842.49	3,793.33	3,770.44	3,759.67
350,000	4,482.91	4,425.55	4,398.85	4,386.28
400,000	5,123.32	5,057.78	5,027.25	5,012.90
450,000	5,763.74	5,690.00	5,655.66	5,639.51
500,000	6,404.15	6,322.22	6,284.07	6,266.12
600,000	7,684.98	7,586.66	7,540.88	7,519.34
700,000	8,965.81	8,851.11	8,797.69	8,772.57
800,000	10,246.64	10,115.55	10,054.51	10,025.79
900,000	11,527.48	11,380.00	11,311.32	11,279.02
1,000,000	12,808.31	12,644.44	12,568.13	12,532.24

Loan Payment

LOAN PAYMENT TABLE
INTEREST RATE: 15.25%
Monthly Payments - Fully Amortized

Loan Amount	15.25%	Term of Loan In Years		
	5	10	15	20
$ 1,000	23.92	16.29	14.17	13.35
5,000	119.61	81.43	70.84	66.76
10,000	239.21	162.87	141.67	133.53
25,000	598.03	407.17	354.19	333.82
40,000	956.85	651.48	566.70	534.12
50,000	1,196.07	814.35	708.37	667.65
75,000	1,794.10	1,221.52	1,062.56	1,001.47
100,000	2,392.14	1,628.69	1,416.75	1,335.30
125,000	2,990.17	2,035.87	1,770.94	1,669.12
150,000	3,588.20	2,443.04	2,125.12	2,002.95
175,000	4,186.24	2,850.21	2,479.31	2,336.77
200,000	4,784.27	3,257.39	2,833.50	2,670.60
225,000	5,382.31	3,664.56	3,187.69	3,004.42
250,000	5,980.34	4,071.73	3,541.87	3,338.25
275,000	6,578.37	4,478.91	3,896.06	3,672.07
300,000	7,176.41	4,886.08	4,250.25	4,005.90
350,000	8,372.48	5,700.43	4,958.62	4,673.55
400,000	9,568.54	6,514.77	5,667.00	5,341.19
450,000	10,764.61	7,329.12	6,375.37	6,008.84
500,000	11,960.68	8,143.47	7,083.75	6,676.49
600,000	14,352.82	9,772.16	8,500.50	8,011.79
700,000	16,744.95	11,400.85	9,917.25	9,347.09
800,000	19,137.09	13,029.55	11,334.00	10,682.39
900,000	21,529.22	14,658.24	12,750.75	12,017.69
1,000,000	23,921.36	16,286.93	14,167.50	13,352.99

Loan Payment

LOAN PAYMENT TABLE
INTEREST RATE: 15.25%
Monthly Payments - Fully Amortized

Loan Amount	15.25% 25	Term of Loan In Years 30	35	40
$ 1,000	13.00	12.84	12.77	12.74
5,000	65.01	64.22	63.86	63.69
10,000	130.03	128.45	127.72	127.38
25,000	325.06	321.11	319.30	318.45
40,000	520.10	513.78	510.87	509.52
50,000	650.13	642.23	638.59	636.90
75,000	975.19	963.34	957.89	955.35
100,000	1,300.26	1,284.46	1,277.18	1,273.80
125,000	1,625.32	1,605.57	1,596.48	1,592.25
150,000	1,950.39	1,926.69	1,915.78	1,910.70
175,000	2,275.45	2,247.80	2,235.07	2,229.15
200,000	2,600.52	2,568.92	2,554.37	2,547.60
225,000	2,925.58	2,890.03	2,873.66	2,866.06
250,000	3,250.65	3,211.15	3,192.96	3,184.51
275,000	3,575.71	3,532.26	3,512.26	3,502.96
300,000	3,900.77	3,853.38	3,831.55	3,821.41
350,000	4,550.90	4,495.60	4,470.14	4,458.31
400,000	5,201.03	5,137.83	5,108.74	5,095.21
450,000	5,851.16	5,780.06	5,747.33	5,732.11
500,000	6,501.29	6,422.29	6,385.92	6,369.01
600,000	7,801.55	7,706.75	7,663.10	7,642.81
700,000	9,101.81	8,991.21	8,940.29	8,916.62
800,000	10,402.07	10,275.67	10,217.47	10,190.42
900,000	11,702.32	11,560.13	11,494.66	11,464.22
1,000,000	13,002.58	12,844.59	12,771.84	12,738.02

Loan Payment

LOAN PAYMENT TABLE
INTEREST RATE: 15.50%
Monthly Payments - Fully Amortized

Loan Amount	15.50%	Term of Loan In Years		
	5	10	15	20
$ 1,000	24.05	16.44	14.34	13.54
5,000	120.27	82.21	71.70	67.69
10,000	240.53	164.41	143.40	135.39
25,000	601.33	411.03	358.50	338.47
40,000	962.13	657.64	573.60	541.55
50,000	1,202.66	822.05	717.00	676.94
75,000	1,803.99	1,233.08	1,075.49	1,015.41
100,000	2,405.32	1,644.11	1,433.99	1,353.88
125,000	3,006.65	2,055.13	1,792.49	1,692.35
150,000	3,607.98	2,466.16	2,150.99	2,030.82
175,000	4,209.31	2,877.18	2,509.48	2,369.29
200,000	4,810.64	3,288.21	2,867.98	2,707.76
225,000	5,411.97	3,699.24	3,226.48	3,046.23
250,000	6,013.30	4,110.26	3,584.98	3,384.70
275,000	6,614.63	4,521.29	3,943.47	3,723.17
300,000	7,215.96	4,932.32	4,301.97	4,061.64
350,000	8,418.62	5,754.37	5,018.97	4,738.58
400,000	9,621.28	6,576.42	5,735.96	5,415.52
450,000	10,823.94	7,398.47	6,452.96	6,092.46
500,000	12,026.60	8,220.53	7,169.95	6,769.40
600,000	14,431.91	9,864.63	8,603.94	8,123.28
700,000	16,837.23	11,508.74	10,037.93	9,477.16
800,000	19,242.55	13,152.84	11,471.92	10,831.05
900,000	21,647.87	14,796.95	12,905.91	12,184.93
1,000,000	24,053.19	16,441.05	14,339.90	13,538.81

LOAN PAYMENT TABLE
INTEREST RATE: 15.50%
Monthly Payments - Fully Amortized

Loan Amount	15.50%	Term of Loan In Years		
	25	30	35	40
$ 1,000	13.20	13.05	12.98	12.94
5,000	65.99	65.23	64.88	64.72
10,000	131.97	130.45	129.76	129.44
25,000	329.94	326.13	324.40	323.60
40,000	527.90	521.81	519.03	517.76
50,000	659.87	652.26	648.79	647.20
75,000	989.81	978.39	973.19	970.80
100,000	1,319.75	1,304.52	1,297.58	1,294.40
125,000	1,649.68	1,630.65	1,621.98	1,618.00
150,000	1,979.62	1,956.78	1,946.38	1,941.60
175,000	2,309.55	2,282.90	2,270.77	2,265.20
200,000	2,639.49	2,609.03	2,595.17	2,588.80
225,000	2,969.43	2,935.16	2,919.57	2,912.40
250,000	3,299.36	3,261.29	3,243.96	3,236.00
275,000	3,629.30	3,587.42	3,568.36	3,559.60
300,000	3,959.24	3,913.55	3,892.75	3,883.20
350,000	4,619.11	4,565.81	4,541.55	4,530.40
400,000	5,278.98	5,218.07	5,190.34	5,177.60
450,000	5,938.85	5,870.33	5,839.13	5,824.80
500,000	6,598.73	6,522.58	6,487.92	6,472.00
600,000	7,918.47	7,827.10	7,785.51	7,766.40
700,000	9,238.22	9,131.62	9,083.09	9,060.80
800,000	10,557.96	10,436.14	10,380.68	10,355.20
900,000	11,877.71	11,740.65	11,678.26	11,649.60
1,000,000	13,197.45	13,045.17	12,975.85	12,944.00

Loan Payment

LOAN PAYMENT TABLE
INTEREST RATE: 15.75%
Monthly Payments - Fully Amortized

Loan Amount	15.75%	Term of Loan In Years		
	5	10	15	20
$ 1,000	24.19	16.60	14.51	13.73
5,000	120.93	82.98	72.57	68.63
10,000	241.85	165.96	145.13	137.25
25,000	604.64	414.90	362.83	343.13
40,000	967.42	663.83	580.52	549.01
50,000	1,209.27	829.79	725.65	686.27
75,000	1,813.91	1,244.69	1,088.48	1,029.40
100,000	2,418.54	1,659.58	1,451.31	1,372.53
125,000	3,023.18	2,074.48	1,814.13	1,715.67
150,000	3,627.81	2,489.38	2,176.96	2,058.80
175,000	4,232.45	2,904.27	2,539.79	2,401.93
200,000	4,837.08	3,319.17	2,902.62	2,745.07
225,000	5,441.72	3,734.07	3,265.44	3,088.20
250,000	6,046.36	4,148.96	3,628.27	3,431.33
275,000	6,650.99	4,563.86	3,991.10	3,774.47
300,000	7,255.63	4,978.75	4,353.92	4,117.60
350,000	8,464.90	5,808.55	5,079.58	4,803.87
400,000	9,674.17	6,638.34	5,805.23	5,490.13
450,000	10,883.44	7,468.13	6,530.88	6,176.40
500,000	12,092.71	8,297.92	7,256.54	6,862.67
600,000	14,511.25	9,957.51	8,707.85	8,235.20
700,000	16,929.80	11,617.09	10,159.15	9,607.74
800,000	19,348.34	13,276.68	11,610.46	10,980.27
900,000	21,766.88	14,936.26	13,061.77	12,352.80
1,000,000	24,185.42	16,595.85	14,513.08	13,725.34

LOAN PAYMENT TABLE
INTEREST RATE: 15.75%
Monthly Payments - Fully Amortized

Loan Amount	15.75%	Term of Loan In Years		
	25	30	35	40
$ 1,000	13.39	13.25	13.18	13.15
5,000	66.96	66.23	65.90	65.75
10,000	133.93	132.46	131.80	131.50
25,000	334.82	331.15	329.50	328.75
40,000	535.72	529.85	527.21	526.01
50,000	669.64	662.31	659.01	657.51
75,000	1,004.47	993.46	988.51	986.26
100,000	1,339.29	1,324.62	1,318.01	1,315.02
125,000	1,674.11	1,655.77	1,647.52	1,643.77
150,000	2,008.93	1,986.93	1,977.02	1,972.52
175,000	2,343.76	2,318.08	2,306.52	2,301.28
200,000	2,678.58	2,649.23	2,636.03	2,630.03
225,000	3,013.40	2,980.39	2,965.53	2,958.79
250,000	3,348.22	3,311.54	3,295.03	3,287.54
275,000	3,683.05	3,642.70	3,624.54	3,616.29
300,000	4,017.87	3,973.85	3,954.04	3,945.05
350,000	4,687.51	4,636.16	4,613.05	4,602.56
400,000	5,357.16	5,298.47	5,272.05	5,260.06
450,000	6,026.80	5,960.78	5,931.06	5,917.57
500,000	6,696.45	6,623.09	6,590.07	6,575.08
600,000	8,035.74	7,947.70	7,908.08	7,890.09
700,000	9,375.03	9,272.32	9,226.10	9,205.11
800,000	10,714.32	10,596.94	10,544.11	10,520.13
900,000	12,053.61	11,921.55	11,862.12	11,835.14
1,000,000	13,392.90	13,246.17	13,180.14	13,150.16

Loan Payment

LOAN PAYMENT TABLE
INTEREST RATE: 16.00%
Monthly Payments - Fully Amortized

Loan Amount	16.00%	Term of Loan In Years		
	5	10	15	20
$ 1,000	24.32	16.75	14.69	13.91
5,000	121.59	83.76	73.44	69.56
10,000	243.18	167.51	146.87	139.13
25,000	607.95	418.78	367.18	347.81
40,000	972.72	670.05	587.48	556.50
50,000	1,215.90	837.57	734.35	695.63
75,000	1,823.85	1,256.35	1,101.53	1,043.44
100,000	2,431.81	1,675.13	1,468.70	1,391.26
125,000	3,039.76	2,093.91	1,835.88	1,739.07
150,000	3,647.71	2,512.70	2,203.05	2,086.88
175,000	4,255.66	2,931.48	2,570.23	2,434.70
200,000	4,863.61	3,350.26	2,937.40	2,782.51
225,000	5,471.56	3,769.05	3,304.58	3,130.33
250,000	6,079.51	4,187.83	3,671.75	3,478.14
275,000	6,687.47	4,606.61	4,038.93	3,825.95
300,000	7,295.42	5,025.39	4,406.10	4,173.77
350,000	8,511.32	5,862.96	5,140.45	4,869.40
400,000	9,727.22	6,700.52	5,874.80	5,565.02
450,000	10,943.13	7,538.09	6,609.15	6,260.65
500,000	12,159.03	8,375.66	7,343.50	6,956.28
600,000	14,590.83	10,050.79	8,812.20	8,347.54
700,000	17,022.64	11,725.92	10,280.91	9,738.79
800,000	19,454.45	13,401.05	11,749.61	11,130.05
900,000	21,886.25	15,076.18	13,218.31	12,521.30
1,000,000	24,318.06	16,751.31	14,687.01	13,912.56

LOAN PAYMENT TABLE
INTEREST RATE: 16.00%
Monthly Payments - Fully Amortized

Loan Amount	16.00%	Term of Loan In Years		
	25	30	35	40
$ 1,000	13.59	13.45	13.38	13.36
5,000	67.94	67.24	66.92	66.78
10,000	135.89	134.48	133.85	133.56
25,000	339.72	336.19	334.62	333.91
40,000	543.56	537.90	535.39	534.26
50,000	679.44	672.38	669.23	667.82
75,000	1,019.17	1,008.57	1,003.85	1,001.74
100,000	1,358.89	1,344.76	1,338.47	1,335.65
125,000	1,698.61	1,680.95	1,673.09	1,669.56
150,000	2,038.33	2,017.14	2,007.70	2,003.47
175,000	2,378.06	2,353.32	2,342.32	2,337.38
200,000	2,717.78	2,689.51	2,676.94	2,671.30
225,000	3,057.50	3,025.70	3,011.56	3,005.21
250,000	3,397.22	3,361.89	3,346.17	3,339.12
275,000	3,736.94	3,698.08	3,680.79	3,673.03
300,000	4,076.67	4,034.27	4,015.41	4,006.95
350,000	4,756.11	4,706.65	4,684.64	4,674.77
400,000	5,435.56	5,379.03	5,353.88	5,342.59
450,000	6,115.00	6,051.41	6,023.11	6,010.42
500,000	6,794.44	6,723.78	6,692.35	6,678.24
600,000	8,153.33	8,068.54	8,030.82	8,013.89
700,000	9,512.22	9,413.30	9,369.29	9,349.54
800,000	10,871.11	10,758.06	10,707.76	10,685.19
900,000	12,230.00	12,102.81	12,046.22	12,020.84
1,000,000	13,588.89	13,447.57	13,384.69	13,356.48

Loan Payment

LOAN PAYMENT TABLE
INTEREST RATE: 16.25%
Monthly Payments - Fully Amortized

Loan Amount	16.25% 5	Term of Loan In Years 10	15	20
$ 1,000	24.45	16.91	14.86	14.10
5,000	122.26	84.54	74.31	70.50
10,000	244.51	169.07	148.62	141.00
25,000	611.28	422.69	371.54	352.51
40,000	978.04	676.30	594.47	564.02
50,000	1,222.55	845.37	743.08	705.02
75,000	1,833.83	1,268.06	1,114.63	1,057.53
100,000	2,445.11	1,690.74	1,486.17	1,410.05
125,000	3,056.39	2,113.43	1,857.71	1,762.56
150,000	3,667.66	2,536.12	2,229.25	2,115.07
175,000	4,278.94	2,958.80	2,600.79	2,467.58
200,000	4,890.22	3,381.49	2,972.34	2,820.09
225,000	5,501.50	3,804.17	3,343.88	3,172.60
250,000	6,112.77	4,226.86	3,715.42	3,525.11
275,000	6,724.05	4,649.55	4,086.96	3,877.63
300,000	7,335.33	5,072.23	4,458.50	4,230.14
350,000	8,557.88	5,917.60	5,201.59	4,935.16
400,000	9,780.44	6,762.98	5,944.67	5,640.18
450,000	11,002.99	7,608.35	6,687.76	6,345.20
500,000	12,225.54	8,453.72	7,430.84	7,050.23
600,000	14,670.65	10,144.46	8,917.01	8,460.27
700,000	17,115.76	11,835.21	10,403.18	9,870.32
800,000	19,560.87	13,525.95	11,889.34	11,280.36
900,000	22,005.98	15,216.70	13,375.51	12,690.41
1,000,000	24,451.09	16,907.44	14,861.68	14,100.46

LOAN PAYMENT TABLE
INTEREST RATE: 16.25%
Monthly Payments - Fully Amortized

Loan Amount	16.25% 25	Term of Loan In Years 30	35	40
$ 1,000	13.79	13.65	13.59	13.56
5,000	68.93	68.25	67.95	67.81
10,000	137.85	136.49	135.89	135.63
25,000	344.64	341.23	339.74	339.07
40,000	551.42	545.97	543.58	542.52
50,000	689.27	682.47	679.47	678.15
75,000	1,033.91	1,023.70	1,019.21	1,017.22
100,000	1,378.54	1,364.93	1,358.95	1,356.30
125,000	1,723.18	1,706.17	1,698.69	1,695.37
150,000	2,067.81	2,047.40	2,038.42	2,034.45
175,000	2,412.45	2,388.64	2,378.16	2,373.52
200,000	2,757.08	2,729.87	2,717.90	2,712.59
225,000	3,101.72	3,071.10	3,057.64	3,051.67
250,000	3,446.35	3,412.34	3,397.37	3,390.74
275,000	3,790.99	3,753.57	3,737.11	3,729.82
300,000	4,135.62	4,094.80	4,076.85	4,068.89
350,000	4,824.89	4,777.27	4,756.32	4,747.04
400,000	5,514.17	5,459.74	5,435.80	5,425.19
450,000	6,203.44	6,142.21	6,115.27	6,103.34
500,000	6,892.71	6,824.67	6,794.75	6,781.48
600,000	8,271.25	8,189.61	8,153.70	8,137.78
700,000	9,649.79	9,554.54	9,512.65	9,494.08
800,000	11,028.33	10,919.48	10,871.60	10,850.37
900,000	12,406.87	12,284.41	12,230.55	12,206.67
1,000,000	13,785.41	13,649.35	13,589.50	13,562.97

Loan Payment

LOAN PAYMENT TABLE
INTEREST RATE: 16.50%
Monthly Payments - Fully Amortized

Loan Amount	16.50%	Term of Loan In Years		
	5	10	15	20
$ 1,000	24.58	17.06	15.04	14.29
5,000	122.92	85.32	75.19	71.45
10,000	245.85	170.64	150.37	142.89
25,000	614.61	426.61	375.93	357.23
40,000	983.38	682.57	601.48	571.56
50,000	1,229.23	853.21	751.85	714.45
75,000	1,843.84	1,279.82	1,127.78	1,071.68
100,000	2,458.45	1,706.42	1,503.71	1,428.90
125,000	3,073.07	2,133.03	1,879.64	1,786.13
150,000	3,687.68	2,559.63	2,255.56	2,143.35
175,000	4,302.29	2,986.24	2,631.49	2,500.58
200,000	4,916.90	3,412.85	3,007.42	2,857.80
225,000	5,531.52	3,839.45	3,383.34	3,215.03
250,000	6,146.13	4,266.06	3,759.27	3,572.25
275,000	6,760.74	4,692.66	4,135.20	3,929.48
300,000	7,375.36	5,119.27	4,511.13	4,286.70
350,000	8,604.58	5,972.48	5,262.98	5,001.15
400,000	9,833.81	6,825.69	6,014.83	5,715.60
450,000	11,063.03	7,678.90	6,766.69	6,430.05
500,000	12,292.26	8,532.11	7,518.54	7,144.50
600,000	14,750.71	10,238.54	9,022.25	8,573.40
700,000	17,209.16	11,944.96	10,525.96	10,002.30
800,000	19,667.62	13,651.38	12,029.67	11,431.21
900,000	22,126.07	15,357.81	13,533.38	12,860.11
1,000,000	24,584.52	17,064.23	15,037.09	14,289.01

LOAN PAYMENT TABLE
INTEREST RATE: 16.50%
Monthly Payments - Fully Amortized

Loan Amount	16.50%	Term of Loan In Years		
	25	30	35	40
$ 1,000	13.98	13.85	13.79	13.77
5,000	69.91	69.26	68.97	68.85
10,000	139.82	138.51	137.95	137.70
25,000	349.56	346.29	344.86	344.24
40,000	559.30	554.06	551.78	550.78
50,000	699.12	692.57	689.73	688.48
75,000	1,048.68	1,038.86	1,034.59	1,032.72
100,000	1,398.24	1,385.15	1,379.45	1,376.96
125,000	1,747.81	1,731.44	1,724.32	1,721.20
150,000	2,097.37	2,077.72	2,069.18	2,065.44
175,000	2,446.93	2,424.01	2,414.04	2,409.68
200,000	2,796.49	2,770.30	2,758.91	2,753.92
225,000	3,146.05	3,116.58	3,103.77	3,098.16
250,000	3,495.61	3,462.87	3,448.63	3,442.40
275,000	3,845.17	3,809.16	3,793.50	3,786.64
300,000	4,194.73	4,155.44	4,138.36	4,130.88
350,000	4,893.86	4,848.02	4,828.09	4,819.36
400,000	5,592.98	5,540.59	5,517.82	5,507.84
450,000	6,292.10	6,233.17	6,207.54	6,196.32
500,000	6,991.22	6,925.74	6,897.27	6,884.80
600,000	8,389.47	8,310.89	8,276.72	8,261.76
700,000	9,787.71	9,696.04	9,656.18	9,638.72
800,000	11,185.96	11,081.18	11,035.63	11,015.67
900,000	12,584.20	12,466.33	12,415.09	12,392.63
1,000,000	13,982.45	13,851.48	13,794.54	13,769.59

Loan Payment

LOAN PAYMENT TABLE
INTEREST RATE: 16.75%
Monthly Payments - Fully Amortized

Loan Amount	16.75% 5	Term of Loan In Years 10	15	20
$ 1,000	24.72	17.22	15.21	14.48
5,000	123.59	86.11	76.07	72.39
10,000	247.18	172.22	152.13	144.78
25,000	617.96	430.54	380.33	361.95
40,000	988.73	688.87	608.53	579.13
50,000	1,235.92	861.08	760.66	723.91
75,000	1,853.88	1,291.63	1,140.99	1,085.86
100,000	2,471.84	1,722.17	1,521.32	1,447.82
125,000	3,089.79	2,152.71	1,901.65	1,809.77
150,000	3,707.75	2,583.25	2,281.98	2,171.73
175,000	4,325.71	3,013.79	2,662.31	2,533.68
200,000	4,943.67	3,444.33	3,042.64	2,895.64
225,000	5,561.63	3,874.68	3,422.97	3,257.59
250,000	6,179.59	4,305.42	3,803.30	3,619.55
275,000	6,797.55	4,735.96	4,183.63	3,981.50
300,000	7,415.51	5,166.50	4,563.96	4,343.46
350,000	8,651.42	6,027.59	5,324.62	5,067.37
400,000	9,887.34	6,888.67	6,085.28	5,791.28
450,000	11,123.26	7,749.75	6,845.94	6,515.19
500,000	12,359.18	8,610.84	7,606.61	7,239.10
600,000	14,831.01	10,333.00	9,127.93	8,686.92
700,000	17,302.85	12,055.17	10,649.25	10,134.74
800,000	19,774.68	13,777.34	12,170.57	11,582.56
900,000	22,246.52	15,499.51	13,691.89	13,030.38
1,000,000	24,718.35	17,221.67	15,213.21	14,478.20

LOAN PAYMENT TABLE
INTEREST RATE: 16.75%
Monthly Payments - Fully Amortized

Loan Amount	16.75%	Term of Loan In Years		
	25	30	35	40
$ 1,000	14.18	14.05	14.00	13.98
5,000	70.90	70.27	70.00	69.88
10,000	141.80	140.54	140.00	139.76
25,000	354.50	351.35	349.99	349.41
40,000	567.20	562.16	559.99	559.05
50,000	709.00	702.70	699.99	698.82
75,000	1,063.50	1,054.05	1,049.98	1,048.23
100,000	1,418.00	1,405.40	1,399.98	1,397.64
125,000	1,772.50	1,756.74	1,749.97	1,747.04
150,000	2,127.00	2,108.09	2,099.97	2,096.45
175,000	2,481.49	2,459.44	2,449.96	2,445.86
200,000	2,835.99	2,810.79	2,799.96	2,795.27
225,000	3,190.49	3,162.14	3,149.95	3,144.68
250,000	3,544.99	3,513.49	3,499.95	3,494.09
275,000	3,899.49	3,864.84	3,849.94	3,843.50
300,000	4,253.99	4,216.19	4,199.94	4,192.91
350,000	4,962.99	4,918.88	4,899.93	4,891.72
400,000	5,671.99	5,621.58	5,599.92	5,590.54
450,000	6,380.99	6,324.28	6,299.91	6,289.36
500,000	7,089.99	7,026.98	6,999.90	6,988.18
600,000	8,507.98	8,432.37	8,399.88	8,385.81
700,000	9,925.98	9,837.77	9,799.86	9,783.45
800,000	11,343.98	11,243.16	11,199.84	11,181.08
900,000	12,761.97	12,648.56	12,599.82	12,578.72
1,000,000	14,179.97	14,053.96	13,999.80	13,976.35

Loan Payment

LOAN PAYMENT TABLE
INTEREST RATE: 17.00%
Monthly Payments - Fully Amortized

Loan Amount	17.00%	Term of Loan In Years		
	5	10	15	20
$ 1,000	24.85	17.38	15.39	14.67
5,000	124.26	86.90	76.95	73.34
10,000	248.53	173.80	153.90	146.68
25,000	621.31	434.49	384.75	366.70
40,000	994.10	695.19	615.60	586.72
50,000	1,242.63	868.99	769.50	733.40
75,000	1,863.94	1,303.48	1,154.25	1,100.10
100,000	2,485.26	1,737.98	1,539.00	1,466.80
125,000	3,106.57	2,172.47	1,923.76	1,833.50
150,000	3,727.89	2,606.96	2,308.51	2,200.20
175,000	4,349.20	3,041.46	2,693.26	2,566.90
200,000	4,970.52	3,475.95	3,078.01	2,933.60
225,000	5,591.83	3,910.45	3,462.76	3,300.30
250,000	6,213.14	4,344.94	3,847.51	3,667.00
275,000	6,834.46	4,779.44	4,232.26	4,033.70
300,000	7,455.77	5,213.93	4,617.01	4,400.40
350,000	8,698.40	6,082.92	5,386.52	5,133.80
400,000	9,941.03	6,951.91	6,156.02	5,867.20
450,000	11,183.66	7,820.89	6,925.52	6,600.60
500,000	12,426.29	8,689.88	7,695.02	7,334.00
600,000	14,911.55	10,427.86	9,234.03	8,800.80
700,000	17,396.80	12,165.84	10,773.03	10,267.60
800,000	19,882.06	13,903.81	12,312.03	11,734.40
900,000	22,367.32	15,641.79	13,851.04	13,201.20
1,000,000	24,852.58	17,379.77	15,390.04	14,668.01

LOAN PAYMENT TABLE
INTEREST RATE: 17.00%
Monthly Payments - Fully Amortized

Loan Amount	17.00%	Term of Loan In Years		
	25	30	35	40
$ 1,000	14.38	14.26	14.21	14.18
5,000	71.89	71.28	71.03	70.92
10,000	143.78	142.57	142.05	141.83
25,000	359.45	356.42	355.13	354.58
40,000	575.12	570.27	568.21	567.33
50,000	718.90	712.84	710.26	709.16
75,000	1,078.35	1,069.26	1,065.39	1,063.74
100,000	1,437.80	1,425.68	1,420.53	1,418.32
125,000	1,797.25	1,782.09	1,775.66	1,772.90
150,000	2,156.69	2,138.51	2,130.79	2,127.49
175,000	2,516.14	2,494.93	2,485.92	2,482.07
200,000	2,875.59	2,851.35	2,841.05	2,836.65
225,000	3,235.04	3,207.77	3,196.18	3,191.23
250,000	3,594.49	3,564.19	3,551.32	3,545.81
275,000	3,953.94	3,920.61	3,906.45	3,900.39
300,000	4,313.39	4,277.03	4,261.58	4,254.97
350,000	5,032.29	4,989.86	4,971.84	4,964.13
400,000	5,751.19	5,702.70	5,682.10	5,673.29
450,000	6,470.08	6,415.54	6,392.37	6,382.46
500,000	7,188.98	7,128.38	7,102.63	7,091.62
600,000	8,626.78	8,554.05	8,523.16	8,509.94
700,000	10,064.58	9,979.73	9,943.68	9,928.26
800,000	11,502.37	11,405.40	11,364.21	11,346.59
900,000	12,940.17	12,831.08	12,784.74	12,764.91
1,000,000	14,377.97	14,256.75	14,205.26	14,183.24

Loan Payment

LOAN PAYMENT TABLE
INTEREST RATE: 17.25%
Monthly Payments - Fully Amortized

Loan Amount	17.25%	Term of Loan In Years		
	5	10	15	20
$ 1,000	24.99	17.54	15.57	14.86
5,000	124.94	87.69	77.84	74.29
10,000	249.87	175.39	155.68	148.58
25,000	624.68	438.46	389.19	371.46
40,000	999.49	701.54	622.70	594.34
50,000	1,249.36	876.93	778.38	742.92
75,000	1,874.04	1,315.39	1,167.57	1,114.38
100,000	2,498.72	1,753.85	1,556.76	1,485.84
125,000	3,123.40	2,192.31	1,945.95	1,857.30
150,000	3,748.08	2,630.78	2,335.14	2,228.76
175,000	4,372.76	3,069.24	2,724.32	2,600.22
200,000	4,997.44	3,507.70	3,113.51	2,971.68
225,000	5,622.12	3,946.16	3,502.70	3,343.14
250,000	6,246.80	4,384.63	3,891.89	3,714.60
275,000	6,871.48	4,823.09	4,281.08	4,086.07
300,000	7,496.16	5,261.55	4,670.27	4,457.53
350,000	8,745.52	6,138.48	5,448.65	5,200.45
400,000	9,994.88	7,015.40	6,227.03	5,943.37
450,000	11,244.24	7,892.33	7,005.41	6,686.29
500,000	12,493.60	8,769.25	7,783.79	7,429.21
600,000	14,992.32	10,523.10	9,340.54	8,915.05
700,000	17,491.04	12,276.95	10,897.30	10,400.89
800,000	19,989.76	14,030.80	12,454.06	11,886.74
900,000	22,488.48	15,784.65	14,010.81	13,372.58
1,000,000	24,987.20	17,538.50	15,567.57	14,858.42

LOAN PAYMENT TABLE
INTEREST RATE: 17.25%
Monthly Payments - Fully Amortized

Loan	17.25%	Term of Loan In Years		
Amount	25	30	35	40
$ 1,000	14.58	14.46	14.41	14.39
5,000	72.88	72.30	72.05	71.95
10,000	145.76	144.60	144.11	143.90
25,000	364.41	361.50	360.27	359.76
40,000	583.06	578.39	576.44	575.61
50,000	728.82	722.99	720.55	719.51
75,000	1,093.23	1,084.49	1,080.82	1,079.27
100,000	1,457.64	1,445.99	1,441.09	1,439.02
125,000	1,822.05	1,807.48	1,801.36	1,798.78
150,000	2,186.46	2,168.98	2,161.64	2,158.53
175,000	2,550.87	2,530.48	2,521.91	2,518.29
200,000	2,915.28	2,891.97	2,882.18	2,878.05
225,000	3,279.69	3,253.47	3,242.46	3,237.80
250,000	3,644.10	3,614.96	3,602.73	3,597.56
275,000	4,008.51	3,976.46	3,963.00	3,957.31
300,000	4,372.92	4,337.96	4,323.28	4,317.07
350,000	5,101.74	5,060.95	5,043.82	5,036.58
400,000	5,830.57	5,783.94	5,764.37	5,756.09
450,000	6,559.39	6,506.94	6,484.91	6,475.60
500,000	7,288.21	7,229.93	7,205.46	7,195.12
600,000	8,745.85	8,675.91	8,646.55	8,634.14
700,000	10,203.49	10,121.90	10,087.64	10,073.16
800,000	11,661.13	11,567.89	11,528.73	11,512.19
900,000	13,118.77	13,013.87	12,969.83	12,951.21
1,000,000	14,576.41	14,459.86	14,410.92	14,390.23

LOAN PAYMENT TABLE
INTEREST RATE: 17.50%
Monthly Payments - Fully Amortized

Loan Amount	17.50% 5	Term of Loan In Years 10	15	20
$ 1,000	25.12	17.70	15.75	15.05
5,000	125.61	88.49	78.73	75.25
10,000	251.22	176.98	157.46	150.49
25,000	628.06	442.45	393.64	376.24
40,000	1,004.89	707.92	629.83	601.98
50,000	1,256.11	884.89	787.29	752.47
75,000	1,884.17	1,327.34	1,180.93	1,128.71
100,000	2,512.22	1,769.79	1,574.58	1,504.94
125,000	3,140.28	2,212.23	1,968.22	1,881.18
150,000	3,768.33	2,654.68	2,361.87	2,257.41
175,000	4,396.39	3,097.13	2,755.51	2,633.65
200,000	5,024.44	3,539.58	3,149.16	3,009.88
225,000	5,652.50	3,982.02	3,542.80	3,386.12
250,000	6,280.55	4,424.47	3,936.45	3,762.35
275,000	6,908.61	4,866.92	4,330.09	4,138.59
300,000	7,536.66	5,309.36	4,723.73	4,514.83
350,000	8,792.77	6,194.26	5,511.02	5,267.30
400,000	10,048.89	7,079.15	6,298.31	6,019.77
450,000	11,305.00	7,964.04	7,085.60	6,772.24
500,000	12,561.11	8,848.94	7,872.89	7,524.71
600,000	15,073.33	10,618.73	9,447.47	9,029.65
700,000	17,585.55	12,388.51	11,022.05	10,534.59
800,000	20,097.77	14,158.30	12,596.63	12,039.54
900,000	22,609.99	15,928.09	14,171.20	13,544.48
1,000,000	25,122.21	17,697.88	15,745.78	15,049.42

LOAN PAYMENT TABLE
INTEREST RATE: 17.50%
Monthly Payments - Fully Amortized

Loan Amount	17.50%	Term of Loan In Years		
	25	30	35	40
$ 1,000	14.78	14.66	14.62	14.60
5,000	73.88	73.32	73.08	72.99
10,000	147.75	146.63	146.17	145.97
25,000	369.38	366.58	365.42	364.93
40,000	591.01	586.53	584.67	583.89
50,000	738.76	733.16	730.84	729.87
75,000	1,108.15	1,099.74	1,096.26	1,094.80
100,000	1,477.53	1,466.33	1,461.68	1,459.73
125,000	1,846.91	1,832.91	1,827.09	1,824.67
150,000	2,216.29	2,199.49	2,192.51	2,189.60
175,000	2,585.68	2,566.07	2,557.93	2,554.53
200,000	2,955.06	2,932.65	2,923.35	2,919.47
225,000	3,324.44	3,299.23	3,288.77	3,284.40
250,000	3,693.82	3,665.81	3,654.19	3,649.33
275,000	4,063.21	4,032.39	4,019.61	4,014.27
300,000	4,432.59	4,398.98	4,385.03	4,379.20
350,000	5,171.35	5,132.14	5,115.86	5,109.07
400,000	5,910.12	5,865.30	5,846.70	5,838.93
450,000	6,648.88	6,598.46	6,577.54	6,568.80
500,000	7,387.65	7,331.63	7,308.38	7,298.67
600,000	8,865.18	8,797.95	8,770.05	8,758.40
700,000	10,342.71	10,264.28	10,231.73	10,218.13
800,000	11,820.24	11,730.60	11,693.40	11,677.87
900,000	13,297.77	13,196.93	13,155.08	13,137.60
1,000,000	14,775.30	14,663.25	14,616.75	14,597.33

Loan Payment

LOAN PAYMENT TABLE
INTEREST RATE: 17.75%
Monthly Payments - Fully Amortized

Loan Amount	17.75%	Term of Loan In Years		
	5	10	15	20
$ 1,000	25.26	17.86	15.92	15.24
5,000	126.29	89.29	79.62	76.20
10,000	252.58	178.58	159.25	152.41
25,000	631.44	446.45	398.12	381.02
40,000	1,010.30	714.32	636.99	609.64
50,000	1,262.88	892.89	796.23	762.05
75,000	1,894.32	1,339.34	1,194.35	1,143.07
100,000	2,525.76	1,785.79	1,592.47	1,524.10
125,000	3,157.20	2,232.24	1,990.58	1,905.12
150,000	3,788.64	2,678.68	2,388.70	2,286.15
175,000	4,420.08	3,125.13	2,786.82	2,667.17
200,000	5,051.52	3,571.58	3,184.93	3,048.20
225,000	5,682.97	4,018.02	3,583.05	3,429.22
250,000	6,314.41	4,464.47	3,981.17	3,810.25
275,000	6,945.85	4,910.92	4,379.28	4,191.27
300,000	7,577.29	5,357.37	4,777.40	4,572.30
350,000	8,840.17	6,250.26	5,573.63	5,334.35
400,000	10,103.05	7,143.15	6,369.87	6,096.40
450,000	11,365.93	8,036.05	7,166.10	6,858.45
500,000	12,628.81	8,928.94	7,962.33	7,620.50
600,000	15,154.57	10,714.73	9,554.80	9,144.59
700,000	17,680.34	12,500.52	11,147.27	10,668.69
800,000	20,206.10	14,286.31	12,739.73	12,192.79
900,000	22,731.86	16,072.10	14,332.20	13,716.89
1,000,000	25,257.62	17,857.88	15,924.67	15,240.99

LOAN PAYMENT TABLE
INTEREST RATE: 17.75%
Monthly Payments - Fully Amortized

Loan Amount	17.75%	Term of Loan In Years		
	25	30	35	40
$ 1,000	14.97	14.87	14.82	14.80
5,000	74.87	74.33	74.11	74.02
10,000	149.75	148.67	148.23	148.05
25,000	374.36	371.67	370.57	370.11
40,000	598.98	594.68	592.91	592.18
50,000	748.73	743.35	741.14	740.23
75,000	1,123.09	1,115.02	1,111.71	1,110.34
100,000	1,497.46	1,486.69	1,482.28	1,480.45
125,000	1,871.82	1,858.37	1,852.84	1,850.57
150,000	2,246.19	2,230.04	2,223.41	2,220.68
175,000	2,620.55	2,601.71	2,593.98	2,590.79
200,000	2,994.92	2,973.38	2,964.55	2,960.91
225,000	3,369.28	3,345.06	3,335.12	3,331.02
250,000	3,743.65	3,716.73	3,705.69	3,701.13
275,000	4,118.01	4,088.40	4,076.26	4,071.25
300,000	4,492.38	4,460.08	4,446.83	4,441.36
350,000	5,241.11	5,203.42	5,187.97	5,181.59
400,000	5,989.84	5,946.77	5,929.10	5,921.81
450,000	6,738.57	6,690.12	6,670.24	6,662.04
500,000	7,487.30	7,433.46	7,411.38	7,402.27
600,000	8,984.76	8,920.15	8,893.65	8,882.72
700,000	10,482.22	10,406.85	10,375.93	10,363.17
800,000	11,979.68	11,893.54	11,858.21	11,843.63
900,000	13,477.14	13,380.23	13,340.48	13,324.08
1,000,000	14,974.60	14,866.92	14,822.76	14,804.53

Loan Payment

LOAN PAYMENT TABLE
INTEREST RATE: 18.00%
Monthly Payments - Fully Amortized

Loan Amount	18.00% 5	Term of Loan In Years 10	15	20
$ 1,000	25.39	18.02	16.10	15.43
5,000	126.97	90.09	80.52	77.17
10,000	253.93	180.19	161.04	154.33
25,000	634.84	450.46	402.61	385.83
40,000	1,015.74	720.74	644.17	617.32
50,000	1,269.67	900.93	805.21	771.66
75,000	1,904.51	1,351.39	1,207.82	1,157.48
100,000	2,539.34	1,801.85	1,610.42	1,543.31
125,000	3,174.18	2,252.31	2,013.03	1,929.14
150,000	3,809.01	2,702.78	2,415.63	2,314.97
175,000	4,443.85	3,153.24	2,818.24	2,700.80
200,000	5,078.69	3,603.70	3,220.84	3,086.62
225,000	5,713.52	4,054.17	3,623.45	3,472.45
250,000	6,348.36	4,504.63	4,026.05	3,858.28
275,000	6,983.19	4,955.09	4,428.66	4,244.11
300,000	7,618.03	5,405.56	4,831.26	4,629.93
350,000	8,887.70	6,306.48	5,636.47	5,401.59
400,000	10,157.37	7,207.41	6,441.68	6,173.25
450,000	11,427.04	8,108.33	7,246.89	6,944.90
500,000	12,696.71	9,009.26	8,052.11	7,716.56
600,000	15,236.06	10,811.11	9,662.53	9,259.87
700,000	17,775.40	12,612.96	11,272.95	10,803.18
800,000	20,314.74	14,414.82	12,883.37	12,346.49
900,000	22,854.08	16,216.67	14,493.79	13,889.80
1,000,000	25,393.43	18,018.52	16,104.21	15,433.12

LOAN PAYMENT TABLE
INTEREST RATE: 18.00%
Monthly Payments - Fully Amortized

Loan Amount	18.00%	Term of Loan In Years		
	25	30	35	40
$ 1,000	15.17	15.07	15.03	15.01
5,000	75.87	75.35	75.14	75.06
10,000	151.74	150.71	150.29	150.12
25,000	379.36	376.77	375.72	375.30
40,000	606.97	602.83	601.16	600.47
50,000	758.71	753.54	751.45	750.59
75,000	1,138.07	1,130.31	1,127.17	1,125.89
100,000	1,517.43	1,507.09	1,502.89	1,501.18
125,000	1,896.79	1,883.86	1,878.61	1,876.48
150,000	2,276.14	2,260.63	2,254.34	2,251.77
175,000	2,655.50	2,637.40	2,630.06	2,627.07
200,000	3,034.86	3,014.17	3,005.78	3,002.36
225,000	3,414.22	3,390.94	3,381.51	3,377.66
250,000	3,793.57	3,767.71	3,757.23	3,752.96
275,000	4,172.93	4,144.48	4,132.95	4,128.25
300,000	4,552.29	4,521.26	4,508.68	4,503.55
350,000	5,311.00	5,274.80	5,260.12	5,254.14
400,000	6,069.72	6,028.34	6,011.57	6,004.73
450,000	6,828.43	6,781.88	6,763.01	6,755.32
500,000	7,587.15	7,535.43	7,514.46	7,505.91
600,000	9,104.58	9,042.51	9,017.35	9,007.09
700,000	10,622.01	10,549.60	10,520.24	10,508.28
800,000	12,139.44	12,056.68	12,023.14	12,009.46
900,000	13,656.87	13,563.77	13,526.03	13,510.64
1,000,000	15,174.30	15,070.85	15,028.92	15,011.82

Loan Payment

LOAN PAYMENT TABLE
INTEREST RATE: 18.25%
Monthly Payments - Fully Amortized

Loan Amount	18.25%	Term of Loan In Years		
	5	10	15	20
$ 1,000	25.53	18.18	16.28	15.63
5,000	127.65	90.90	81.42	78.13
10,000	255.30	181.80	162.84	156.26
25,000	638.24	454.49	407.11	390.64
40,000	1,021.18	727.19	651.38	625.03
50,000	1,276.48	908.99	814.22	781.29
75,000	1,914.72	1,363.48	1,221.33	1,171.93
100,000	2,552.96	1,817.98	1,628.44	1,562.58
125,000	3,191.20	2,272.47	2,035.55	1,953.22
150,000	3,829.44	2,726.97	2,442.66	2,343.87
175,000	4,467.68	3,181.46	2,849.77	2,734.51
200,000	5,105.92	3,635.96	3,256.88	3,125.16
225,000	5,744.17	4,090.45	3,663.99	3,515.80
250,000	6,382.41	4,544.94	4,071.10	3,906.44
275,000	7,020.65	4,999.44	4,478.21	4,297.09
300,000	7,658.89	5,453.93	4,885.32	4,687.73
350,000	8,935.37	6,362.92	5,699.54	5,469.02
400,000	10,211.85	7,271.91	6,513.76	6,250.31
450,000	11,488.33	8,180.90	7,327.98	7,031.60
500,000	12,764.81	9,089.89	8,142.20	7,812.89
600,000	15,317.77	10,907.87	9,770.64	9,375.47
700,000	17,870.74	12,725.84	11,399.08	10,938.05
800,000	20,423.70	14,543.82	13,027.52	12,500.62
900,000	22,976.66	16,361.80	14,655.96	14,063.20
1,000,000	25,529.62	18,179.78	16,284.40	15,625.78

Loan Payment

LOAN PAYMENT TABLE
INTEREST RATE: 18.25%
Monthly Payments - Fully Amortized

Loan Amount	18.25%	Term of Loan In Years		
	25	30	35	40
$ 1,000	15.37	15.28	15.24	15.22
5,000	76.87	76.38	76.18	76.10
10,000	153.74	152.75	152.35	152.19
25,000	384.36	381.88	380.88	380.48
40,000	614.98	611.00	609.41	608.77
50,000	768.72	763.75	761.76	760.96
75,000	1,153.08	1,145.63	1,142.64	1,141.44
100,000	1,537.44	1,527.50	1,523.52	1,521.92
125,000	1,921.80	1,909.38	1,904.40	1,902.40
150,000	2,306.16	2,291.25	2,285.28	2,282.88
175,000	2,690.52	2,673.13	2,666.17	2,663.36
200,000	3,074.88	3,055.01	3,047.05	3,043.84
225,000	3,459.24	3,436.88	3,427.93	3,424.32
250,000	3,843.60	3,818.76	3,808.81	3,804.80
275,000	4,227.96	4,200.63	4,189.69	4,185.28
300,000	4,612.32	4,582.51	4,570.57	4,565.76
350,000	5,381.04	5,346.26	5,332.33	5,326.72
400,000	6,149.75	6,110.01	6,094.09	6,087.68
450,000	6,918.47	6,873.76	6,855.85	6,848.64
500,000	7,687.19	7,637.52	7,617.61	7,609.60
600,000	9,224.63	9,165.02	9,141.14	9,131.52
700,000	10,762.07	10,692.52	10,664.66	10,653.44
800,000	12,299.51	12,220.03	12,188.18	12,175.36
900,000	13,836.95	13,747.53	13,711.71	13,697.28
1,000,000	15,374.39	15,275.03	15,235.23	15,219.20

Loan Payment

LOAN PAYMENT TABLE
INTEREST RATE: 18.50%
Monthly Payments - Fully Amortized

Loan Amount	18.50% 5	Term of Loan In Years 10	15	20
$ 1,000	25.67	18.34	16.47	15.82
5,000	128.33	91.71	82.33	79.09
10,000	256.66	183.42	164.65	158.19
25,000	641.66	458.54	411.63	395.47
40,000	1,026.65	733.67	658.61	632.76
50,000	1,283.31	917.08	823.26	790.95
75,000	1,924.97	1,375.62	1,234.89	1,186.42
100,000	2,566.62	1,834.17	1,646.52	1,581.90
125,000	3,208.28	2,292.71	2,058.15	1,977.37
150,000	3,849.93	2,751.25	2,469.79	2,372.84
175,000	4,491.59	3,209.79	2,881.42	2,768.32
200,000	5,133.24	3,668.33	3,293.05	3,163.79
225,000	5,774.90	4,126.87	3,704.68	3,559.27
250,000	6,416.55	4,585.41	4,116.31	3,954.74
275,000	7,058.21	5,043.95	4,527.94	4,350.22
300,000	7,699.86	5,502.50	4,939.57	4,745.69
350,000	8,983.17	6,419.58	5,762.83	5,536.64
400,000	10,266.48	7,336.66	6,586.09	6,327.59
450,000	11,549.79	8,253.74	7,409.36	7,118.53
500,000	12,833.10	9,170.83	8,232.62	7,909.48
600,000	15,399.73	11,004.99	9,879.14	9,491.38
700,000	17,966.35	12,839.16	11,525.66	11,073.28
800,000	20,532.97	14,673.32	13,172.19	12,655.17
900,000	23,099.59	16,507.49	14,818.71	14,237.07
1,000,000	25,666.21	18,341.65	16,465.23	15,818.97

LOAN PAYMENT TABLE
INTEREST RATE: 18.50%
Monthly Payments - Fully Amortized

Loan Amount	18.50%	Term of Loan In Years		
	25	30	35	40
$ 1,000	15.57	15.48	15.44	15.43
5,000	77.87	77.40	77.21	77.13
10,000	155.75	154.79	154.42	154.27
25,000	389.37	386.99	386.04	385.67
40,000	622.99	619.18	617.67	617.07
50,000	778.74	773.97	772.08	771.33
75,000	1,168.11	1,160.96	1,158.13	1,157.00
100,000	1,557.48	1,547.94	1,544.17	1,542.66
125,000	1,946.86	1,934.93	1,930.21	1,928.33
150,000	2,336.23	2,321.92	2,316.25	2,314.00
175,000	2,725.60	2,708.90	2,702.29	2,699.66
200,000	3,114.97	3,095.89	3,088.34	3,085.33
225,000	3,504.34	3,482.88	3,474.38	3,470.99
250,000	3,893.71	3,869.86	3,860.42	3,856.66
275,000	4,283.08	4,256.85	4,246.46	4,242.33
300,000	4,672.45	4,643.83	4,632.50	4,627.99
350,000	5,451.19	5,417.81	5,404.59	5,399.33
400,000	6,229.94	6,191.78	6,176.67	6,170.66
450,000	7,008.68	6,965.75	6,948.75	6,941.99
500,000	7,787.42	7,739.72	7,720.84	7,713.32
600,000	9,344.90	9,287.67	9,265.01	9,255.99
700,000	10,902.39	10,835.61	10,809.17	10,798.65
800,000	12,459.87	12,383.56	12,353.34	12,341.32
900,000	14,017.36	13,931.50	13,897.51	13,883.98
1,000,000	15,574.84	15,479.45	15,441.68	15,426.64

Loan Payment

LOAN PAYMENT TABLE
INTEREST RATE: 18.75%
Monthly Payments - Fully Amortized

Loan Amount	18.75% 5	Term of Loan In Years 10	15	20
$ 1,000	25.80	18.50	16.65	16.01
5,000	129.02	92.52	83.23	80.06
10,000	258.03	185.04	166.47	160.13
25,000	645.08	462.60	416.17	400.32
40,000	1,032.13	740.17	665.87	640.51
50,000	1,290.16	925.21	832.33	800.63
75,000	1,935.24	1,387.81	1,248.50	1,200.95
100,000	2,580.32	1,850.41	1,664.67	1,601.27
125,000	3,225.40	2,313.02	2,080.84	2,001.58
150,000	3,870.48	2,775.62	2,497.00	2,401.90
175,000	4,515.56	3,238.22	2,913.17	2,802.22
200,000	5,160.64	3,700.83	3,329.34	3,202.53
225,000	5,805.72	4,163.43	3,745.51	3,602.85
250,000	6,450.80	4,626.04	4,161.67	4,003.17
275,000	7,095.88	5,088.64	4,577.84	4,403.48
300,000	7,740.96	5,551.24	4,994.01	4,803.80
350,000	9,031.11	6,476.45	5,826.34	5,604.43
400,000	10,321.27	7,401.66	6,658.68	6,405.06
450,000	11,611.43	8,326.86	7,491.01	7,205.70
500,000	12,901.59	9,252.07	8,323.34	8,006.33
600,000	15,481.91	11,102.48	9,988.01	9,607.60
700,000	18,062.23	12,952.90	11,652.68	11,208.86
800,000	20,642.55	14,803.31	13,317.35	12,810.13
900,000	23,222.87	16,653.73	14,982.02	14,411.39
1,000,000	25,803.19	18,504.14	16,646.69	16,012.66

Loan Payment

LOAN PAYMENT TABLE
INTEREST RATE: 18.75%
Monthly Payments - Fully Amortized

Loan Amount	18.75%	Term of Loan In Years		
	25	30	35	40
$ 1,000	15.78	15.68	15.65	15.63
5,000	78.88	78.42	78.24	78.17
10,000	157.76	156.84	156.48	156.34
25,000	394.39	392.10	391.21	390.85
40,000	631.03	627.36	625.93	625.37
50,000	788.78	784.20	782.41	781.71
75,000	1,183.17	1,176.31	1,173.62	1,172.56
100,000	1,577.57	1,568.41	1,564.83	1,563.42
125,000	1,971.96	1,960.51	1,956.03	1,954.27
150,000	2,366.35	2,352.61	2,347.24	2,345.12
175,000	2,760.74	2,744.71	2,738.44	2,735.98
200,000	3,155.13	3,136.82	3,129.65	3,126.83
225,000	3,549.52	3,528.92	3,520.86	3,517.69
250,000	3,943.91	3,921.02	3,912.06	3,908.54
275,000	4,338.30	4,313.12	4,303.27	4,299.39
300,000	4,732.70	4,705.22	4,694.48	4,690.25
350,000	5,521.48	5,489.43	5,476.89	5,471.96
400,000	6,310.26	6,273.63	6,259.30	6,253.67
450,000	7,099.04	7,057.84	7,041.71	7,035.37
500,000	7,887.83	7,842.04	7,824.13	7,817.08
600,000	9,465.39	9,410.45	9,388.95	9,380.50
700,000	11,042.96	10,978.86	10,953.78	10,943.91
800,000	12,620.52	12,547.26	12,518.60	12,507.33
900,000	14,198.09	14,115.67	14,083.43	14,070.75
1,000,000	15,775.65	15,684.08	15,648.26	15,634.16

Loan Payment

LOAN PAYMENT TABLE
INTEREST RATE: 19.00%
Monthly Payments - Fully Amortized

Loan Amount	19.00% 5	Term of Loan In Years 10	15	20
$ 1,000	25.94	18.67	16.83	16.21
5,000	129.70	93.34	84.14	81.03
10,000	259.41	186.67	168.29	162.07
25,000	648.51	466.68	420.72	405.17
40,000	1,037.62	746.69	673.15	648.27
50,000	1,297.03	933.36	841.44	810.34
75,000	1,945.54	1,400.04	1,262.16	1,215.51
100,000	2,594.06	1,866.72	1,682.88	1,620.68
125,000	3,242.57	2,333.40	2,103.60	2,025.86
150,000	3,891.08	2,800.09	2,524.31	2,431.03
175,000	4,539.60	3,266.77	2,945.03	2,836.20
200,000	5,188.11	3,733.45	3,365.75	3,241.37
225,000	5,836.62	4,200.13	3,786.47	3,646.54
250,000	6,485.14	4,666.81	4,207.19	4,051.71
275,000	7,133.65	5,133.49	4,627.91	4,456.88
300,000	7,782.17	5,600.17	5,048.63	4,862.05
350,000	9,079.19	6,533.53	5,890.07	5,672.40
400,000	10,376.22	7,466.89	6,731.50	6,482.74
450,000	11,673.25	8,400.26	7,572.94	7,293.08
500,000	12,970.28	9,333.62	8,414.38	8,103.42
600,000	15,564.33	11,200.34	10,097.26	9,724.11
700,000	18,158.39	13,067.06	11,780.13	11,344.79
800,000	20,752.44	14,933.79	13,463.01	12,965.48
900,000	23,346.50	16,800.51	15,145.88	14,586.16
1,000,000	25,940.55	18,667.24	16,828.76	16,206.85

LOAN PAYMENT TABLE
INTEREST RATE: 19.00%
Monthly Payments - Fully Amortized

Loan Amount	19.00%	Term of Loan In Years		
	25	30	35	40
$ 1,000	15.98	15.89	15.85	15.84
5,000	79.88	79.44	79.27	79.21
10,000	159.77	158.89	158.55	158.42
25,000	399.42	397.22	396.37	396.04
40,000	639.07	635.56	634.20	633.67
50,000	798.84	794.45	792.75	792.09
75,000	1,198.26	1,191.67	1,189.12	1,188.13
100,000	1,597.68	1,588.89	1,585.49	1,584.17
125,000	1,997.10	1,986.12	1,981.87	1,980.22
150,000	2,396.52	2,383.34	2,378.24	2,376.26
175,000	2,795.94	2,780.56	2,774.62	2,772.31
200,000	3,195.36	3,177.78	3,170.99	3,168.35
225,000	3,594.78	3,575.01	3,567.36	3,564.39
250,000	3,994.20	3,972.23	3,963.74	3,960.44
275,000	4,393.62	4,369.45	4,360.11	4,356.48
300,000	4,793.04	4,766.68	4,756.48	4,752.52
350,000	5,591.88	5,561.12	5,549.23	5,544.61
400,000	6,390.72	6,355.57	6,341.98	6,336.70
450,000	7,189.56	7,150.02	7,134.73	7,128.79
500,000	7,988.40	7,944.46	7,927.47	7,920.87
600,000	9,586.08	9,533.35	9,512.97	9,505.05
700,000	11,183.76	11,122.25	11,098.46	11,089.22
800,000	12,781.44	12,711.14	12,683.96	12,673.40
900,000	14,379.12	14,300.03	14,269.45	14,257.57
1,000,000	15,976.80	15,888.92	15,854.95	15,841.75

LOAN PAYMENT TABLE
INTEREST RATE: 19.25%
Monthly Payments - Fully Amortized

Loan	19.25%	Term of Loan In Years		
Amount	5	10	15	20
$ 1,000	26.08	18.83	17.01	16.40
5,000	130.39	94.15	85.06	82.01
10,000	260.78	188.31	170.11	164.02
25,000	651.96	470.77	425.29	410.04
40,000	1,043.13	753.24	680.46	656.06
50,000	1,303.92	941.55	850.57	820.08
75,000	1,955.87	1,412.32	1,275.86	1,230.11
100,000	2,607.83	1,883.09	1,701.14	1,640.15
125,000	3,259.79	2,353.87	2,126.43	2,050.19
150,000	3,911.75	2,824.64	2,551.72	2,460.23
175,000	4,563.70	3,295.41	2,977.00	2,870.27
200,000	5,215.66	3,766.19	3,402.29	3,280.30
225,000	5,867.62	4,236.96	3,827.57	3,690.34
250,000	6,519.58	4,707.73	4,252.86	4,100.38
275,000	7,171.53	5,178.51	4,678.14	4,510.42
300,000	7,823.49	5,649.28	5,103.43	4,920.45
350,000	9,127.41	6,590.83	5,954.00	5,740.53
400,000	10,431.32	7,532.37	6,804.57	6,560.61
450,000	11,735.24	8,473.92	7,655.15	7,380.68
500,000	13,039.15	9,415.47	8,505.72	8,200.76
600,000	15,646.98	11,298.56	10,206.86	9,840.91
700,000	18,254.81	13,181.65	11,908.00	11,481.06
800,000	20,862.64	15,064.74	13,609.15	13,121.21
900,000	23,470.47	16,947.84	15,310.29	14,761.36
1,000,000	26,078.30	18,830.93	17,011.43	16,401.52

LOAN PAYMENT TABLE
INTEREST RATE: 19.25%
Monthly Payments - Fully Amortized

Loan Amount	19.25%	Term of Loan In Years		
	25	30	35	40
$ 1,000	16.18	16.09	16.06	16.05
5,000	80.89	80.47	80.31	80.25
10,000	161.78	160.94	160.62	160.49
25,000	404.46	402.35	401.54	401.23
40,000	647.13	643.76	642.47	641.98
50,000	808.91	804.70	803.09	802.47
75,000	1,213.37	1,207.05	1,204.63	1,203.70
100,000	1,617.83	1,609.40	1,606.18	1,604.94
125,000	2,022.28	2,011.75	2,007.72	2,006.17
150,000	2,426.74	2,414.10	2,409.26	2,407.41
175,000	2,831.20	2,816.44	2,810.81	2,808.64
200,000	3,235.65	3,218.79	3,212.35	3,209.88
225,000	3,640.11	3,621.14	3,613.89	3,611.11
250,000	4,044.57	4,023.49	4,015.44	4,012.35
275,000	4,449.03	4,425.84	4,416.98	4,413.58
300,000	4,853.48	4,828.19	4,818.53	4,814.82
350,000	5,662.40	5,632.89	5,621.61	5,617.29
400,000	6,471.31	6,437.59	6,424.70	6,419.76
450,000	7,280.22	7,242.29	7,227.79	7,222.23
500,000	8,089.14	8,046.98	8,030.88	8,024.70
600,000	9,706.96	9,656.38	9,637.05	9,629.64
700,000	11,324.79	11,265.78	11,243.23	11,234.57
800,000	12,942.62	12,875.17	12,849.40	12,839.51
900,000	14,560.45	14,484.57	14,455.58	14,444.45
1,000,000	16,178.27	16,093.97	16,061.76	16,049.39

Loan Payment

LOAN PAYMENT TABLE
INTEREST RATE: 19.50%
Monthly Payments - Fully Amortized

Loan Amount	19.50% 5	Term of Loan In Years 10	15	20
$ 1,000	26.22	19.00	17.19	16.60
5,000	131.08	94.98	85.97	82.98
10,000	262.16	189.95	171.95	165.97
25,000	655.41	474.88	429.87	414.92
40,000	1,048.66	759.81	687.79	663.87
50,000	1,310.82	949.76	859.74	829.83
75,000	1,966.23	1,424.64	1,289.60	1,244.75
100,000	2,621.64	1,899.52	1,719.47	1,659.66
125,000	3,277.06	2,374.40	2,149.34	2,074.58
150,000	3,932.47	2,849.28	2,579.21	2,489.50
175,000	4,587.88	3,324.16	3,009.07	2,904.41
200,000	5,243.29	3,799.04	3,438.94	3,319.33
225,000	5,898.70	4,273.92	3,868.81	3,734.25
250,000	6,554.11	4,748.81	4,298.68	4,149.16
275,000	7,209.52	5,223.69	4,728.54	4,564.08
300,000	7,864.93	5,698.57	5,158.41	4,978.99
350,000	9,175.76	6,648.33	6,018.15	5,808.83
400,000	10,486.58	7,598.09	6,877.88	6,638.66
450,000	11,797.40	8,547.85	7,737.62	7,468.49
500,000	13,108.22	9,497.61	8,597.35	8,298.32
600,000	15,729.87	11,397.13	10,316.82	9,957.99
700,000	18,351.51	13,296.65	12,036.29	11,617.65
800,000	20,973.16	15,196.18	13,755.76	13,277.32
900,000	23,594.80	17,095.70	15,475.23	14,936.98
1,000,000	26,216.45	18,995.22	17,194.70	16,596.65

LOAN PAYMENT TABLE
INTEREST RATE: 19.50%
Monthly Payments - Fully Amortized

Loan Amount	19.50% 25	Term of Loan In Years 30	35	40
$ 1,000	16.38	16.30	16.27	16.26
5,000	81.90	81.50	81.34	81.29
10,000	163.80	162.99	162.69	162.57
25,000	409.50	407.48	406.72	406.43
40,000	655.20	651.97	650.75	650.28
50,000	819.00	814.96	813.43	812.85
75,000	1,228.50	1,222.44	1,220.15	1,219.28
100,000	1,638.01	1,629.92	1,626.87	1,625.71
125,000	2,047.51	2,037.40	2,033.58	2,032.14
150,000	2,457.01	2,444.88	2,440.30	2,438.56
175,000	2,866.51	2,852.36	2,847.02	2,844.99
200,000	3,276.01	3,259.84	3,253.73	3,251.42
225,000	3,685.51	3,667.32	3,660.45	3,657.85
250,000	4,095.02	4,074.80	4,067.17	4,064.27
275,000	4,504.52	4,482.28	4,473.88	4,470.70
300,000	4,914.02	4,889.76	4,880.60	4,877.13
350,000	5,733.02	5,704.72	5,694.03	5,689.98
400,000	6,552.02	6,519.68	6,507.47	6,502.84
450,000	7,371.03	7,334.64	7,320.90	7,315.69
500,000	8,190.03	8,149.60	8,134.33	8,128.55
600,000	9,828.04	9,779.52	9,761.20	9,754.26
700,000	11,466.04	11,409.44	11,388.07	11,379.96
800,000	13,104.05	13,039.36	13,014.94	13,005.67
900,000	14,742.06	14,669.28	14,641.80	14,631.38
1,000,000	16,380.06	16,299.20	16,268.67	16,257.09

Loan Payment

LOAN PAYMENT TABLE
INTEREST RATE: 19.75%
Monthly Payments - Fully Amortized

Loan Amount	19.75% 5	Term of Loan In Years 10	15	20
$ 1,000	26.35	19.16	17.38	16.79
5,000	131.77	95.80	86.89	83.96
10,000	263.55	191.60	173.79	167.92
25,000	658.87	479.00	434.46	419.81
40,000	1,054.20	766.40	695.14	671.69
50,000	1,317.75	958.01	868.93	839.61
75,000	1,976.62	1,437.01	1,303.39	1,259.42
100,000	2,635.50	1,916.01	1,737.85	1,679.22
125,000	3,294.37	2,395.01	2,172.32	2,099.03
150,000	3,953.25	2,874.02	2,606.78	2,518.83
175,000	4,612.12	3,353.02	3,041.25	2,938.64
200,000	5,270.99	3,832.02	3,475.71	3,358.45
225,000	5,929.87	4,311.02	3,910.17	3,778.25
250,000	6,588.74	4,790.03	4,344.64	4,198.06
275,000	7,247.62	5,269.03	4,779.10	4,617.86
300,000	7,906.49	5,748.03	5,213.56	5,037.67
350,000	9,224.24	6,706.04	6,082.49	5,877.28
400,000	10,541.99	7,664.04	6,951.42	6,716.89
450,000	11,859.74	8,622.05	7,820.35	7,556.50
500,000	13,177.49	9,580.05	8,689.27	8,396.11
600,000	15,812.98	11,496.06	10,427.13	10,075.34
700,000	18,448.48	13,412.07	12,164.98	11,754.56
800,000	21,083.98	15,328.08	13,902.84	13,433.78
900,000	23,719.47	17,244.09	15,640.69	15,113.00
1,000,000	26,354.97	19,160.10	17,378.55	16,792.23

LOAN PAYMENT TABLE
INTEREST RATE: 19.75%
Monthly Payments - Fully Amortized

Loan Amount	19.75%	Term of Loan In Years		
	25	30	35	40
$ 1,000	16.58	16.50	16.48	16.46
5,000	82.91	82.52	82.38	82.32
10,000	165.82	165.05	164.76	164.65
25,000	414.55	412.62	411.89	411.62
40,000	663.29	660.18	659.03	658.59
50,000	829.11	825.23	823.78	823.24
75,000	1,243.66	1,237.85	1,235.68	1,234.86
100,000	1,658.21	1,650.46	1,647.57	1,646.48
125,000	2,072.77	2,063.08	2,059.46	2,058.11
150,000	2,487.32	2,475.69	2,471.35	2,469.73
175,000	2,901.88	2,888.31	2,883.24	2,881.35
200,000	3,316.43	3,300.92	3,295.14	3,292.97
225,000	3,730.98	3,713.54	3,707.03	3,704.59
250,000	4,145.54	4,126.15	4,118.92	4,116.21
275,000	4,560.09	4,538.77	4,530.81	4,527.83
300,000	4,974.64	4,951.38	4,942.70	4,939.45
350,000	5,803.75	5,776.61	5,766.49	5,762.70
400,000	6,632.86	6,601.84	6,590.27	6,585.94
450,000	7,461.97	7,427.07	7,414.06	7,409.18
500,000	8,291.07	8,252.30	8,237.84	8,232.42
600,000	9,949.29	9,902.77	9,885.41	9,878.91
700,000	11,607.50	11,553.23	11,532.98	11,525.39
800,000	13,265.72	13,203.69	13,180.54	13,171.87
900,000	14,923.93	14,854.15	14,828.11	14,818.36
1,000,000	16,582.15	16,504.61	16,475.68	16,464.84

LOAN PAYMENT TABLE
INTEREST RATE: 20.00%
Monthly Payments - Fully Amortized

Loan Amount	20.00% 5	Term of Loan In Years 10	15	20
$ 1,000	26.49	19.33	17.56	16.99
5,000	132.47	96.63	87.81	84.94
10,000	264.94	193.26	175.63	169.88
25,000	662.35	483.14	439.07	424.71
40,000	1,059.76	773.02	702.52	679.53
50,000	1,324.69	966.28	878.15	849.41
75,000	1,987.04	1,449.42	1,317.22	1,274.12
100,000	2,649.39	1,932.56	1,756.30	1,698.82
125,000	3,311.74	2,415.70	2,195.37	2,123.53
150,000	3,974.08	2,898.84	2,634.44	2,548.24
175,000	4,636.43	3,381.97	3,073.52	2,972.94
200,000	5,298.78	3,865.11	3,512.59	3,397.65
225,000	5,961.12	4,348.25	3,951.67	3,822.36
250,000	6,623.47	4,831.39	4,390.74	4,247.06
275,000	7,285.82	5,314.53	4,829.82	4,671.77
300,000	7,948.17	5,797.67	5,268.89	5,096.47
350,000	9,272.86	6,763.95	6,147.04	5,945.89
400,000	10,597.55	7,730.23	7,025.19	6,795.30
450,000	11,922.25	8,696.51	7,903.33	7,644.71
500,000	13,246.94	9,662.78	8,781.48	8,494.12
600,000	15,896.33	11,595.34	10,537.78	10,192.95
700,000	18,545.72	13,527.90	12,294.08	11,891.77
800,000	21,195.11	15,460.45	14,050.37	13,590.60
900,000	23,844.50	17,393.01	15,806.67	15,289.42
1,000,000	26,493.88	19,325.57	17,562.97	16,988.25

LOAN PAYMENT TABLE
INTEREST RATE: 20.00%
Monthly Payments - Fully Amortized

Loan Amount	20.00%	Term of Loan In Years		
	25	30	35	40
$ 1,000	16.78	16.71	16.68	16.67
5,000	83.92	83.55	83.41	83.36
10,000	167.85	167.10	166.83	166.73
25,000	419.61	417.75	417.07	416.82
40,000	671.38	668.41	667.31	666.91
50,000	839.23	835.51	834.14	833.63
75,000	1,258.84	1,253.26	1,251.21	1,250.45
100,000	1,678.45	1,671.02	1,668.28	1,667.26
125,000	2,098.06	2,088.77	2,085.35	2,084.08
150,000	2,517.68	2,506.53	2,502.42	2,500.90
175,000	2,937.29	2,924.28	2,919.49	2,917.71
200,000	3,356.90	3,342.04	3,336.56	3,334.53
225,000	3,776.52	3,759.79	3,753.63	3,751.34
250,000	4,196.13	4,177.55	4,170.70	4,168.16
275,000	4,615.74	4,595.30	4,587.77	4,584.98
300,000	5,035.36	5,013.06	5,004.83	5,001.79
350,000	5,874.58	5,848.57	5,838.97	5,835.42
400,000	6,713.81	6,684.07	6,673.11	6,669.06
450,000	7,553.03	7,519.58	7,507.25	7,502.69
500,000	8,392.26	8,355.09	8,341.39	8,336.32
600,000	10,070.71	10,026.11	10,009.67	10,003.58
700,000	11,749.16	11,697.13	11,677.95	11,670.85
800,000	13,427.61	13,368.15	13,346.23	13,338.11
900,000	15,106.07	15,039.17	15,014.50	15,005.38
1,000,000	16,784.52	16,710.19	16,682.78	16,672.64

Loan Payment

EFFECTIVE LOAN INTEREST RATE
INCLUSIVE OF POINTS
10 YEAR TERM - HELD TO MATURITY

10 Year Contract Rate	Points				
	1	2	3	4	5
5.00%	5.22	5.43	5.65	5.86	6.07
5.25%	5.47	5.68	5.90	6.11	6.32
5.50%	5.72	5.94	6.15	6.37	6.58
5.75%	5.97	6.19	6.40	6.62	6.83
6.00%	6.22	6.44	6.66	6.87	7.09
6.25%	6.47	6.69	6.91	7.13	7.34
6.50%	6.72	6.94	7.16	7.38	7.60
6.75%	6.97	7.20	7.42	7.64	7.86
7.00%	7.22	7.45	7.67	7.89	8.11
7.25%	7.48	7.70	7.92	8.15	8.37
7.50%	7.73	7.95	8.18	8.40	8.62
7.75%	7.98	8.20	8.43	8.65	8.88
8.00%	8.23	8.46	8.68	8.91	9.13
8.25%	8.48	8.71	8.94	9.16	9.39
8.50%	8.73	8.96	9.19	9.42	9.64
8.75%	8.98	9.21	9.44	9.67	9.90
9.00%	9.23	9.47	9.70	9.93	10.15
9.25%	9.48	9.72	9.95	10.18	10.41
9.50%	9.74	9.97	10.20	10.44	10.67
9.75%	9.99	10.22	10.46	10.69	10.92
10.00%	10.24	10.47	10.71	10.94	11.18
10.25%	10.49	10.73	10.96	11.20	11.43
10.50%	10.74	10.98	11.22	11.45	11.69
10.75%	10.99	11.23	11.47	11.71	11.95

EFFECTIVE LOAN INTEREST RATE
INCLUSIVE OF POINTS
10 YEAR TERM - HELD TO MATURITY

10 Year Contract Rate	Points				
	1	2	3	4	5
11.00%	11.24	11.48	11.72	11.96	12.20
11.25%	11.49	11.74	11.98	12.22	12.46
11.50%	11.75	11.99	12.23	12.47	12.71
11.75%	12.00	12.24	12.49	12.73	12.97
12.00%	12.25	12.49	12.74	12.98	13.23
12.25%	12.50	12.75	12.99	13.24	13.48
12.50%	12.75	13.00	13.25	13.49	13.74
12.75%	13.00	13.25	13.50	13.75	13.99
13.00%	13.25	13.50	13.75	14.00	14.25
13.25%	13.50	13.76	14.01	14.26	14.51
13.50%	13.76	14.01	14.26	14.51	14.76
13.75%	14.01	14.26	14.52	14.77	15.02
14.00%	14.26	14.51	14.77	15.02	15.28
14.25%	14.51	14.77	15.02	15.28	15.53
14.50%	14.76	15.02	15.28	15.53	15.79
14.75%	15.01	15.27	15.53	15.79	16.05
15.00%	15.26	15.52	15.78	16.04	16.30
15.25%	15.51	15.78	16.04	16.30	16.56
15.50%	15.77	16.03	16.29	16.55	16.82
15.75%	16.02	16.28	16.55	16.81	17.07
16.00%	16.27	16.54	16.80	17.07	17.33
16.25%	16.52	16.79	17.06	17.32	17.59
16.50%	16.77	17.04	17.31	17.58	17.84
16.75%	17.02	17.29	17.56	17.83	18.10

Interest Rate With Points

EFFECTIVE LOAN INTEREST RATE
INCLUSIVE OF POINTS
10 YEAR TERM - HELD TO MATURITY

10 Year Contract Rate	Points				
	1	2	3	4	5
17.00%	17.27	17.55	17.82	18.09	18.36
17.25%	17.53	17.80	18.07	18.34	18.61
17.50%	17.78	18.05	18.33	18.60	18.87
17.75%	18.03	18.30	18.58	18.85	19.13
18.00%	18.28	18.56	18.83	19.11	19.38
18.25%	18.53	18.81	19.09	19.37	19.64
18.50%	18.78	19.06	19.34	19.62	19.90
18.75%	19.03	19.32	19.60	19.88	20.16
19.00%	19.29	19.57	19.85	20.13	20.41
19.25%	19.54	19.82	20.11	20.39	20.67
19.50%	19.79	20.07	20.36	20.64	20.93
19.75%	20.04	20.33	20.61	20.90	21.19
20.00%	20.29	20.58	20.87	21.16	21.44
20.25%	20.54	20.83	21.12	21.41	21.70
20.50%	20.79	21.09	21.38	21.67	21.96
20.75%	21.05	21.34	21.63	21.92	22.22
21.00%	21.30	21.59	21.89	22.18	22.47
21.25%	21.55	21.85	22.14	22.44	22.73
21.50%	21.80	22.10	22.40	22.69	22.99
21.75%	22.05	22.35	22.65	22.95	23.25
22.00%	22.30	22.60	22.91	23.21	23.50
22.25%	22.55	22.86	23.16	23.46	23.76
22.50%	22.81	23.11	23.41	23.72	24.02
22.75%	23.06	23.36	23.67	23.97	24.28

EFFECTIVE LOAN INTEREST RATE
INCLUSIVE OF POINTS
15 YEAR TERM - HELD TO MATURITY

15 Year Contract Rate	Points				
	1	2	3	4	5
5.00%	5.15	5.30	5.45	5.60	5.75
5.25%	5.40	5.55	5.70	5.85	6.00
5.50%	5.65	5.81	5.96	6.11	6.26
5.75%	5.90	6.06	6.21	6.36	6.51
6.00%	6.16	6.31	6.46	6.62	6.77
6.25%	6.41	6.56	6.72	6.87	7.03
6.50%	6.66	6.82	6.97	7.13	7.28
6.75%	6.91	7.07	7.23	7.38	7.54
7.00%	7.16	7.32	7.48	7.64	7.79
7.25%	7.41	7.57	7.73	7.89	8.05
7.50%	7.66	7.82	7.99	8.15	8.31
7.75%	7.91	8.08	8.24	8.40	8.56
8.00%	8.17	8.33	8.49	8.66	8.82
8.25%	8.42	8.58	8.75	8.91	9.07
8.50%	8.67	8.83	9.00	9.17	9.33
8.75%	8.92	9.09	9.25	9.42	9.59
9.00%	9.17	9.34	9.51	9.68	9.84
9.25%	9.42	9.59	9.76	9.93	10.10
9.50%	9.67	9.84	10.02	10.19	10.36
9.75%	9.92	10.10	10.27	10.44	10.61
10.00%	10.18	10.35	10.52	10.70	10.87
10.25%	10.43	10.60	10.78	10.95	11.12
10.50%	10.68	10.85	11.03	11.21	11.38
10.75%	10.93	11.11	11.29	11.46	11.64

Interest Rate With Points

EFFECTIVE LOAN INTEREST RATE
INCLUSIVE OF POINTS
15 YEAR TERM - HELD TO MATURITY

15 Year Contract Rate	Points				
	1	2	3	4	5
11.00%	11.18	11.36	11.54	11.72	11.90
11.25%	11.43	11.61	11.79	11.97	12.15
11.50%	11.68	11.87	12.05	12.23	12.41
11.75%	11.93	12.12	12.30	12.48	12.67
12.00%	12.19	12.37	12.56	12.74	12.92
12.25%	12.44	12.62	12.81	13.00	13.18
12.50%	12.69	12.88	13.06	13.25	13.44
12.75%	12.94	13.13	13.32	13.51	13.69
13.00%	13.19	13.38	13.57	13.76	13.95
13.25%	13.44	13.64	13.83	14.02	14.21
13.50%	13.69	13.89	14.08	14.27	14.47
13.75%	13.95	14.14	14.34	14.53	14.72
14.00%	14.20	14.39	14.59	14.79	14.98
14.25%	14.45	14.65	14.85	15.04	15.24
14.50%	14.70	14.90	15.10	15.30	15.50
14.75%	14.95	15.15	15.35	15.56	15.75
15.00%	15.20	15.41	15.61	15.81	16.01
15.25%	15.46	15.66	15.86	16.07	16.27
15.50%	15.71	15.91	16.12	16.32	16.53
15.75%	15.96	16.17	16.37	16.58	16.79
16.00%	16.21	16.42	16.63	16.84	17.04
16.25%	16.46	16.67	16.88	17.09	17.30
16.50%	16.71	16.93	17.14	17.35	17.56
16.75%	16.97	17.18	17.39	17.61	17.82

Interest Rate With Points

EFFECTIVE LOAN INTEREST RATE
INCLUSIVE OF POINTS
15 YEAR TERM - HELD TO MATURITY

15 Year Contract Rate	Points				
	1	2	3	4	5
17.00%	17.22	17.43	17.65	17.86	18.08
17.25%	17.47	17.69	17.90	18.12	18.34
17.50%	17.72	17.94	18.16	18.38	18.59
17.75%	17.97	18.19	18.41	18.63	18.85
18.00%	18.22	18.45	18.67	18.89	19.11
18.25%	18.48	18.70	18.92	19.15	19.37
18.50%	18.73	18.95	19.18	19.40	19.63
18.75%	18.98	19.21	19.43	19.66	19.89
19.00%	19.23	19.46	19.69	19.92	20.15
19.25%	19.48	19.71	19.94	20.17	20.40
19.50%	19.73	19.97	20.20	20.43	20.66
19.75%	19.99	20.22	20.45	20.69	20.92
20.00%	20.24	20.47	20.71	20.95	21.18
20.25%	20.49	20.73	20.97	21.20	21.44
20.50%	20.74	20.98	21.22	21.46	21.70
20.75%	20.99	21.23	21.48	21.72	21.96
21.00%	21.24	21.49	21.73	21.97	22.22
21.25%	21.50	21.74	21.99	22.23	22.48
21.50%	21.75	22.00	22.24	22.49	22.74
21.75%	22.00	22.25	22.50	22.75	22.99
22.00%	22.25	22.50	22.75	23.00	23.25
22.25%	22.50	22.76	23.01	23.26	23.51
22.50%	22.76	23.01	23.27	23.52	23.77
22.75%	23.01	23.26	23.52	23.78	24.03

Interest Rate With Points

EFFECTIVE LOAN INTEREST RATE
INCLUSIVE OF POINTS
20 YEAR TERM - HELD TO MATURITY

20 Year Contract Rate	Points				
	1	2	3	4	5
5.00%	5.12	5.24	5.36	5.47	5.59
5.25%	5.37	5.49	5.61	5.73	5.85
5.50%	5.62	5.74	5.86	5.98	6.10
5.75%	5.87	5.99	6.12	6.24	6.36
6.00%	6.12	6.25	6.37	6.49	6.61
6.25%	6.38	6.50	6.62	6.75	6.87
6.50%	6.63	6.75	6.88	7.00	7.13
6.75%	6.88	7.00	7.13	7.26	7.38
7.00%	7.13	7.26	7.38	7.51	7.64
7.25%	7.38	7.51	7.64	7.77	7.89
7.50%	7.63	7.76	7.89	8.02	8.15
7.75%	7.88	8.01	8.15	8.28	8.41
8.00%	8.13	8.27	8.40	8.53	8.66
8.25%	8.39	8.52	8.65	8.79	8.92
8.50%	8.64	8.77	8.91	9.04	9.18
8.75%	8.89	9.03	9.16	9.30	9.44
9.00%	9.14	9.28	9.42	9.55	9.69
9.25%	9.39	9.53	9.67	9.81	9.95
9.50%	9.64	9.78	9.93	10.07	10.21
9.75%	9.89	10.04	10.18	10.32	10.46
10.00%	10.15	10.29	10.43	10.58	10.72
10.25%	10.40	10.54	10.69	10.83	10.98
10.50%	10.65	10.80	10.94	11.09	11.24
10.75%	10.90	11.05	11.20	11.35	11.49

EFFECTIVE LOAN INTEREST RATE
INCLUSIVE OF POINTS
20 YEAR TERM - HELD TO MATURITY

20 Year Contract Rate	Points				
	1	2	3	4	5
11.00%	11.15	11.30	11.45	11.60	11.75
11.25%	11.40	11.56	11.71	11.86	12.01
11.50%	11.65	11.81	11.96	12.11	12.27
11.75%	11.91	12.06	12.22	12.37	12.52
12.00%	12.16	12.31	12.47	12.63	12.78
12.25%	12.41	12.57	12.73	12.88	13.04
12.50%	12.66	12.82	12.98	13.14	13.30
12.75%	12.91	13.07	13.24	13.40	13.56
13.00%	13.16	13.33	13.49	13.65	13.82
13.25%	13.42	13.58	13.75	13.91	14.07
13.50%	13.67	13.83	14.00	14.17	14.33
13.75%	13.92	14.09	14.26	14.42	14.59
14.00%	14.17	14.34	14.51	14.68	14.85
14.25%	14.42	14.59	14.77	14.94	15.11
14.50%	14.67	14.85	15.02	15.19	15.37
14.75%	14.93	15.10	15.28	15.45	15.63
15.00%	15.18	15.36	15.53	15.71	15.88
15.25%	15.43	15.61	15.79	15.97	16.14
15.50%	15.68	15.86	16.04	16.22	16.40
15.75%	15.93	16.12	16.30	16.48	16.66
16.00%	16.19	16.37	16.55	16.74	16.92
16.25%	16.44	16.62	16.81	17.00	17.18
16.50%	16.69	16.88	17.07	17.25	17.44
16.75%	16.94	17.13	17.32	17.51	17.70

Interest Rate With Points

EFFECTIVE LOAN INTEREST RATE
INCLUSIVE OF POINTS
20 YEAR TERM - HELD TO MATURITY

20 Year Contract Rate	Points 1	2	3	4	5
17.00%	17.19	17.38	17.58	17.77	17.96
17.25%	17.44	17.64	17.83	18.03	18.22
17.50%	17.70	17.89	18.09	18.28	18.48
17.75%	17.95	18.15	18.34	18.54	18.74
18.00%	18.20	18.40	18.60	18.80	19.00
18.25%	18.45	18.65	18.86	19.06	19.26
18.50%	18.70	18.91	19.11	19.31	19.52
18.75%	18.96	19.16	19.37	19.57	19.78
19.00%	19.21	19.42	19.62	19.83	20.04
19.25%	19.46	19.67	19.88	20.09	20.30
19.50%	19.71	19.92	20.14	20.35	20.56
19.75%	19.96	20.18	20.39	20.60	20.82
20.00%	20.22	20.43	20.65	20.86	21.08
20.25%	20.47	20.69	20.90	21.12	21.34
20.50%	20.72	20.94	21.16	21.38	21.60
20.75%	20.97	21.19	21.42	21.64	21.86
21.00%	21.22	21.45	21.67	21.90	22.12
21.25%	21.48	21.70	21.93	22.15	22.38
21.50%	21.73	21.96	22.18	22.41	22.64
21.75%	21.98	22.21	22.44	22.67	22.90
22.00%	22.23	22.47	22.70	22.93	23.16
22.25%	22.48	22.72	22.95	23.19	23.42
22.50%	22.74	22.97	23.21	23.45	23.68
22.75%	22.99	23.23	23.47	23.71	23.94

EFFECTIVE LOAN INTEREST RATE
INCLUSIVE OF POINTS
25 YEAR TERM - HELD TO MATURITY

25 Year Contract Rate	Points				
	1	2	3	4	5
5.00%	5.10	5.20	5.30	5.40	5.50
5.25%	5.35	5.45	5.55	5.65	5.75
5.50%	5.60	5.70	5.81	5.91	6.01
5.75%	5.85	5.96	6.06	6.16	6.26
6.00%	6.11	6.21	6.31	6.42	6.52
6.25%	6.36	6.46	6.57	6.67	6.78
6.50%	6.61	6.72	6.82	6.93	7.03
6.75%	6.86	6.97	7.08	7.18	7.29
7.00%	7.11	7.22	7.33	7.44	7.55
7.25%	7.36	7.47	7.58	7.69	7.81
7.50%	7.61	7.73	7.84	7.95	8.06
7.75%	7.86	7.98	8.09	8.21	8.32
8.00%	8.12	8.23	8.35	8.46	8.58
8.25%	8.37	8.49	8.60	8.72	8.83
8.50%	8.62	8.74	8.86	8.97	9.09
8.75%	8.87	8.99	9.11	9.23	9.35
9.00%	9.12	9.24	9.37	9.49	9.61
9.25%	9.37	9.50	9.62	9.74	9.86
9.50%	9.63	9.75	9.88	10.00	10.12
9.75%	9.88	10.00	10.13	10.26	10.38
10.00%	10.13	10.26	10.38	10.51	10.64
10.25%	10.38	10.51	10.64	10.77	10.90
10.50%	10.63	10.76	10.89	11.03	11.16
10.75%	10.88	11.02	11.15	11.28	11.41

Interest Rate With Points

EFFECTIVE LOAN INTEREST RATE
INCLUSIVE OF POINTS
25 YEAR TERM - HELD TO MATURITY

25 Year Contract Rate	Points				
	1	2	3	4	5
11.00%	11.14	11.27	11.40	11.54	11.67
11.25%	11.39	11.52	11.66	11.80	11.93
11.50%	11.64	11.78	11.92	12.05	12.19
11.75%	11.89	12.03	12.17	12.31	12.45
12.00%	12.14	12.28	12.43	12.57	12.71
12.25%	12.39	12.54	12.68	12.82	12.97
12.50%	12.65	12.79	12.94	13.08	13.23
12.75%	12.90	13.05	13.19	13.34	13.48
13.00%	13.15	13.30	13.45	13.60	13.74
13.25%	13.40	13.55	13.70	13.85	14.00
13.50%	13.65	13.81	13.96	14.11	14.26
13.75%	13.91	14.06	14.21	14.37	14.52
14.00%	14.16	14.31	14.47	14.63	14.78
14.25%	14.41	14.57	14.73	14.88	15.04
14.50%	14.66	14.82	14.98	15.14	15.30
14.75%	14.91	15.08	15.24	15.40	15.56
15.00%	15.16	15.33	15.49	15.66	15.82
15.25%	15.42	15.58	15.75	15.92	16.08
15.50%	15.67	15.84	16.01	16.17	16.34
15.75%	15.92	16.09	16.26	16.43	16.60
16.00%	16.17	16.35	16.52	16.69	16.86
16.25%	16.42	16.60	16.77	16.95	17.12
16.50%	16.68	16.85	17.03	17.21	17.38
16.75%	16.93	17.11	17.29	17.46	17.64

Interest Rate With Points

EFFECTIVE LOAN INTEREST RATE
INCLUSIVE OF POINTS
25 YEAR TERM - HELD TO MATURITY

25 Year Contract Rate	Points				
	1	2	3	4	5
17.00%	17.18	17.36	17.54	17.72	17.90
17.25%	17.43	17.62	17.80	17.98	18.16
17.50%	17.69	17.87	18.06	18.24	18.42
17.75%	17.94	18.12	18.31	18.50	18.68
18.00%	18.19	18.38	18.57	18.76	18.95
18.25%	18.44	18.63	18.82	19.02	19.21
18.50%	18.69	18.89	19.08	19.27	19.47
18.75%	18.95	19.14	19.34	19.53	19.73
19.00%	19.20	19.40	19.59	19.79	19.99
19.25%	19.45	19.65	19.85	20.05	20.25
19.50%	19.70	19.91	20.11	20.31	20.51
19.75%	19.95	20.16	20.36	20.57	20.77
20.00%	20.21	20.41	20.62	20.83	21.03
20.25%	20.46	20.67	20.88	21.09	21.29
20.50%	20.71	20.92	21.13	21.34	21.56
20.75%	20.96	21.18	21.39	21.60	21.82
21.00%	21.22	21.43	21.65	21.86	22.08
21.25%	21.47	21.69	21.90	22.12	22.34
21.50%	21.72	21.94	22.16	22.38	22.60
21.75%	21.97	22.20	22.42	22.64	22.86
22.00%	22.23	22.45	22.67	22.90	23.12
22.25%	22.48	22.70	22.93	23.16	23.39
22.50%	22.73	22.96	23.19	23.42	23.65
22.75%	22.98	23.21	23.45	23.68	23.91

Interest Rate With Points

EFFECTIVE LOAN INTEREST RATE
INCLUSIVE OF POINTS
30 YEAR TERM - HELD TO MATURITY

30 Year Contract Rate	Points				
	1	2	3	4	5
5.00%	5.09	5.17	5.26	5.35	5.43
5.25%	5.34	5.43	5.52	5.60	5.69
5.50%	5.59	5.68	5.77	5.86	5.95
5.75%	5.84	5.93	6.02	6.11	6.20
6.00%	6.09	6.19	6.28	6.37	6.46
6.25%	6.34	6.44	6.53	6.63	6.72
6.50%	6.60	6.69	6.79	6.88	6.98
6.75%	6.85	6.94	7.04	7.14	7.23
7.00%	7.10	7.20	7.30	7.39	7.49
7.25%	7.35	7.45	7.55	7.65	7.75
7.50%	7.60	7.70	7.80	7.91	8.01
7.75%	7.85	7.96	8.06	8.16	8.26
8.00%	8.11	8.21	8.31	8.42	8.52
8.25%	8.36	8.46	8.57	8.67	8.78
8.50%	8.61	8.72	8.82	8.93	9.04
8.75%	8.86	8.97	9.08	9.19	9.30
9.00%	9.11	9.22	9.33	9.44	9.55
9.25%	9.36	9.48	9.59	9.70	9.81
9.50%	9.62	9.73	9.84	9.96	10.07
9.75%	9.87	9.98	10.10	10.22	10.33
10.00%	10.12	10.24	10.35	10.47	10.59
10.25%	10.37	10.49	10.61	10.73	10.85
10.50%	10.62	10.74	10.87	10.99	11.11
10.75%	10.87	11.00	11.12	11.24	11.37

EFFECTIVE LOAN INTEREST RATE
INCLUSIVE OF POINTS
30 YEAR TERM - HELD TO MATURITY

30 Year Contract Rate	Points				
	1	2	3	4	5
11.00%	11.13	11.25	11.38	11.50	11.63
11.25%	11.38	11.51	11.63	11.76	11.89
11.50%	11.63	11.76	11.89	12.02	12.15
11.75%	11.88	12.01	12.14	12.27	12.40
12.00%	12.13	12.27	12.40	12.53	12.66
12.25%	12.39	12.52	12.66	12.79	12.92
12.50%	12.64	12.77	12.91	13.05	13.18
12.75%	12.89	13.03	13.17	13.31	13.44
13.00%	13.14	13.28	13.42	13.56	13.70
13.25%	13.39	13.54	13.68	13.82	13.96
13.50%	13.65	13.79	13.94	14.08	14.22
13.75%	13.90	14.04	14.19	14.34	14.49
14.00%	14.15	14.30	14.45	14.60	14.75
14.25%	14.40	14.55	14.70	14.86	15.01
14.50%	14.65	14.81	14.96	15.11	15.27
14.75%	14.91	15.06	15.22	15.37	15.53
15.00%	15.16	15.32	15.47	15.63	15.79
15.25%	15.41	15.57	15.73	15.89	16.05
15.50%	15.66	15.82	15.99	16.15	16.31
15.75%	15.91	16.08	16.24	16.41	16.57
16.00%	16.17	16.33	16.50	16.67	16.83
16.25%	16.42	16.59	16.76	16.92	17.09
16.50%	16.67	16.84	17.01	17.18	17.35
16.75%	16.92	17.10	17.27	17.44	17.61

Interest Rate With Points

EFFECTIVE LOAN INTEREST RATE
INCLUSIVE OF POINTS
30 YEAR TERM - HELD TO MATURITY

30 Year Contract Rate	Points				
	1	2	3	4	5
17.00%	17.18	17.35	17.53	17.70	17.88
17.25%	17.43	17.61	17.78	17.96	18.14
17.50%	17.68	17.86	18.04	18.22	18.40
17.75%	17.93	18.11	18.30	18.48	18.66
18.00%	18.18	18.37	18.55	18.74	18.92
18.25%	18.44	18.62	18.81	19.00	19.18
18.50%	18.69	18.88	19.07	19.26	19.44
18.75%	18.94	19.13	19.32	19.51	19.71
19.00%	19.19	19.39	19.58	19.77	19.97
19.25%	19.45	19.64	19.84	20.03	20.23
19.50%	19.70	19.90	20.09	20.29	20.49
19.75%	19.95	20.15	20.35	20.55	20.75
20.00%	20.20	20.41	20.61	20.81	21.01
20.25%	20.46	20.66	20.87	21.07	21.28
20.50%	20.71	20.92	21.12	21.33	21.54
20.75%	20.96	21.17	21.38	21.59	21.80
21.00%	21.21	21.42	21.64	21.85	22.06
21.25%	21.46	21.68	21.89	22.11	22.32
21.50%	21.72	21.93	22.15	22.37	22.59
21.75%	21.97	22.19	22.41	22.63	22.85
22.00%	22.22	22.44	22.67	22.89	23.11
22.25%	22.47	22.70	22.92	23.15	23.37
22.50%	22.73	22.95	23.18	23.41	23.63
22.75%	22.98	23.21	23.44	23.67	23.90

EFFECTIVE LOAN INTEREST RATE
INCLUSIVE OF POINTS
35 YEAR TERM - HELD TO MATURITY

35 Year Contract Rate	Points				
	1	2	3	4	5
5.00%	5.08	5.16	5.24	5.31	5.39
5.25%	5.33	5.41	5.49	5.57	5.65
5.50%	5.58	5.66	5.74	5.83	5.91
5.75%	5.83	5.92	6.00	6.08	6.16
6.00%	6.08	6.17	6.25	6.34	6.42
6.25%	6.34	6.42	6.51	6.59	6.68
6.50%	6.59	6.68	6.76	6.85	6.94
6.75%	6.84	6.93	7.02	7.11	7.19
7.00%	7.09	7.18	7.27	7.36	7.45
7.25%	7.34	7.43	7.53	7.62	7.71
7.50%	7.59	7.69	7.78	7.88	7.97
7.75%	7.85	7.94	8.04	8.13	8.23
8.00%	8.10	8.19	8.29	8.39	8.49
8.25%	8.35	8.45	8.55	8.65	8.74
8.50%	8.60	8.70	8.80	8.90	9.00
8.75%	8.85	8.96	9.06	9.16	9.26
9.00%	9.10	9.21	9.31	9.42	9.52
9.25%	9.36	9.46	9.57	9.67	9.78
9.50%	9.61	9.72	9.82	9.93	10.04
9.75%	9.86	9.97	10.08	10.19	10.30
10.00%	10.11	10.22	10.34	10.45	10.56
10.25%	10.36	10.48	10.59	10.70	10.82
10.50%	10.62	10.73	10.85	10.96	11.08
10.75%	10.87	10.99	11.10	11.22	11.34

Interest Rate With Points

EFFECTIVE LOAN INTEREST RATE
INCLUSIVE OF POINTS
35 YEAR TERM - HELD TO MATURITY

35 Year Contract Rate	Points				
	1	2	3	4	5
11.00%	11.12	11.24	11.36	11.48	11.60
11.25%	11.37	11.49	11.62	11.74	11.86
11.50%	11.62	11.75	11.87	11.99	12.12
11.75%	11.88	12.00	12.13	12.25	12.38
12.00%	12.13	12.26	12.38	12.51	12.64
12.25%	12.38	12.51	12.64	12.77	12.90
12.50%	12.63	12.76	12.90	13.03	13.16
12.75%	12.88	13.02	13.15	13.29	13.42
13.00%	13.14	13.27	13.41	13.55	13.68
13.25%	13.39	13.53	13.67	13.80	13.94
13.50%	13.64	13.78	13.92	14.06	14.20
13.75%	13.89	14.04	14.18	14.32	14.46
14.00%	14.15	14.29	14.44	14.58	14.73
14.25%	14.40	14.54	14.69	14.84	14.99
14.50%	14.65	14.80	14.95	15.10	15.25
14.75%	14.90	15.05	15.21	15.36	15.51
15.00%	15.15	15.31	15.46	15.62	15.77
15.25%	15.41	15.56	15.72	15.88	16.03
15.50%	15.66	15.82	15.98	16.13	16.29
15.75%	15.91	16.07	16.23	16.39	16.55
16.00%	16.16	16.33	16.49	16.65	16.82
16.25%	16.42	16.58	16.75	16.91	17.08
16.50%	16.67	16.84	17.00	17.17	17.34
16.75%	16.92	17.09	17.26	17.43	17.60

EFFECTIVE LOAN INTEREST RATE
INCLUSIVE OF POINTS
35 YEAR TERM - HELD TO MATURITY

35 Year Contract Rate	Points				
	1	2	3	4	5
17.00%	17.17	17.35	17.52	17.69	17.86
17.25%	17.43	17.60	17.77	17.95	18.12
17.50%	17.68	17.85	18.03	18.21	18.39
17.75%	17.93	18.11	18.29	18.47	18.65
18.00%	18.18	18.36	18.55	18.73	18.91
18.25%	18.43	18.62	18.80	18.99	19.17
18.50%	18.69	18.87	19.06	19.25	19.43
18.75%	18.94	19.13	19.32	19.51	19.70
19.00%	19.19	19.38	19.57	19.77	19.96
19.25%	19.44	19.64	19.83	20.03	20.22
19.50%	19.70	19.89	20.09	20.29	20.48
19.75%	19.95	20.15	20.35	20.55	20.74
20.00%	20.20	20.40	20.60	20.80	21.01
20.25%	20.45	20.66	20.86	21.06	21.27
20.50%	20.71	20.91	21.12	21.32	21.53
20.75%	20.96	21.17	21.38	21.58	21.79
21.00%	21.21	21.42	21.63	21.84	22.05
21.25%	21.46	21.68	21.89	22.10	22.32
21.50%	21.72	21.93	22.15	22.36	22.58
21.75%	21.97	22.19	22.40	22.62	22.84
22.00%	22.22	22.44	22.66	22.88	23.10
22.25%	22.47	22.70	22.92	23.14	23.37
22.50%	22.73	22.95	23.18	23.40	23.63
22.75%	22.98	23.21	23.43	23.66	23.89

Interest Rate With Points

EFFECTIVE LOAN INTEREST RATE
INCLUSIVE OF POINTS
40 YEAR TERM - HELD TO MATURITY

40 Year Contract Rate	Points				
	1	2	3	4	5
5.00%	5.07	5.15	5.22	5.29	5.36
5.25%	5.32	5.40	5.47	5.54	5.62
5.50%	5.58	5.65	5.73	5.80	5.88
5.75%	5.83	5.90	5.98	6.06	6.13
6.00%	6.08	6.16	6.24	6.31	6.39
6.25%	6.33	6.41	6.49	6.57	6.65
6.50%	6.58	6.66	6.75	6.83	6.91
6.75%	6.83	6.92	7.00	7.08	7.17
7.00%	7.09	7.17	7.26	7.34	7.42
7.25%	7.34	7.42	7.51	7.60	7.68
7.50%	7.59	7.68	7.77	7.85	7.94
7.75%	7.84	7.93	8.02	8.11	8.20
8.00%	8.09	8.18	8.28	8.37	8.46
8.25%	8.34	8.44	8.53	8.63	8.72
8.50%	8.60	8.69	8.79	8.88	8.98
8.75%	8.85	8.95	9.04	9.14	9.24
9.00%	9.10	9.20	9.30	9.40	9.50
9.25%	9.35	9.45	9.56	9.66	9.76
9.50%	9.60	9.71	9.81	9.91	10.02
9.75%	9.86	9.96	10.07	10.17	10.28
10.00%	10.11	10.22	10.32	10.43	10.54
10.25%	10.36	10.47	10.58	10.69	10.80
10.50%	10.61	10.72	10.84	10.95	11.06
10.75%	10.86	10.98	11.09	11.21	11.32

EFFECTIVE LOAN INTEREST RATE
INCLUSIVE OF POINTS
40 YEAR TERM - HELD TO MATURITY

40 Year Contract Rate	Points				
	1	2	3	4	5
11.00%	11.12	11.23	11.35	11.46	11.58
11.25%	11.37	11.49	11.60	11.72	11.84
11.50%	11.62	11.74	11.86	11.98	12.10
11.75%	11.87	12.00	12.12	12.24	12.36
12.00%	12.12	12.25	12.37	12.50	12.62
12.25%	12.38	12.50	12.63	12.76	12.88
12.50%	12.63	12.76	12.89	13.02	13.15
12.75%	12.88	13.01	13.14	13.28	13.41
13.00%	13.13	13.27	13.40	13.53	13.67
13.25%	13.39	13.52	13.66	13.79	13.93
13.50%	13.64	13.78	13.91	14.05	14.19
13.75%	13.89	14.03	14.17	14.31	14.45
14.00%	14.14	14.29	14.43	14.57	14.71
14.25%	14.40	14.54	14.69	14.83	14.98
14.50%	14.65	14.80	14.94	15.09	15.24
14.75%	14.90	15.05	15.20	15.35	15.50
15.00%	15.15	15.30	15.46	15.61	15.76
15.25%	15.40	15.56	15.71	15.87	16.02
15.50%	15.66	15.81	15.97	16.13	16.28
15.75%	15.91	16.07	16.23	16.39	16.55
16.00%	16.16	16.32	16.48	16.65	16.81
16.25%	16.41	16.58	16.74	16.91	17.07
16.50%	16.67	16.83	17.00	17.17	17.33
16.75%	16.92	17.09	17.26	17.43	17.59

Interest Rate With Points

EFFECTIVE LOAN INTEREST RATE
INCLUSIVE OF POINTS
40 YEAR TERM - HELD TO MATURITY

40 Year Contract Rate	Points				
	1	2	3	4	5
17.00%	17.17	17.34	17.51	17.68	17.86
17.25%	17.42	17.60	17.77	17.94	18.12
17.50%	17.68	17.85	18.03	18.20	18.38
17.75%	17.93	18.11	18.29	18.46	18.64
18.00%	18.18	18.36	18.54	18.72	18.90
18.25%	18.43	18.62	18.80	18.98	19.17
18.50%	18.69	18.87	19.06	19.24	19.43
18.75%	18.94	19.13	19.31	19.50	19.69
19.00%	19.19	19.38	19.57	19.76	19.95
19.25%	19.44	19.64	19.83	20.02	20.22
19.50%	19.70	19.89	20.09	20.28	20.48
19.75%	19.95	20.15	20.34	20.54	20.74
20.00%	20.20	20.40	20.60	20.80	21.00
20.25%	20.45	20.66	20.86	21.06	21.26
20.50%	20.71	20.91	21.12	21.32	21.53
20.75%	20.96	21.17	21.37	21.58	21.79
21.00%	21.21	21.42	21.63	21.84	22.05
21.25%	21.46	21.68	21.89	22.10	22.31
21.50%	21.72	21.93	22.15	22.36	22.58
21.75%	21.97	22.19	22.40	22.62	22.84
22.00%	22.22	22.44	22.66	22.88	23.10
22.25%	22.47	22.70	22.92	23.14	23.36
22.50%	22.73	22.95	23.18	23.40	23.63
22.75%	22.98	23.21	23.43	23.66	23.89

Constant Annual Percent Table

CONSTANT ANNUAL PERCENT TABLE
Fully Amortized, Based Upon Monthly Payments

TERM (YEARS)	5	10	15	20
RATE				
6.00%	23.1994	13.3225	10.1263	8.5972
6.25%	23.3391	13.4736	10.2891	8.7711
6.50%	23.4794	13.6258	10.4533	8.9469
6.75%	23.6202	13.7789	10.6189	9.1244
7.00%	23.7614	13.9330	10.7859	9.3036
7.25%	23.9032	14.0881	10.9544	9.4845
7.50%	24.0455	14.2442	11.1241	9.6671
7.75%	24.1884	14.4013	11.2953	9.8514
8.00%	24.3317	14.5593	11.4678	10.0373
8.25%	24.4755	14.7183	11.6417	10.2248
8.50%	24.6198	14.8783	11.8169	10.4139
8.75%	24.7647	15.0392	11.9934	10.6045
9.00%	24.9100	15.2011	12.1712	10.7967
9.25%	25.0559	15.3639	12.3503	10.9904
9.50%	25.2022	15.5277	12.5307	11.1856
9.75%	25.3491	15.6924	12.7124	11.3822
10.00%	25.4965	15.8581	12.8953	11.5803
10.25%	25.6443	16.0247	13.0794	11.7797
10.50%	25.7927	16.1922	13.2648	11.9806
10.75%	25.9415	16.3606	13.4514	12.1827

Find the interest rate in the left column and read
across to the term in years. This is the mortgage
constant expressed as a percent of the loan.
Example: A $1,000,000 loan for 30 years at 10.5%
interest: $1,000,000 @ 10.9769% = $109,770 annual
payment, or $9,147 monthly payment.

	25	30	35	40
RATE				
6.00%	7.7316	7.1946	6.8423	6.6026
6.25%	7.9160	7.3886	7.0449	6.8129
6.50%	8.1025	7.5848	7.2499	7.0255
6.75%	8.2909	7.7832	7.4570	7.2403
7.00%	8.4814	7.9836	7.6663	7.4572
7.25%	8.6737	8.1861	7.8776	7.6761
7.50%	8.8679	8.3906	8.0909	7.8968
7.75%	9.0639	8.5969	8.3061	8.1194
8.00%	9.2618	8.8052	8.5231	8.3437
8.25%	9.4614	9.0152	8.7419	8.5697
8.50%	9.6627	9.2270	8.9623	8.7971
8.75%	9.8657	9.4404	9.1844	9.0260
9.00%	10.0704	9.6555	9.4079	9.2563
9.25%	10.2766	9.8721	9.6329	9.4879
9.50%	10.4844	10.0903	9.8593	9.7207
9.75%	10.6936	10.3099	10.0871	9.9547
10.00%	10.9044	10.5309	10.3161	10.1898
10.25%	11.1166	10.7532	10.5463	10.4258
10.50%	11.3302	10.9769	10.7776	10.6628
10.75%	11.5451	11.2018	11.0100	10.9008

Constant Annual Percent Table

CONSTANT ANNUAL PERCENT TABLE
Fully Amortized, Based Upon Monthly Payments

TERM (YEARS)	5	10	15	20
RATE				
11.00%	26.0909	16.5300	13.6392	12.3863
11.25%	26.2408	16.7003	13.8281	12.5911
11.50%	26.3911	16.8715	14.0183	12.7972
11.75%	26.5420	17.0435	14.2096	13.0045
12.00%	26.6933	17.2165	14.4020	13.2130
12.25%	26.8452	17.3904	14.5956	13.4228
12.50%	26.9975	17.5651	14.7903	13.6337
12.75%	27.1504	17.7408	14.9860	13.8457
13.00%	27.3037	17.9173	15.1829	14.0589
13.25%	27.4575	18.0947	15.3808	14.2732
13.50%	27.6118	18.2729	15.5798	14.4885
13.75%	27.7666	18.4520	15.7798	14.7049
14.00%	27.9219	18.6320	15.9809	14.9222
14.25%	28.0777	18.8128	16.1830	15.1406
14.50%	28.2339	18.9944	16.3860	15.3600
14.75%	28.3907	19.1769	16.5900	15.5803
15.00%	28.5479	19.3602	16.7950	15.8015
15.25%	28.7056	19.5443	17.0010	16.0236
15.50%	28.8638	19.7293	17.2079	16.2466
15.75%	29.0225	19.9150	17.4157	16.4704
16.00%	29.1817	20.1016	17.6244	16.6951

Find the interest rate in the left column and read across to the term in years. This is the mortgage constant expressed as a percent of the loan. Example: A $1,000,000 loan for 30 years at 10.5% interest: $1,000,000 @ 10.9769% = $109,770 annual payment, or $9,147 monthly payment.

RATE	25	30	35	40
11.00%	11.7614	11.4279	11.2435	11.1395
11.25%	11.9789	11.6551	11.4779	11.3791
11.50%	12.1976	11.8835	11.7133	11.6194
11.75%	12.4176	12.1129	11.9495	11.8604
12.00%	12.6387	12.3434	12.1866	12.1020
12.25%	12.8609	12.5748	12.4245	12.3442
12.50%	13.0842	12.8071	12.6631	12.5870
12.75%	13.3086	13.0403	12.9024	12.8304
13.00%	13.5340	13.2744	13.1423	13.0742
13.25%	13.7604	13.5093	13.3829	13.3184
13.50%	13.9877	13.7449	13.6241	13.5631
13.75%	14.2160	13.9814	13.8658	13.8082
14.00%	14.4451	14.2185	14.1081	14.0537
14.25%	14.6751	14.4562	14.3508	14.2995
14.50%	14.9060	14.6947	14.5940	14.5456
14.75%	15.1376	14.9337	14.8377	14.7920
15.00%	15.3700	15.1733	15.0818	15.0387
15.25%	15.6031	15.4135	15.3262	15.2856
15.50%	15.8369	15.6542	15.5710	15.5328
15.75%	16.0715	15.8954	15.8162	15.7802
16.00%	16.3067	16.1371	16.0616	16.0278

Constant Annual Percent Table

INDEX

Index

Index

Index

Index

Index

Index

ABOUT THE AUTHOR

Randall Bell is one of the foremost real estate experts in the nation. His career has been profiled in the WALL STREET JOURNAL, PEOPLE MAGAZINE and TODAY'S REALTOR. He has been interviewed by the ABC, CBS, NBC, FOX, CNN and BBC Television Networks.

A Southern California native, Mr. Bell earned an MBA Degree in Real Estate from UCLA; holds the MAI Designation from, and is an instructor for, the Appraisal Institute. He has testified as an expert witness on numerous court cases involving real estate and holds both real estate appraisal and broker licenses.

Mr. Bell is experienced in the valuation of commercial and industrial properties, apartment complexes, subdivisions, and single-family dwellings. His specialty is *diminution in value* issues involving construction defects, environmental contamination, eminent domain, crime scene stigma, natural disasters and other detrimental conditions. His clients include federal and state governmental agencies, major banks, developers, law firms, insurance companies and brokerage firms.

A prolific writer and speaker, his articles have been published in ENVIRONMENTAL CLAIMS JOURNAL, URBAN LAND MAGAZINE, RIGHT OF WAY and the APPRAISAL JOURNAL. He has addressed the BROWNSFIELD SYMPOSIUM in Irvine California, the NATIONAL SYMPOSIUM OF THE APPRAISAL INSTITUTE in Washington, DC and the NATIONAL CONFERENCE OF REAL ESTATE JOURNALISTS in Las Vegas, Nevada.

Mr. Bell's consulting assignments have involved several high-profile situations and some of the largest properties in the country. These situations have earned him considerable notoriety. His studies have been cited by the ASSOCIATED PRESS, USA TODAY, THE NEW YORK TIMES, THE LOS ANGELES TIMES, and the SAN FRANCISCO CHRONICLE.

Based upon his experience and knowledge, this handbook is of benefit to anyone who owns, rents, leases or is otherwise involved with real estate...from developers, builders, bankers, attorneys, investors, and brokers to homeowners and students.

David Derby
Publisher

USER COMMENTS

Bell's Guides, first edition, have been recognized as a standard quick-reference source for professionals and homeowners alike. They are used by universities, law firms, title companies, brokerage firms, escrow companies...and by property owners. Here is a sample of what users of **Bell's Guides** have to say about them:

I manage a portfolio of offices, gas stations, retail stores and athletic clubs. I have used Bell's Guides in both my career and as a homeowner. In my opinion, Bell's Guides are the most powerful real estate reference tool that I have ever seen. I am really amazed by how much information they have.
C A / Property Manager
Washington, DC

I have used Bell's Guides as exhibits in Superior Court. They are an outstanding tool for explaining complex real estate concepts to a jury.
D F / Attorney
Los Angeles, California

In my office, we have a standard policy that when someone has a real estate question, they refer to Bell's Guides first. That usually takes care of things.

M S / Escrow Officer
Orlando, Florida

I have been using Bell's Guides for several years in my title company business. They are by far the most outstanding real estate reference guide in the industry. I give them an A+.
J K / Account Executive
San Francisco, California